About the Editor

Ivan Strenski is North American Editor-in-Chief of the international journal, *Religion* and a member of the faculty of the department of Religious Studies at the University of California, Santa Barbara. His *Four Theories of Myth in Twentieth-Century History* (London and Iowa City: Macmillan and Iowa University Press, 1987), won the 1989 national Award for Excellence in History from the American Academy of Religion. His *Religion in Relation: Method, Application and Moral Location* will appear in 1992 (London: Macmillan). He has twice been the recipient of research fellowships from the National Endowment for the Humanities for his work in religious studies. His recent publications include articles on the members of the Durkheimian group such as Henri Hubert and Marcel Mauss, and the work of Louis Dumont. He is currently completing a history of theories of civic and ritual sacrifice.

MALINOWSKI AND
THE WORK OF MYTH

MALINOWSKI AND THE WORK OF MYTH

*Selected and Introduced
by Ivan Strenski*

PRINCETON UNIVERSITY PRESS

PRINCETON, NEW JERSEY

PUBLISHED BY PRINCETON UNIVERSITY PRESS, 41 WILLIAM STREET,
PRINCETON, NEW JERSEY 08540

IN THE UNITED KINGDOM, PRINCETON UNIVERSITY PRESS, OXFORD

LIBRARY OF CONGRESS CATALOGING-IN-PUBLICATION DATA

MALINOWSKI, BRONISLAW, 1884–1942.

MALINOWSKI AND THE WORK OF MYTH / SELECTED AND INTRODUCED BY
IVAN STRENSKI.

P. CM.—(MYTHOS)

INCLUDES BIBLIOGRAPHICAL REFERENCES AND INDEX.

ISBN 0-691-07414-3 (ALK. PAPER)

ISBN 0-691-02077-9 (PBK. : ALK. PAPER)

1. ETHNOLOGY. 2. MYTH. 3. ETHNOPSYCHOLOGY. 4. MALINOWSKI,
BRONISLAW, 1884–1942. I. STRENSKI, IVAN. II. TITLE. III. SERIES:
MYTHOS (PRINCETON, N.J.)

GN304.M36 1992   291.1'3—DC20   91-38250

THIS BOOK HAS BEEN COMPOSED IN LINOTRON CALEDONIA

PRINCETON UNIVERSITY PRESS BOOKS ARE PRINTED ON ACID-FREE PAPER,
AND MEET THE GUIDELINES FOR PERMANENCE AND DURABILITY OF THE
COMMITTEE ON PRODUCTION GUIDELINES FOR BOOK LONGEVITY OF THE
COUNCIL ON LIBRARY RESOURCES

1 3 5 7 9 10 8 6 4 2

PRINTED IN THE UNITED STATES OF AMERICA

FRONTISPIECE AND COVER DETAIL: PAUL GAUGUIN, *WHERE DO WE COME FROM?*
WHAT ARE WE? WHERE ARE WE GOING? (D'OÙ VENONS-NOUS?
QUE SOMMES-NOUS? OÙ ALLONS-NOUS), 1897. TOMPKINS COLLECTION.
COURTESY MUSEUM OF FINE ARTS, BOSTON.

Ninian Smart
"Dullabho purisājañño,
na so sabbattha jāyati"
(*Dhammapada*: 193.)

CONTENTS

ACKNOWLEDGMENTS

THE INDIVIDUAL CHAPTERS of this edition are reprinted from the following sources with the kind cooperation of Mrs. Helena Wayne (Malinowska), and by permission of the Malinowski Estate. Chapter 1, "In Tewara and Sanaroa—Mythology of the Kula," *Argonauts of the Western Pacific* [1922] (New York: E. P. Dutton, 1961), pp. 290–330. Chapter 2, "Ethnology and the Study of Society," *Economica* 2 (1921): 208–19. Chapter 3, "Psychology and Anthropology," *Nature* (1924): 650–51, reprinted in *Sex, Culture and Myth* (New York City: Harcourt, Brace & World, 1962), pp. 114–16. Chapter 4, "Obscenity and Myth," *Sex and Repression in Savage Society* (London: Routledge and Kegan Paul, 1927), pp 104–34. Chapter 5, "Myth in Primitive Psychology" (1926) in *Magic, Science and Religion*, Robert Redfield, ed. (New York: Doubleday, 1954). Chapter 6, "Myth as a Dramatic Development of Dogma" (n.d.), reprinted in *Sex, Culture and Myth* (New York: Harcourt, Brace & World, 1962), pp. 245–65. Chapter 7, "The Foundations of Faith and Morals" (Oxford: Oxford University Press, 1936), reprinted in *Sex, Culture and Myth* (New York: Harcourt, Brace & World, 1962), pp. 295–336.

My thanks above all to Robert Segal, stalwart colleague, cherished friend.

INTRODUCTION: *MALINOWSKI AND MYTH*

Why Read Malinowski on Myth?

N EARLY SEVENTY-FIVE YEARS have passed since Bronislaw Malinowski (1884–1942) first wrote about myth. Can Malinowski still teach us anything important about myth today? Since Malinowski's time, much work has been done on the theory of myth by Claude Lévi-Strauss, Mircea Eliade, Carl Jung, Joseph Campbell, and many others. Did Malinowski say anything that these theorists did not say better? Why should we still read Malinowski at all?

The best reason for continuing to read Malinowski on myth is simply that many of his insights remain important. These fall into four categories: function and practice, context and meaning, anthropology and psychoanalysis, and conceptual marking.

First, Malinowski articulated as never before, or since, a program of seeing myths as part of the functional, pragmatic, or *performed* dimension of culture—that is, as part of activities which *do* certain tasks for particular human communities.[1] Second, he created sensitivity for the critical role of context in interpreting the meaning of myths. Myths do not have intrinsic meaning; their meaning is given by their home context of situation. Myths are thus not primarily texts, or isolated pieces of literature; they are texts merged with contexts. Third, Malinowski was a pioneer in applying the lessons of psychoanalysis to the study of culture. At the same time, he usefully attempted to correct the generalizations of psychoanalysis with the cross-cultural researches of ethnology. Fourth, he showed exemplary conceptual self-awareness about the epistemological status of the category of myth. He knew that to call something a 'myth' is to *mark* it as special, to separate it off from things considered to be of a different nature. To do so means taking responsibility for the categories of inquiry, and not to imagine that we could excuse our theoretical moves by appealing to some objective and given nature of myth.

A final reason to read Malinowski on myth is for the sheer interest and pleasure of it. Malinowski was a remarkably catholic thinker whose mind explored many fields and whose ideas enriched just as many. His own original training was done in Poland in physics and mathematics, with a

---

[1] Contemporary practitioners of approaches to culture that emphasize performance, practice, and function number S. J. Tambiah, "The Magical Power of Words," *Man* 3 (1968): 175–208; Pierre Bourdieu, *Outlines of a Theory of Practice* (Cambridge: Cambridge University Press, 1977); and Mary Douglas, *How Institutions Think* (Syracuse: Syracuse University Press, 1986).

strong component of philosophy, at the University of Krakow. There, Malinowski took a Ph.D. (1906) with a *rigorosum* (a form of academic distinction) in both physics and philosophy.[2] Then followed a year of studies with the experimental psychologist and philosopher Wilhelm Wundt and economist Karl Bücher at the University of Leipzig, where Malinowski's father had studied. But these interests in the hard sciences in part gave way to a growing professional preoccupation with so-called primitive cultures, perhaps encouraged by Wundt's development of a *Völkerpsychologie*. Malinowski moved to London in 1910 to pursue a program of study in anthropology at the London School of Economics under the direction of Charles Seligman and Edward Westermarck. Shortly before the outbreak of the First World War, Malinowski set out for Australia, and from there on his now famous field studies in New Guinea (1914–1918). These years of field study became the basis of Malinowski's extensive writings on myth.

The work that Malinowski produced as a result of his field studies revealed a man who was much more than a fact-finding ethnographer. He was a genuine intellectual. Beyond his training in ethnology, his writings on myth ventured into debates within the fields of folklore, literary criticism, linguistics, philosophy, psychology, psychoanalysis, religion, and sexuality studies. Malinowski took his place in the intellectual world of interwar London, moving in the fashionable circles frequented by figures ranging from Bertrand Russell to Havelock Ellis. He held forth at the London School of Economics for nearly two decades, leaving England only a year or so before his death to accept a post at Yale. Having lived through two personally disruptive world wars and the rapid transformation of the western world during the early twentieth century, Malinowski was passionate about applying the lessons of anthropology to contemporary social problems—war, aggression, sexual mores, crime and punishment. Malinowski was thus an exciting and provocative thinker, one who tried to combine scientific styles of thinking with the big issues of life and death, our so-called existential human problems. So for these reasons, we can make a case for giving Malinowski's theory of myth another good hard look. This introduction will concentrate on the lasting value of Ma-

[2] "Bronislaw Malinowski's Cracow Doctorate," Andrzej Flis, ed., *Malinowski between Two Worlds: The Polish Roots of an Anthropological Tradition*, Roy Ellen, Ernest Gellner, Grazyna Kubica, and Janusz Mucha, eds. (Cambridge: Cambridge University Press, 1988), p. 195. See also Andrzej K. Paluch, "Introduction: Bronislaw Malinowski and Cracow Anthropology," *Malinowski between Two Worlds*, pp. 1–11 for a general discussion of Malinowski's academic biography. For relations between the thought of Ernst Mach and Malinowski, see Ernest Gellner, " 'Zeno of Cracow' or 'Revolution at Nemi' or 'The Polish Revenge: A Drama in Three Acts,' " *Malinowski between Two Worlds*, pp. 164–94.

linowski's views about myth—on what *has* survived and what *ought* to survive.

What Should Survive of Malinowski's Theory of Myth?

Their "Lili'u" Is Really Our "Myth"

Malinowski did what every myth theorist ought to do but which few, if any, have done. He understood that using the word "myth" is to mark a category of story.[3] "Myth" is not just the name of any story. The term "myth" singles out a class of story, just as the terms "art" or "literature" do the same for their referents. Thus, using the word "myth" is a way of evaluating stories, or of describing them as special or important stories.

In addition to myth theorists' general obliviousness to the marking process, the main problem in the development of a theory of myth has been that myth theorists broadly disagree about at least two things: First, what should make up the content, function, or structure of the marked category "myth"? For example, do myths have to contain some reference to gods, heroes, creation, origins, spirits, and so on? Or must they *function* religiously, to evoke mystery and to create existential realizations, or socially, to charter institutions? Second, to which particular stories should we apply this term "myth"? Is the story of Adam and Eve myth or is it revelation? Are the gospel stories of the life of Jesus myth or are they history, legend, or an heroic tale?

What makes something a work of art or literature? Is art distinctive because of what it *depicts* (e.g., satyrs and nymphs, rather than humble peasants), or the way it *functions* (e.g., to create the feeling of the sublime)? But having agreed, for the sake of demonstration, that art must create the feeling of the sublime, we might disagree that a certain *depiction* in a portrait or landscape does so. The Naturalist painters created precisely this kind of dilemma by trying to create a sense of the sublime while depicting objects not previously thought capable of creating intense emotional reactions. For this reason, a good myth theorist, like a theorist of art or literature in a comparable situation, will have to defend why they think a certain story should be called myth. Myth theorists have to take responsibility for their concept of myth by recognizing that in calling something a myth, they are marking that something off as a distinct category.

Malinowski operates with some awareness that he is involved in a

---

[3] See especially Bronislaw Malinowski, *Argonauts of the Western Pacific* (1922), pp. 299 (pp. 10–11 this volume), 301–3, and "Myth in Primitive Psychology," *Magic, Science and Religion*, Robert Redfield, ed., p. 107f (p. 86ff this volume), and "The Foundations of Faith and Morals," *Sex, Culture and Myth*, p. 304f (pp. 140–41 this volume).

marking process when he deals with "myths." In "Myth in Primitive Psychology" Malinowski writes that "the most important point of the thesis which I am urging" is that "I maintain that there exists a class of stories"[4] that he calls myths.

How did Malinowski determine what a myth was? How did he decide what fit the category? What did "myth" mean for him, even before he arrived in the Trobriand Islands?

We might begin by recognizing that the term "myth" had a rich and controversial history in Malinowski's Europe. In this context, myth primarily meant a radiant and important story. The Romantic culture which Malinowski inherited in late nineteenth- and early twentieth-century Polish society had to some degree overcome the Enlightenment's disparagement of myths as simpleminded false stories.

As a recent Polish study of Malinowski's romantic background concludes: "Even Malinowski's biography turned out to be a model biography of Polish romanticism."[5] Even more, Malinowski's sensibilities were shaped specifically by a local Polish version of the European "modernist" or neoromantic movement.[6] The original British and German romantics of the late eighteenth and early nineteenth centuries did much to collect and popularize the stories of ancient Greece and Rome, as well as those of the northern peoples, the Scandinavian Eddas or the German stories collected by the brothers Grimm or those put into epic operatic form in the Ring Cycle of Richard Wagner. In like manner, the Polish neoromantics expressed their sensibilities in scientific, ethnographic, and folklorist work. During the last quarter of the nineteenth century, Malinowski's own linguist father and his academic friends formed a loosely connected intellectual circle in Krakow devoted to such interests as local ethnology and Polish folk culture.[7] High on the list of things that interested these neoromantic intellectuals of Malinowski's milieu were stories; these stories were routinely called "myths."

Malinowski was drawn to stories in part because, like all anthropologists who harbored empirical and "scientific" aspirations, he needed data. Now, stories are relatively easy to convert into data. In large part, they are publicly available for recording in the notebook of the anthropologist. This distinguishes them from many of our cultural beliefs, which often are presumed, but not explicitly available to consciousness. Further, sto-

---

[4] Malinowski, "Myth in Primitive Psychology," p. 108 (p. 87 this volume).

[5] Jan Jerschina, "Polish Culture of Modernism and Malinowski's Personality," *Malinowski between Two Worlds*, p. 136.

[6] Ibid., pp. 128–48, esp. 128, 130, 136. Ivan Strenski, "Malinowski: Second Positivism, Second Romanticism," *Man* 17 (1982): 766–71.

[7] Paluch, "Malinowski and Cracow Anthropology," p. 5, and Grazyna Kubica, "Malinowski's Years in Poland," pp. 88–89, 94 in *Malinowski between Two Worlds*.

ries are "portable" and their removal does not really make much of an impact upon the cultural environment of the society in question, compared with the legion of problems—even in the heyday of imperialism when Malinowski flourished—in collecting so-called "primitive art," and the problems of making it "data." In many cases, statues or masks are not portable simply because of their size, but equally they often cannot be taken away (secretly or openly) for display and discussion because of cultural restrictions. They are holy objects, the removal of which would be inconvenient or conspicuous, and moreover a grave wrong to the people being studied. While it is true that many stories are sacred in this sense, many are not subject to restrictions (nor even the possibility of enforcing them) against retelling them or writing them down.

Malinowski was drawn to the stories his hosts in the southwestern Pacific told among themselves and, sometimes, to him, But why call these stories "myth" rather than "literature" or "art"? These stories were different from each other and had many indigenous names (but none of these names was of course "myth"). The Trobrianders had what Malinowski just called "stories."[8] But they also had their "*lili'u*," "*libogwo*," "*kukwanebu*," "*wosi*," "*vinavina*," "*megwa*," and "*yopa*."[9] How should Malinowski talk about these classes of stories? Should he just use these raw terms unfamiliar to his readers, or should he try to invent equivalents in Western culture, and then translate the names of the different kinds of native stories into terms his readers might better understand? And which native story, if any, was equivalent to our notion of "myth" which Malinowski and others took for granted as a result of their European romantic nurture?

In trying to answer this question, Malinowski assumes what most of our theorists of myth assume as well, yet in ways that show a somewhat higher degree of self-awareness about what he was doing. What makes Malinowski somewhat admirable, and thus what should contribute to the survival of his approach to myth, is that he chose deliberately to try to convey the sense of the unfamiliar by the familiar, the new by the old, by having recourse to the *marking process*. He knew that in labeling a story a "myth," he was marking it in a particular way—just as surely as when we call a painting "art," or a novel "literature." This is one reason it is instructive to read Malinowski on myth, and to look at his effort to render native stories intelligible to Western readers.

As a Romantic, Malinowski assumed that the stories he should study and feature as "myths" were those stories especially marked as "sacred" among the Trobrianders. In doing this, rightly or wrongly, he imported

---

[8] Malinowski, *Argonauts*, pp. 291–95 (pp. 3–6 this volume).
[9] Ibid., p. 299 (pp. 10–11 this volume).

fundamental assumptions from Western culture which almost all theorists of myth do as well. We have given importance to certain stories, such as the Greek myths, the Bible stories, the folktales of northern Europe; we have tended to call them all "myths," and have linked them with religion. They are the "sacred" narratives, even when "myth" is taken pejoratively to mean "false story."[10] In this case, typically its falsity is itself important. Attempts to debunk biblical narrative as merely mythical are so fervent partly because critics believe that these stories have done real damage in leading people astray. Malinowski assumed that the Trobrianders mark off some stories for special religious reasons, and that they would name them as well.

This then leads Malinowski to seek out a class of stories for special treatment among the Trobrianders. He chose the Trobriand "*lili'u*," and equated them straightaway with our (originally Greek) term, "myth." Why? Malinowski says that the *lili'u* are the "most important class" of stories—adding that this is "reproducing *prima facie* the natives' own classification and nomenclature".[11] Identifying it with "myth," Malinowski notes that the *lili'u* is "true, venerable and sacred," and plays a "highly important cultural part".[12] Thus it is because both are the important or sacred stories of a given society, that we can speak of their "*lili'u*" as equivalent to our "myth."

I am not uncritically celebrating this equating of terms from different cultures in the way Malinowski does. In many ways, his approach could be indicted for engaging in a massive imperialist projection of Western romantic notions upon the Trobrianders. Our word, "myth," henceforth swallows up their word, "*lili'u*," without any sense that "*lili'u*" might contain different non-Western features. More than that, from here on, Malinowski assumes both that stories have an equally special value in all societies, and that "myth" swallows up all non-Western "important narratives."

Nevertheless, Malinowski is to be commended for being as explicit as he was about the marking process. His example, rightly read, enables us to see that all talk about "myth" across cultures involves the kinds of conceptual marking of choice features of the cultures of others. Since there is no accepted definition of "myth" and since "myth" is our word—not theirs—whenever we want to talk about another culture, we will inevitably need to work out acceptable ways of using terms familiar to our readers. Malinowski was very far from perfect in this regard, but he at least opens the door a crack, allowing us to see further.

---

[10] Malinowski, "The Foundations of Faith and Morals," p. 312 (p. 148 this volume).

[11] Malinowski, "Myth in Primitive Psychology," p. 107 (p. 86 this volume).

[12] Ibid., p. 107 (p. 86 this volume).

Functionalism: Myth Is as Myth Does

If any word is always associated with Malinowski, it is "functionalism." Despite many critical attacks on Malinowski's functional theory, it continues to hold many adherents. But what is functionalism in respect to myth? How can we understand why it has managed to retain the interest and devotion of students of myth and religion? An inquiry into Malinowski's functionalism is doubly important, because he held different functionalist positions at different times in his life. Let us start simply by asking what central claims are embedded in Malinowski's functionalism.

First, there is generic or "broad" functionalism. To be this kind of functionalist means little more than to view society as an interdependent organic whole.[13] This generic functionalism calls attention to the ways culture or society coheres, hangs together, works—how it *functions*. Here Malinowski does not differ significantly from Durkheim or even Aristotle. On this view, such functionalists view myth as a part of the social or cultural whole, a piece of the mechanism of society performing its tasks in maintaining the whole. In particular, Malinowski says that the job of myth is "a warrant, a charter, and even a practical guide to the activities with which it is connected." Myths are not actually meant to be read as explanations, but are active parts of culture like commands, deeds, or guarantees, certifying that some sort of social arrangement is legitimate; they are the "backbone of primitive culture."[14] They maintain the legitimacy of our social arrangements. The story of Adam and Eve, for example, may or may not be literally true, but its literal truth is irrelevant to its *function*. The story has functioned in the past, among other things, to charter the institutions of wearing clothes, bearing children in pain, or working by the "sweat of our brows."

But a second, riskier, and more interesting, sense of functionalism can also be found in Malinowski.[15] It has two parts as well. Malinowski asserts, first, that myth functions *unconsciously* as far as the actors in question are concerned. Second, myth functions as "an indispensable ingredient of all culture";[16] it fulfills objective, even biological, needs essential to the survival of the culture in question.

What distinguishes Malinowski's second pragmatic sense of functionalism from the first broad or generic variety is the idea that *all* the elements of a cultural whole serve a *necessary* practical function for the survival of the institution. *Everything* in society functions to fulfill basic

---

[13] Malinowski, "The Foundations of Faith and Morals," p. 324 (p. 160 this volume).

[14] Malinowski, "Myth in Primitive Psychology," p. 108 (p. 87 this volume).

[15] A. Pierce, "Durkheim and Functionalism," in K. Wolff, ed., *Essays on Sociology and Philosophy* (New York: Harper and Row, 1964), p. 154.

[16] Malinowski, "Myth in Primitive Psychology," p. 146 (p. 115 this volume).

needs. And when Malinowski speaks of the "basic needs," he has biology in mind—so much so that he speaks of the "biological utility" of culturally functioning institutions.[17] This extreme biological functionalist interpretation of human culture developed gradually for Malinowski. Early in his career, Malinowski argued that only so-called "primitive" culture was exclusively pragmatic. Thus at one point Malinowski believed that even language was used in exclusively pragmatic ways: "primitive" cultures simply had no other choice, since they lived precarious existences and needed to make everything in their culture count. As Malinowski says, "language in its primitive function and original form has an essentially pragmatic character . . . [It is] a mode of behavior, an indispensable element of concerted human action."[18]

Myth thus follows the lead of language. The so-called "primitive" is "an eager actor, playing his part for his own benefit, trying to use all the means in his power towards the attainment of his various needs and desires. . . . He is interested in all things which subserve these ends and are thus immediately useful. Round these he develops not only his magic . . . but also his myths."[19]

This assertion occurred in the context of Malinowski's point that "primitive" folk were not idle and ignorant.[20] Their cultures showed admirably that they worked with a hardheaded practicality. But to some extent Malinowski also disparaged practicality—native or otherwise—as sign of a certain lack of refinement or aristocratic cultivation. At the same time as he was saying that primitive language was essentially pragmatic, he believed that Western scientific language rose above practicality and moved in realms of pure thought.

But later in *Coral Gardens* (1935) Malinowski changed his mind. He extended his pragmatic reading of "primitive" culture to "us" "moderns" as well. "Even literary and scientific language" is subject to the same pragmatic interpretation as primitive language:

in one of my previous writings [above], I opposed civilized and scientific to primitive speech, and argued as if the theoretical uses of words in modern philosophic and scientific writings were completely detached from their pragmatic sources. This was an error, and a serious one at that. Between the savage use of words and the most abstract and theoretical one, there is only

[17] Bronislaw Malinowski, "The Problem of Meaning in Primitive Languages," Special Appendix to C. K. Ogden and I. A. Richards, *The Meaning of Meaning* (London: Kegan, Paul, Trench and Trubner, 1923), p. 332.

[18] Ibid., p. 316.

[19] Bronislaw Malinowski, "On Sir James Frazer," *Sex, Culture and Myth* (New York: Harcourt, Brace and World, 1962), p. 272.

[20] Malinowski, *Argonauts*, p. 166.

a difference of degree. Ultimately all the meaning of all the words is derived from bodily experience.[21]

Pragmatism is everywhere.

As for myth, it is here in this fundamental, biological, and universal human pragmatism, that we find the origins of myth. Myth for Malinowski is "indispensable" and "vital"[22]—something a society needs—and without which it cannot materially persist. Tradition here takes a special role in this indispensable job which myth performs for culture: "Myth expresses, enhances and codifies belief; it safeguards and enforces morality; it vouches for the efficiency of ritual and contains practical rules for the guidance of men . . . a pragmatic charter of primitive faith and moral wisdom.[23] Myth is thus a "hard-worked active force," covering the "whole pragmatic reaction of man towards disease and death" and expressing "his emotions, his foreboding."[24] For Malinowski, myth is practically linked with our basic biological needs.

As if this pragmatic biological sense of functionalism were not radical enough, Malinowski also claimed that the actors in question were *unconsciously* serving these functions.[25] Myths work on us subrationally, below our threshold of awareness. We may be moved by stories of the return of a dead loved one such as in the play *Blithe Spirit*. Malinowski would say that this is not because we consciously recognize the truth of these accounts, and rationally conclude that they are so. Rather, the promise of neverending life and the desire to avoid death, which are embodied in such a play, speak directly to us, straight to our organism as Malinowski might say. Our will to believe myths of life beyond the grave testify to the natural built-in drives and instincts of our animal nature. These visceral reactions translate into emotions which overwhelm our rational critical calculating mind, and thus make believers out of every one of us— all without our being necessarily aware of it. "There are no atheists in foxholes," the saying goes. Thus Malinowski can earnestly assert that myth is "born from the innermost and emotional reaction to the most formidable and haunting idea"[26]—death.

Whatever doubts we may have about Malinowski's viewpoint, there is power in this position—the power of the "bottom line." Malinowski forces us to measure myths by what they can really seem able to

---

[21] Bronislaw Malinowski, *Coral Gardens* (London: Allen & Unwin, 1935), vol. 2, p. 58, quoted by D. T. Langendoen, *London School of Linguistics* (Cambridge: MIT, 1968), p. 34.

[22] Malinowski, "Myth in Primitive Psychology," p. 101 (p. 82 this volume).

[23] Ibid., p. 101 (p. 82 this volume).

[24] Ibid., p. 132 (p. 105 this volume).

[25] Pierce, "Durkheim and Functionalism," p. 157.

[26] Malinowski, "Myth in Primitive Psychology," p. 110 (p. 89 this volume).

achieve—by their observable effects. Thus at one level, myths may provide access to the stated beliefs of people. They are "founts of ethnographic information,"[27] as Malinowski calls them. But if we take them literally, we will soon become baffled. For example, what are we to make of tales of miracles, ghosts, or persons surviving death to live in another world? If we take the storytellers at their literal word, we would have to conclude either that they knew about the mysterious technology of living forever or, since people die and do not seem to live forever, that they were not telling the truth. Either way, we arrive at a dead end. The technology of life eternal would probably transcend our understanding, leaving us dumbfounded and unable to make intelligent comments or, if untrue, such a narrative simply shuts us out.

Malinowski's answer to this difficulty is to say that what people really mean in relating such narratives was not what they literally (or symbolically) said. Rather, what they meant could be discovered in what the stories did for them. Telling myths about life everlasting does not really give a report about life in another state; rather, these stories are about how they affect an audience—how they demonstrably make people feel better about their inevitable fates. The bottom line about such a myth is what it *does*—it boosts our morale. Malinowski's perspective turns attention to the behavioral consequences of certain stories, rather than their literal meaning: if we really want to understand myths, look at what myths *do*, not what they *say*.

A lie? Maybe. But in Malinowski's view it was a noble lie—one which does some good for people in a situation in which there may really be nothing to be done. Speaking of his informants in the Trobriands, Malinowski reports that

> in his actual emotional attitude towards death, whether his own or that of his loved ones, the native is not completely guided by his belief and mythological ideas. His intense fear of death, his strong desire to postpone it and his deep sorrow at the departure of beloved relatives belie the optimistic creed . . . inherent in native customs, ideas and rituals. . . . But again the same people would clutch at the hope given to them by their beliefs. They would *screen, with the vivid texture of their myths, stories and beliefs about the spirit world, the vast emotional void gaping beyond them.*[28]

Speaking for himself and his own times, Malinowski tells the audience of his 1936 Riddell lectures much the same thing. "The rationalist and agnostic must admit that even if he himself cannot accept these truths

[27] Bronislaw Malinowski, "Baloma," *Magic, Science and Religion*, p. 239, and *Argonauts*, p. 317 (p. 25 this volume).

[28] Malinowski, "Myth in Primitive Psychology," p. 138 (pp. 108–9 this volume), my emphasis.

[myth and religion], he must at least admit them as indispensable pragmatic figments without which civilization cannot exist."[29] And so we must
keep up appearances, so to speak, and leave myth undisturbed in modern society. Without myth, the practical job which it does would not be
fulfilled, and without the fulfillment of these vital functions, society
would fall into chaos. Society is better off if people believe what myths
like *Blithe Spirit* portray—even if false—than if people had no hope in
reunion with lost loved ones. Such myths keep alive human hope, and
with it human society. To the extent that Malinowski's paternal viewpoint
is true, so long as people actually do need the noble lies which he equates
with myths, so long as people live through self-deception—and the success of a play like *Blithe Spirit* suggests that many of us do—then so long
must we take his words to heart.

Context Holds the Key to the Real Meaning of Myths

Sensitivity to the context of situation is a third reason why Malinowski's
theory of myth can be recommended to today's readers.

There are two parts to Malinowski's appreciation of context that are
worth considering. First, Malinowski breaks the monopoly of the text.
Questions about myths may need to go beyond the literary level of a
myth, beyond the text, to the situation and *intentions* of their collective
or individual creation. For Malinowski, myths are not mere "texts"; they
are at least texts in contexts. Myths are narratives which occur within a
society, a culture; they cannot therefore fully be appreciated unless we
have access to that living culture which gives them birth and in which
they are current. Says Malinowski, "To understand [a particular society's]
myth, you must have a good knowledge of their sociology, religion, customs, and outlook. *Then, and only then*, can you appreciate what this
story means to the natives and how it can live in their life."[30] Second, this
leads naturally to the idea that questions of meaning, function, and the
like can now be answered not simply in terms of the intentions of the
mythmaker, but also in terms of the varieties of context—the differences
in the audiences in which myths *perform*. Accordingly, Malinowski calls
for the study of myth within its "context of living faith, social organization
. . . morals . . . and customs."[31]

Taken together these two points give the fieldworking anthropologist a
unique advantage over any deskbound literary student of myth. Having

[29] P. K. Feyerabend, "Explanation, Reduction and Empiricism," in H. Feigl and G. Max-
well, eds., *Minnesota Studies in the Philosophy of Science*, vol. 3 (Minneapolis: University
of Minnesota, 1962), p. 29.

[30] Malinowski, "Myth in Primitive Psychology," p. 113 (p. 90 this volume), my emphasis.

[31] Ibid., p. 100 (p. 82 this volume).

"the mythmaker at his elbow" Malinowski believes he can get at the intentions behind the story. Similarly, by being on the scene the fieldworker can to some extent see how the audience reacts to the story, how the myth means and functions in its environments of origin and currency.

Consider the "Christopher Columbus" story or myth. In trying to understand it, we might refer simply to a literary text of the story—"1492 and all that," for example. In doing so, we might come up with something having to do with a narrative of discovery, adventure, Spanish imperialism, "first contact," Italian renaissance navigation, geography, personal courage, and so on. But clearly one sort of meaning would be as good as another. It would depend on the point of view. Yet we could make some progress, whatever it was worth, if we were able to appeal to what the original narrator *intended* to convey by telling the "Christopher Columbus" story.

But however much an improvement it would be to know what the "mythmaker at his elbow" had to say about his intentions about the myth, the anthropologist would want to go further. After all, the original storyteller does not own the story. The mythmaker puts it into the ears of others, "puts it into circulation." And like money put into circulation in a market, the myth is received in different ways and affects people differently. Then it is "spent" again, circulated anew, as its present holders choose and as its new audiences "choose" to hear it. Thus, beyond this level of original authorial and intended meaning, Malinowski felt that a deeper, perhaps more potent, level of meaning existed. These meanings come not from the mythmaker, but from how what is spoken is received or understood, how the myth affects its audience—how it *functions*. Malinowski insists that these understandings will vary with the social and cultural nature of the audience. When we say things in public, our words are inevitably heard from the point of view of our audience. So the Christopher Columbus story means "1492 and all that" to so-called mainstream Americans schooled in the "myths" of the foundation of their predominantly northern European–derived nation. The Christopher Columbus story would thus charter the view that this is rightfully a nation based upon the values of the heroic peoples who settled it from their bases in western Europe. Yet in these days of ethnic diversity, we can expect that the Christopher Columbus story will mean quite another thing when the interests of special audiences are brought to bear—even when the same words are used. Thus when someone tells the story of Christopher Columbus at the annual convention of the AIM (the American Indian Movement), its meaning will differ drastically from its meaning as related to our so-called mainstream Americans or, even at a gathering of IAM (an Italian-American ethnic organization). The story will function in quite another way. For AIM partisans, it certifies their sense of having been victimized by Europeans; for Italian-Americans, ironically also the butt of ethnic jibes directed at them from WASPs, telling the Columbus story certifies that Italian-Americans are even more legitimately Americans than WASPs: after all, years before the *Mayflower*, an Italian navigator discovered the entire Western hemisphere! The meanings, and thus functions, differ because of the different social and cultural context in which the story is situated. In his theory of myth Malinowski is trying to sensitize us to that level of meaning which is determined by the context.[32]

Malinowski took this view of meaning to extremes. Rather early in his career, he became a behaviorist, and tried to understand all mental language in terms of stimuli and response behaviors.[33] Words were understood as stimuli; their meanings were the response behaviors induced by them. In his article "Culture" (1931) Malinowski puts his sentiments into explicitly behaviorist language: "The meaning of words consists in what they achieve by concerted action, the indirect handling of the environment through the direct action on other organisms."[34] In his 1935 *Coral Gardens and Their Magic*, Malinowski speaks of "reducing Durkheimian theory to the terms of Behavioristic psychology," and thus of "deriving of the meaning of words from bodily experience."[35]

Whatever its drawbacks, the strength of this position lies in its attempts to make meaning a matter of public inquiry, rather than an occult mental entity. The advantage of allowing us to speak about meaning by appealing to things we can observe is great. To return to an earlier example of a play like *Blithe Spirit*, Malinowski is saying that we could learn a great deal more from seeing how the play affected audiences in a certain context, rather than just by studying the play on its own, or even by asking about the intentions of its creator. After all, the play really touched deep places in people that perhaps no one could have predicted. Beyond its existence on the stage, *Blithe Spirit* took on a "life" of its own, to use a beloved word of Malinowski's. It was that "life of myth" which Malinowski wanted to highlight. Moreover, such an approach renders the data of the meaning of myths public and alive in a cultural setting; it makes myths open to dispute. We can raise questions about it, debate the matter with others, and reach consensus in these matters by intellec-

---

[32] More than that in fact. Malinowski is asserting that when we know what "1492 and all that" means in different contexts, we will know the truly significant meanings of the Christopher Columbus story.

[33] Malinowski says that a word is a "significant reaction" and a "definition" is a "sound-reaction." Malinowski, "The Problem of Meaning in Primitive Languages," p. 332.

[34] Bronislaw Malinowski, "Culture," *Encyclopedia of the Social Sciences*, vol. 4 (1931), p. 622.

[35] Malinowski, *Coral Gardens*, vol. 2, p. 236.

tual give and take. We can, under the conditions that Malinowski's approach favored, actually imagine progressing in our knowledge of myths.

Psychoanalysis and Anthropology: "Our" Hidden Mind Meets "Their" Cultural Data

The fourth and final matter recommending Malinowski's approach to myth has to do with his engagement with psychoanalysis.[36] Although he was not original in linking these two discourses,[37] Malinowski did make a serious effort to bridge the gaps separating different fields of inquiry. He might therefore provide an excellent model for readers tempted to similar aspirations.

Malinowski was by nature rigorously introspective. At about eighteen, he first took note of Freud and apparently always thought of himself as a kind of Freudian throughout his life.[38] As did Freud with dreams, Malinowski believed that myths provided access to the desires and beliefs of the mythmakers. And again like Freud, Malinowski held that sometimes what people wanted and believed lay at a great depth, beyond what they were usually aware of at a given moment. Whether this conviction antedated his acquaintance with Freudian psychoanalysis or not, we do not know. We do know that in the early 1920s, Malinowski engaged psychoanalytic literature in his own work, and in his life as well. What makes Malinowski's work interesting is that he dared to merge parts of his private introspective life with his public career as a student of culture. He felt both that anthropology had things to learn from psychoanalysis, and that psychoanalysis should pay heed to the lessons learned in the field from anthropology.

An example of this linking comes in his writings of the 1920s and 1930s. There Malinowski addressed some of the generalizations about universal human nature sponsored by Freud with the aim of showing what anthropology could teach psychoanalysis. Most notably Malinowski attempted to revise the Freudian theory of the universality of the Oedipus complex.[39] Freud's claims were culturally provincial, Malinowski thought, since they were at odds with ethnography. This was a serious charge, since psychoanalysis had ambitions to be a universal scientific method of psychological healing. As such, it needed to square its claims with data that reflected the whole range of human cultural situations. These data

---

[36] George W. Stocking, Jr., "Anthropology and the Science of the Irrational," *Malinowski, Rivers, Benedict and Others: Essays on Culture and Personality*, George W. Stocking, Jr., ed. (Madison: University of Wisconsin Press, 1986): 13–49. See also chapters three and four in this edition.

[37] Ibid., p. 31.

[38] Ibid.

[39] Ibid., pp. 13–49. See also chapters three and four in this edition.

are what the ethnographer could provide, and what should shape the generalizations they made about what it means to be human. But in Malinowski's eyes, Freud had either overlooked or not known about critical cases. In New Guinea, for example, the mother, not the father, was the figure of ferocity and power; likewise, castration desires were directed at the mother's brother, not the father.[40] Indeed, in many societies of this region, the father was thought to have no role in procreation at all, and thus young sons could not (oedipally) wish to replace their father as their mother's lover.

Whether or not Malinowski was finally right in his debate with Freud does not ultimately matter for our purposes.[41] What is worth pointing out with approval is Malinowski's intellectual ambition, his good sense in seeing that psychoanalysis needed to address itself to a broader range of material than once thought. In service to any budding human science claiming to speak for all humanity, Malinowski simply insisted that we should look at all sorts of data before claiming that our intuitions or culturally specific ideas are generally true for all.

As for the influence of psychoanalysis on anthropology, critics have argued two broad points. First, psychoanalysis convinced Malinowski that beyond the obvious surface of human life, another realm may exist with its own distinct rationality. This seems among the first, if not the very first, examples of a systematic embrace by anthropology of this part of psychoanalytic method. Second, Malinowski likewise seemed to accept that this hidden level of activity was the realm of our basically biological drives and instincts. For the study of myth, this appropriation of psychoanalytic notions meant that Malinowski would be encouraged to seek the hidden, unconscious functions which we discussed earlier. It also meant that when these unconscious levels were peeled back, as we noted earlier, we would see humanity grappling with its most elemental biological problems.

Whether cultural problems can be equated in the end with biological ones and whether they can be read from myths remains today a matter of some dispute. To the degree that Malinowski's analysis of myth confirms contemporary tendencies toward biological analyses in anthropology, one can find in Malinowski a real pioneer.[42]

[40] Bronislaw Malinowski, "Psychoanalysis and Anthropology," *Nature* 112 (1923): 650–51, reprinted in *Sex, Culture and Myth* (New York: Harcourt, Brace and World, 1962), pp. 114–15 (pp. 55–57 this volume).

[41] See Melford E. Spiro's defense of the oedipal interpretation of Trobriand incest proscriptions, *Oedipus in the Trobriands* (Chicago: University of Chicago Press, 1982).

[42] Here one might cite the cultural ecology movement identified often with the work of Marvin Harris. See Harris's complimentary words for Malinowski's concern with material needs in *The Rise of Anthropological Theory* (New York: Columbia University Press, 1968), pp. 548, 549–51.

Failing that identification, we should nonetheless take note of the methodological strategy of seeking "hidden" functions which Malinowski seemed to have borrowed from Freud. As an hermeneutic device, the Freudian claim about unconscious functions has had wide popularity in the human sciences. Carl Jung, Claude Lévi-Strauss, and Mircea Eliade are theorists who employ this interpretive strategy in the study of myth. Its popularity, however, has nothing to do with whether such an interpretive strategy should be recommended.

On the one side, it could be said that to claim the existence of "hidden" and unconscious determining levels beneath people's awareness is to deprive people of part of their humanity. If we assume that self-deception (and/or ignorance of self) is complete and total, we will have to reckon with a radical shift in our sense of what it is to be human—one with ramifications for our entire legal system. How can culprits be held responsible for criminal acts if they could plausibly argue at every turn that they were driven by unconscious forces within their personality? Self-deception and lack of introspective skills are common enough for us to take such things seriously, but to generalize these traits to all conduct and to the phenomenon of myth would itself be a dangerous self-deception. What kind of culture would it be if the functions of myth were totally opaque to all consciousness in the culture? Some members of a society will always tend to be more insightful than others, and thus provide better access to what may be happening than others. The entire phenomenon of informants requires this, as does the ethnographer's experience of meeting exceptional individuals who are conscious of what often passes by many of their fellows.

To assume with Malinowski that he occupies a privileged position in divining the secret unconscious functions of myths of another culture also raises the myth theorist to a superhuman level. People don't really know what is going on in their myths, but the doctor does! Again a dangerous half-truth lurks beneath such assumptions. A student of another culture, given sufficient time, resources, and intelligence will often be able to see more than the indigenous folk. This is simply because the anthropologist may amass more data than most folk. Malinowski might, for example, generalize better about the themes in Trobriand myths than a native Trobriander if Malinowski happened to know more myths than the Trobrianders—which he may well have because of his greater mobility around the islands and his diligence at recording myths. But this is not to say that Malinowski or any student of Trobriand myth would *necessarily* know more, and thus be in a position to speak with the authority he implicitly claims in his theory of myth. But in any case, both the anthropologist and the native Trobriander will have to prove that they know more! No facile claim to scientific objectivity on the part of the anthropologist will do, nor will self-serving claims about the privileged position of the Trobriander insider do either. Both sides will have to pass before the bar of evidence and proof. Position does not guarantee privilege in matters of knowledge.

Having warned against the excesses of psychoanalytic methods in anthropology, it would be well to give credit where it is due in Malinowski's theory of myth. At the very least, to posit something unconscious is often a useful hermeneutic device. There are such things, after all! Saying this begins the job of looking to see if such claims are true, and with the pursuit of hidden things many interesting matters may come to light. Has not our entire culture been enriched by psychoanalysis—even if it proves to be utterly untrue in any of its incarnations? We must simply remember to back up our claims, and resist "playing doctor." This in particular means that we need to stipulate in advance what would make us take back or modify our claims about unconscious things. Likewise, what would make the doctor reject or modify a diagnosis? If nothing, then the doctor has donned the robes of a priest or guru, and our health care has entered mysterious domains best left to those who care little for their own health. Although Malinowski has too often played "doctor knows best" with myth, we are richer despite his having done so.

The Plan of This Reader

This anthology arranges a selection of Malinowski's classic statements on myth into four major parts: one, the early ethnological work and the beginnings of functionalism; two, myth and psychoanalysis; three, classic functionalist account of myth; four, the subversive role of the functionalist interpretation of myth and culture.

These are all, one way or another, statements about what myth is, claims about how it should be studied, and reflections on what lessons for understanding human society and culture follow from Malinowski's thinking about myth. These selections from Malinowski's work span his entire career, and are arrayed in approximate chronological order. Readers will find here a remarkable continuity over the years, and at the same time subtle, though important, shifts in emphasis. Thus both persistence and development—or at least gradual emergence—are apparent in Malinowski's theory of myth. This collection accordingly traces his thinking about myth through some of his less well-known publications, never before anthologized, as well as through the widely read and cited classic statements for which Malinowski has become justly famous.

Part 1: Argonauts *and beyond*

The anthology beings with an excerpt from Malinowski's first major book, *Argonauts of the Western Pacific* (1922).[43] Contrary to what we have come to expect from Malinowski the scientist, we meet here someone of classically humanist temper, calling to mind Clifford Geertz.[44] The romantic spirit of *Argonauts* is neatly expressed in Malinowski's statement of his ambitions there:

> to grasp the native's point of view, his relation to life, to realize his vision of *his* world . . . We must study what concerns *him* most, ultimately, that is, the hold which life has on him.[45]

> I have tried to pave my account with fact and details . . . But at the same time, my conviction as expressed over and over again, is that what matters really is not the detail, not the fact, but the scientific use we make of it. Thus, the details and technicalities acquire their meaning in so far only as they express some central attitude of mind of the natives. . . .
>   What interests me really in the study of the native is his outlook on things, his *Weltanschauung*, the breath of life and reality which he breathes and by which he lives . . . a definite vision of the world, a definite zest of life.[46]

This selection also features some of the finest textual content analyses of myth in the entire Malinowski corpus as well as passing observations, reminiscent of Lévi-Strauss, that some myths can be treated as "variants" or "transformations"[47] of each other. But insofar as the treatment of myth goes here, Malinowski is eclectic and indecisive. Myths reassert "heroic" and natural values in a threatened native culture.[48] They celebrate "the glorious past,"[49] and "enliven" the land by giving meaning to certain locales.[50] Durkheim's influence can be seen here as well in Malinowski's assessment of myth in explicitly "sociological" terms.[51] The *lili'u* accord-

[43] Bronislaw Malinowski, "In Tewara and Sanaroa—Mythology of the Kula," *Argonauts*, pp. 290–330 (ch. 1 this volume).

[44] I have in mind here Clifford Geertz's " 'From the Native's Point of View': On the Nature of Anthropological Understanding," *Local Knowledge*, C. Geertz, ed. (New York: Harper, 1983), pp. 55–72. On Malinowski's 'romanticism' see Strenski, "Malinowski: Second Positivism, Second Romanticism," 766–71; Ivan Strenski, *Four Theories of Myth in Twentieth-Century History* (London and Iowa City: Macmillan and Iowa University Press, 1987), pp. 42–69. Jan Jerschina, "Polish Culture of Modernism and Malinowski's Personality," *Malinowski between Two Worlds*, pp. 132–36, 138–39.

[45] Malinowski, *Argonauts*, p. 25.

[46] Ibid., p. 517.

[47] Ibid., pp. 326 (p. 33 this volume), 333.

[48] Ibid., pp. 297, 319 (pp. 9, 27 this volume).

[49] Ibid., p. 301 (p. 12 this volume).

[50] Ibid., p. 298 (p. 10 this volume).

[51] Ibid., p. 326 (p. 33 this volume).

ingly are defined as socially important stories; they bear "an enormous social weight,"[52] or work an immense "normative influence."[53] Indeed, as Durkheim would have it, these myths/*lili'u* are essentially religious: they are "deeply believed" and "held in reverence."[54] Malinowski's approach to myth in *Argonauts* also can be said to be functionalist in the Durkheimian sense of the word—myth is a functioning part of a social totality.[55]

The trajectory of Malinowski's thought then publicly takes (or resumes) a path toward an increasingly pragmatic, material, and even biological conception of the nature of myth and culture at large. This emerges first in a remarkable programmatic essay, "Ethnology and the Study of Society,"[56] here reprinted and anthologized for the first time. This was Malinowski's first extended argument on behalf of his "practical anthropology,"[57] the main lines of which have been sketched above. This was also part of a program placing anthropology at the disposal of colonial administrations, while also seeking to protect the native populations against European intrusions. Malinowski argued that successful colonial management rests on scientific knowledge of native cultures—which only a "scientific" anthropology such as his now biologically based pragmatic functionalism could offer:

> When therefore the legislator and administrator, in a burst of uncalled-for reformatory zeal, further prune and uproot much of the native's tree of life— is there no urgent need to stop and think? To invoke the advice of dispassionate study and scientific expert opinion?[58]

Part 2: Psychoanalysis and Societies

The two pieces included here date from about 1923 or so,[59] and were later published in a complete work devoted to psychological themes, *Sex*

---

[52] Ibid., p. 327 (p. 34 this volume).

[53] Ibid., p. 328 (pp. 34–35 this volume) parallels E. Durkheim, *Elementary Forms of the Religious Life* (Glencoe: Free Press, 1963), p. 102.

[54] Ibid., p. 299 (p. 11 this volume) parallels Durkheim, *Elementary Forms of the Religious Life*, p. 101.

[55] K. Symmons-Symonolewicz, "Bronislaw Malinowski: Formative Influences and Theoretical Evolution," *The Polish Review* 4 (1959): 40; and R. Firth, "Introduction: Malinowski as Scientist and as Man," *Man and Culture: An Evaluation of the Work of Bronislaw Malinowski*, R. Firth, ed. (London: Routledge and Kegan Paul, 1957), pp. 1–14.

[56] Bronislaw Malinowski, "Ethnology and the Study of Society," *Economica* 2 (1921): 208–19 (ch. 2 this volume).

[57] Ibid. This is followed by two pieces in *Africa*, "Practical Anthropology," 2 (1929): 22–38 and "The Rationalization of Anthropology and Administration," 3 (1930): 405–29.

[58] Malinowski, "Ethnology and the Study of Society," 214 (p. 47 this volume).

[59] Stocking, "Anthropology and the Science of the Irrational," pp. 13–49.

and Represssion in Savage Society (1927).[60] As we have seen, Malinowski's gradual interest in psychoanalysis came out of growing conviction of the importance of instinctual and unconscious determinants of human behavior.[61] These are well reflected in the themes and language of these selections. Here in "Psychoanalysis and Anthropology,"[62] Malinowski explicitly salutes Freud for having "given us the first concrete theory about the relation between instinctive life and social institutions," not to mention the "doctrine of repression." "Obscenity and Myth" shows Malinowski at work with his newly found interests in an anthropology enlivened by psychoanalysis. Myths tip us off to the deep repressed desires of the people telling them—just as Freud urged that insulting, abusive, or obscene language did. Part of the repressed psychological material in the myths Malinowski discusses here is the role of women and matriarchy in origin stories. "Obscenity and Myth" is an especially useful text for seeing how Malinowski bridged gaps in his rapidly evolving work. Readers may find instructive Malinowski's ample references to his earlier work on myths in *Argonauts* and his then most recent discussion of myth, "Myth in Primitive Psychology."

Part 3: Myth in Primitive Psychology

Taken together with Malinowski's fieldwork expertise, his psychoanalytic interests culminated in his classic functionalist statement on myth of 1926, "Myth in Primitive Psychology."[63] There, Malinowski boasted of his years in the field, observing the ways myth acts in a context as a "hard-worked active force . . . a pragmatic charter of primitive culture."[64]

In "Myth in Primitive Psychology" one may also recognize other elements retained from *Argonauts*: In both, myth is a "lived reality,"[65] has "sociological" functions,[66] and acts as a warrant for certain institutions. Once again, Malinowski identifies the Trobriand *lili'u* with our term

---

[60] Bronislaw Malinowski, *Sex and Repression in Savage Society* (London: Routledge and Kegan Paul, 1927).

[61] Malinowski, "Psychoanalysis and Anthropology," in *Sex, Culture and Myth*, pp. 114–16 (pp. 55–57 this volume), and "Obscenity and Myth," *Sex and Repression in Savage Society* (London: Routledge and Kegan Paul, 1927), pp. 104–34 (pp. 58–73 this volume).

[62] Stocking, "Anthropology and the Science of the Irrational," pp. 13–49.

[63] Malinowski, "Myth in Primitive Psychology." Some of the historical survey of theories of myth in "Myth in Primitive Psychology" is supplemented by "Myth as a Dramatic Development of Dogma" (n.d.), *Sex, Culture and Myth* (New York: Harcourt, Brace and World, 1962), pp. 245–65 (pp. 117–27 this volume).

[64] Malinowski, "Myth in Primitive Psychology," p. 101 (p. 82 this volume).

[65] Ibid., pp. 100, 101 (pp. 81, 82 this volume).

[66] Ibid., p. 106 (p. 86 this volume).

"myth." But, in these cases Malinowski does not merely repeat previous positions. When Malinowski speaks of "life" in this new work, he not only means something robust and romantic, as he meant in *Argonauts*, he also wants to convey the materialist, utilitarian, and emotionalist message that myth is a "hard-worked active force," covering the "whole pragmatic reaction of man towards disease and death" and expressing "his emotions, his forebodings."[67] Myth, like language, is an action which cannot be understood outside its "context of situation"—"the context of living faith . . . social organization . . . morals . . . and customs."[68] And even linking this notion of context to the biological level of organic being (as he does in *Coral Gardens*) we hear that myth is "born from the innermost and emotional reaction to the most formidable and haunting idea"—death.[69]

Similarly, when Malinowski speaks of the "sociological function" of myth, he now runs together Durkheim's idea of the causal potential of an element of culture, like myth, with the concept of "need," which Durkheim (and the Malinowski of *Argonauts*) had kept distinct. Myth is now "indispensable" and "vital"[70]—something a society needs, and without which it cannot persist. Tradition here takes a special role in this indispensable job which myth performs for culture:

> Myth . . . expresses, enhances and codifies belief; it safeguards and enforces morality; it vouches for the efficiency of ritual and contains practical rules for the guidance of men. . . . a pragmatic charter of primitive faith and moral wisdom.[71]

Part 4: Religion and Myth in Modern Times

"Myth as a Dramatic Development of Dogma" (n.d.), provides a transition from Malinowski's assertion of supremacy in theorizing about myth in "Myth in Primitive Psychology" (1926) to the pronouncements typical of the public intellectual which emerge in our final selection, "The Foundations of Faith and Morals." In this undated piece, addressed to an audience of Christians, Malinowski reviews the history of the study of myth, amplifying what he wrote in this vein in "Myth in Primitive Psychology." But to the usual analysis of "primitive" materials, he adds examples from present-day Christianity. These examples suggest, as already adumbrated in the conclusion to "Myth in Primitive Psychology," that Malinowski's analysis of myth and religion was meant to apply to

---

[67] Ibid., p. 132 (p. 105 this volume).
[68] Ibid., pp. 100–101 (p. 82 this volume).
[69] Ibid., p. 110 (p. 89 this volume).
[70] Ibid., p. 101 (p. 82 this volume).
[71] Ibid (p. 82 this volume).

us—especially to modern Christianity—as well as to the "primitive" "them." Accordingly, this later period in Malinowski's career also saw him writing about contemporary public policy issues, such as freedom, civilization, war, aggression, and world federalism.[72]

Malinowski propagandized intensely on the basis of his success in the mid-1920s, and soon took aim at various targets on the cultural scene. Turning to the public political domain Malinowski not only reviewed the main lines of his classic statements about myth but, in his Riddell lectures of 1936, "The Foundations of Faith and Morals,"[73] extended them to the "modern savagery" of the totalitarian ideologies poised for battle in the years just prior to World War II.

Although Malinowski sought to undermine all religions—not just the modern political ones—he did so ambiguously and under an ironic cover. He refers in his conclusion to the "Pathology of Religion." Religion holds society together in time of disintegration, and so from Malinowski's viewpoint is good. Yet it does so on the bases of mythical beliefs and magical rituals, which a self-admitted agnostic, like Malinowski, could not accept as cognitively sound. "Myths" were latter-day "noble lies," but ones without which common folk would be unable to cope with the final meaninglessness of human existence. Thus although myths are functionally or pragmatically useful in stilling human fears—mere biological palliatives— they are utterly without basis in reality. Myths act in this unconscious and direct way, speaking subrationally to our deepest instincts for survival, fueled by our will to believe. Myths are literally untrue, but they nevertheless perform essential cultural tasks in chartering all sorts of human institutions and practices. In the end, they work to insure human biological integrity by contributing to cultural stability.

[72] Bronislaw Malinowski, *Freedom and Civilization* (New York: Roy, 1944); "The Deadly Issue," *Atlantic Monthly* 158 (1936): 659–69, "An Anthropological Analysis of War," *American Journal of Sociology* 46 (1941): 521–50.

[73] Malinowski, "The Foundations of Faith and Morals," pp. 295–336 (pp. 131–72 this volume).

PART ONE

ARGONAUTS AND BEYOND

1

IN TEWARA AND SANAROA—

MYTHOLOGY OF THE KULA

I

AT DAYBREAK the party leave the Amphletts. This is the stage when the parting gifts, the *talo'i* are given. The clay pots, the several kinds of produce of the islands and of the Koya, which had been laid aside the previous day, are now brought to the canoes. Neither the giver nor the main receiver, the *toliwaga*, take much notice of the proceedings, great nonchalance about give and take being the correct attitude prescribed by good manners. Children bring the objects, and the junior members of the crew stow them away. The general behaviour of the crowds, ashore and in the canoes, is as unostentatious at this moment of parting as it was at the arrival. No more farewells than greetings are spoken or shouted, nor are there any visible or formal signs of grief, or of hope of meeting again, or of any other emotions. The busy, self-absorbed crews push off stolidly, step the mast, set sail, and glide away.

They now approach the broad front of Koyatabu, which with a favourable wind, they might reach within two hours or so. They probably sail near enough to get a clear view of the big trees standing on the edge of the jungle, and of the long waterfall dividing the mountain's flank right down the middle; of the triangular patches under cultivation, covered with the vine of yams and big leaves of taro. They could also perceive here and there smoke curling out of the jungle where, hidden under the trees, there lies a village, composed of a few miserable huts. Nowadays these villages have come down to the water's edge, in order to supplement their garden yield with fish. In olden days they were all high up on the slope, and their huts hardly ever visible from the sea.

The inhabitants of these small and ramshackle villages are shy and timid, though in olden days they would have been dangerous to the Trobrianders. They speak a language which differs from that of Dobu and is usually called by the natives 'the Basima talk.' There seem to be about four or five various languages on the island of Fergusson, besides that of Dobu. My acquaintance with the Basima natives is very small, due only to two forced landings in their district. They struck me as being physically of a different type from the Dobuans, though this is only an impression. They have got no boats, and do the little sailing they require on small rafts of three or five logs tied together. Their houses are smaller and less well-made than those in Dobu. Further investigation of these natives would be very interesting, and probably also very difficult, as is always the case when studying very small communities, living at the same time right out of touch with any white man.

This land must remain, for the present anyhow, veiled for ourselves, as it also is for the Trobriand natives. For these, indeed, the few attempts which they occasionally made to come into contact with these natives, and the few mishaps which brought them to their shores, were all far from encouraging in results, and only strengthened the traditional superstitious fear of them. Several generations ago, a canoe or two from Burakwa, in the island of Kayeula, made an exploring trip to the district of Gabu, lying in a wide bay under the North-West flank of Koyatabu. The natives of Gabu, receiving them at first with a show of interest, and pretending to enter into commercial relations, afterwards fell on them treacherously and slew the chief Toraya and all his companions. This story has become famous, and indeed one of the outstanding historical events of the Trobriands, because Tomakam, the slain chief's younger brother, went to the Koya of Gabu, and killed the head man of one of the villages, avenging thus his brother's death. He then composed a song and a dance which is performed to this day in Kiriwina, and has indeed one of the finest melodies in the islands.

This is the verbatim account of the story as it was told to me by To'uluwa himself, the chief of Omarakana, who at present 'owns' this Gumagabu dance, his ancestors having acquired it from the descendants of Tomakam by a *laga* payment.* It is a commentary to the song, and begins only with the avenging expedition of Tomakam, which is also the theme of the song.

The Story of Gumagabu

"Tomakam got a new *waga*. He blew the conch shell and went to the Koya. He spoke to his mother" (that is, before leaving), " 'My mother, you remain, I shall sail. One conch shell you hear, it will be a conch shell of a necklace.' " (That is, it will be a sign that he has been successful in getting a good Kula necklace). " 'The second conch shell will be the conch shell of the dead man; the sign that I have already carried out my revenge. I shall sail, I shall anchor, I shall sleep. The second day I shall sail, I shall anchor, I shall sleep. The third day I shall anchor in a village, having already arrived in the Mountain. The fourth day I shall give *pari*, the *Kinana* (the Southern foreigner) will come, I shall hit him. The fifth day I shall return. I shall sail fast, till

* See Chapter VI, Division VI.

night grows on the sea. The next day I shall anchor at Burakwa. You hear the conch shell, you sleep in the house, arise. One blow you hear of the shell—the blow of the *bagi* (necklace). Two blows you hear, the blow of the dead man! Then the men of Burakwa will say: 'Two conch shells, two necklaces,' then, you come out of the house, you speak: 'Men of Burakwa, from one side of the village and from the other; indeed you mocked my son, Tomakam. Your speech was—go, carry out thy vendetta in Gabu. The first conch shell is that of the necklace, the second conch shell is that of the dead man. I have spoken!' " (Here ends the speech of Tomakam to his mother.)

"He anchored in the village in the Koya. He told his younger brother: 'Go, tell the *Kinana* men these words: Your friend has a sore leg, well, if we together go to the canoe he will give the *pari!*' The younger brother went and spoke those words to the head-man of the *Kinana*: 'Some green coco-nuts, some betel-nut, some pig, bring this to us and we shall give you *pari*. Your arm-shells, your big stone blade, your boar's tusk, your whale-bone spatula await you in the canoe. The message for you is that your friend has a sore leg and cannot walk.' Says the *Kinana* man: 'Well, let us go!' "

"He caught a pig, he collected betel-nut, sugar cane, bananas, necklaces, betel-pod, he said: 'Well, let us go together to the canoe.' *Pu'u* he gives the necklace; *pu'u*, the pig; then he gave the coco-nut, the betel-nut, the sugar cane, the bananas. Tomakam lay on one side; his leg he wrapped up in a white, soft pandanus mat. Before he had spoken to his younger brother": (i.e., he gave him this instruction also, when he sent him to meet the people of Gabu): " 'You all come with the *Kinana* man. Do not remain in the village.' Then" (after the first gifts were exchanged) "the *Kinana* man stood up in the canoe. His betel-pod fell down. Spoke Tomakam, addressing the *Kinana* man: 'My friend, pick up the betel-pod. It fell and went down into the canoe.' The *Kinana* man bent down, he took the betel-pod. Tomakam saw that the *Kinana* bent down, he took an axe, and sitting he made a stroke at him. He cut off his neck. Then Tomakam took the head, threw the body into the sea. The head he stuck on a stick of his canoe. They sailed, they arrived in their village. He caught a pig, prepared a taro pudding, cut sugar cane, they had a big feast, he invented this song."

Such was the story told me by the chief of Omarakana about the song and dance of Gumagabu, which at that time they were singing and performing in his village. I have adduced it in full, in an almost literal translation from the native text, in order to show it side by side with the song. The narrative thus reproduced shows characteristic gaps, and it does not cover even the incidents of the song.

The following is a free translation of the song, which, in its original native text, is very condensed and impressionistic. A word or two indicates rather than describes whole scenes and incidents, and the tradi-

tional commentary, handed on in a native community side by side with
the song, is necessary for a full understanding.

The Gumabagu Song

I

The stranger of Gumagabu sits on the top of the mountain.
'Go on top of the mountain, the towering mountain. . . .'
——They cry for Toraya. . . . .——
The stranger of Gumagabu sits on the slope of the mountain.
——The fringe of small clouds lifts above Boyowa;
The mother cries for Toraya——
'I shall take my revenge.'
The mother cries for Toraya.

II

Our mother, Dibwaruna, dreams on the mat.
She dreams about the killing.
'Revenge the wailing;
Anchor; hit the Gabu strangers!'
——The stranger comes out;
The chief gives him the *pari*;
'I shall give you the *doga*;
Bring me things from the mountain to the canoe!'

III

We exchange our *vaygu'a*;
The rumour of my arrival spreads through the Koya
We talk and talk.
He bends and is killed.
His companions run away;
His body is thrown into the sea;
The companions of the *Kinana* run away,
We sail home.

IV

Next day, the sea foams up,
The chief's canoe stops on the reef;
The storm approaches;
The chief is afraid of drowning.
The conch shell is blown:
It sounds in the mountain.
They all weep on the reef.

V

They paddle in the chief's canoe;
They circle round the point of Bewara.
'I have hung my basket.
I have met him.'
So cries the chief,
So cries repeatedly the chief.

VI

Women in festive decoration
Walk on the beach.
Nawaruva puts on her turtle rings;
She puts on her *luluga'u* skirt.
In the village of my fathers, in Burakwa.
There is plenty of food;
Plenty is brought in for distribution.

The character of this song is extremely elliptic, one might even say futuristic, since several scenes are crowded simultaneously into the picture. In the first strophe we see the *Kinana*, by which word all the tribesmen from the d'Entrecasteaux Archipelago are designated in Boyowa, on the top of his Mountain in Gabu. Immediately afterwards, we are informed of the intentions of Tomakam to ascend the mountain, while the women cry for Toraya, for the slain chief—probably his kinswomen and widows. The next picture again spans over the wide seas, and on the one shore we see the Gabuan sitting on the slopes of his hill and far away on the other, under the fringe of small clouds lifting above Boyowa, the mother cries for her son, the murdered chief. Tomakam takes a resolve, 'I shall take my revenge,' hearing her cry.

In the second strophe, the mother dreams about the expedition; the words about revenge to be taken on the Gabu men and the directions to anchor and hit him are probably taken from her dream. Then suddenly we are transported right across to the mountain, the expedition having arrived there already. The strangers, the *Kinana* are coming down to the canoe, and we assist at the words spoken between them and the people at Burakwa.

Then in the third strophe, we arrive at the culminating scene of the drama; even here, however, the hero, who is also his own bard, could not help introducing a few boastful words about his renown resounding in the Koya. In a few words the tragedy is described: the *Kinana* bends down, is killed, and his body is thrown into the water. About his head we hear nothing in this verse.

In the next one, a storm overtakes the returning party. Signals of distress are re-echoed by the mountain, and like Homeric heroes, our party are not ashamed to weep in fear and anguish. Somehow they escape, however, and in the next verse, they are already near their village and Tomakam, their leader, bursts into a pæan of triumph. It is not quite clear what the allusion to the basket means, whether he keeps there his Kula trophies or the slain enemy's head; this latter, in contradiction to what we heard in the prose story of its being impaled. The song ends with a description of a feast. The woman mentioned there is Tomakam's daughter, who puts on festive attire in order to welcome her father.

Comparing now the song with the story, we see that they do not quite tally. In the story, there is the dramatic interest of the mother's intervention. We gather from it that Tomakam, goaded by the aspersions of his fellow-villagers, wishes to make his return as effective as possible. He arranges the signals of the two conch shell blasts with his mother, and asks her to harangue the people at the moment of his return. All this finds no expression in the song. The ruse of the chief's sore leg is also omitted from there, which, however, does not mean that the hero was ashamed of it. On the other hand, the storm described in the song is omitted from the story, and there is a discrepancy about the head of the Gabu man, and we do not know whether it really is conveyed in a basket as the song has it or impaled, as the store relates!

I have adduced in detail the story and the song, because they are a good illustration of the native's attitude towards the dangers, and towards the heroic romance of the Koya. They are also interesting as documents, showing which salient points would strike the natives' imagination in such a dramatic occurrence. Both in the story and in the song, we find emphasised the motives of social duty, of satisfied self-regard and ambition; again, the dangers on the reef, the subterfuge in killing, finally the festivities on return home. Much that would interest us in the whole story is omitted, as anyone can see for himself.

Other stories, though not made illustrious through being set into a song, are told about the Koya. I met myself an old man in the island of Vakuta, who, as a boy, had been captured with a whole party by a village community of Dobu-speaking people on Normanby Island. The men and another small boy of the party were killed and eaten, but some women took pity on him, and he was spared, to be brought up amongst them. There is another man, either alive or recently dead in Kavataria, who had a similar experience in Fergusson Island. Another man called Kaypoyla, from the small island of Kuyawa in the Western Trobriands, was stranded with his crew somewhere in the West of Fergusson Island, but not in the district where they used to trade. His companions were killed and eaten. He was taken alive and kept to fatten for a proximate feast. His host, or rather the host of the feast in which he was going to furnish the *pièce de résistance*, was away inland, to invite the guests, while the host's wife went for a moment behind the house, sweeping the ground. Kaypoyla jumped up and ran to the shore. Being chased by some other men from the settlement, he concealed himself in the branches of a big tree standing on the beach, and was not found by his pursuers. At night he came down, took a canoe or a raft, and paddled along the coast. He used to sleep on shore during the night, and paddle on in day time. One night he slept among some sago-palms, and, awakening in the morning, found himself, to his terror, surrounded by *Kinana* men. What was his joyful surprise after all, when he recognised among them his friend and Kula partner, with whom he always used to trade! After some time, he was sent back home in his partner's canoe.

Many such stories have a wide currency, and they supply one of the heroic elements in tribal life, an element which now, with the establishment of white man's influence, has vanished. Yet even now the gloomy shores which our party are leaving to the right, the tall jungle, the deep valleys, the hill-tops darkened with trailing clouds, all this is a dim mysterious background, adding to the awe and solemnity of the Kula, though not entering into it. The sphere of activities of our traders lies at the foot of the high mountains, there, where a chain of rocks and islands lies scattered along the coast. Some of them are passed immediately after leaving Gumasila. Then, after a good distance, a small rock, called Gurewaya, is met, remarkable for the taboos associated with it. Close behind it, two islands, Tewara and Uwama, are separated by a narrow passage, the mythical straits of Kadimwatu. There is a village on the first-mentioned, and the natives of this make gardens on both islands. The village is not very big; it may have some sixty to eighty inhabitants, as it can man three canoes for the Kula. It has no commercial or industrial importance, but is notable because of its mythological associations. This island is the home of the mythological hero, Kasabwaybwayreta, whose story is one of the most important legends of the Kula. Here indeed, in Tewara, we are right within the mythological heart of the Kula. In fact, we entered its legendary area with the moment the Sinaketan fleet sailed out of the Lagoon into the deep waters of Pilolu.

II

Once more we must pause, this time in an attempt to grasp the natives' mental attitude towards the mythological aspect of the Kula. Right through this account it has been our constant endeavour to realise the vision of the world, as it is reflected in the minds of the natives. The frequent references to the scenery have not been given only to enliven the narrative, or even to enable the reader to visualise the setting of the native customs. I have attempted to show how the scene of his actions appears actually to the native, to describe his impressions and feelings with regard to it, as I was able to read them in his folk-lore, in his conversations at home, and in his behaviour when passing through this scenery itself.

Here we must try to reconstruct the influence of myth upon this vast landscape, as it colours it, gives it meaning, and transforms it into something live and familiar. What was a mere rock, now becomes a personality; what was a speck on the horizon becomes a beacon, hallowed by romantic associations with heroes; a meaningless configuration of landscape acquires a significance, obscure no doubt, but full of intense emotion. Sailing with natives, especially with novices to the Kula, I often observed how deep was their interest in sections of landscape impregnated with legendary meaning, how the elder ones would point and explain, the younger would gaze and wonder, while the talk was full of mythological names. It is the addition of the human interest to the natural features, possessing in themselves less power of appealing to a native man than to us, which makes the difference for him in looking at the scenery. A stone hurled by one of the heroes into the sea after an escaping canoe; a sea passage broken between two islands by a magical canoe; here two people turned into rock; there a petrified *waga*—all this makes the landscape represent a continuous story or else the culminating dramatic incident of a familiar legend. This power of transforming the landscape, the visible environment, is one only of the many influences which myth exercises upon the general outlook of the natives. Although here we are studying myth only in its connection with the Kula, even within these narrow limits some of its broader connections will be apparent, notably its influence upon sociology, magic and ceremonial.

The question which presents itself first, in trying to grasp the native outlook on the subject is: what is myth to the natives? How do they conceive and define it? Have they any line of demarcation between the mythical and the actual reality, and if so, how do they draw this line?

Their folk-lore, that is, the verbal tradition, the store of tales, legends, and texts handed on by previous generations, is composed of the following classes: first of all, there is what the natives call *libogwo*, 'old talk,' but which we would call tradition; secondly, *kukwanebu*, fairy tales, recited for amusement, at definite seasons, and relating avowedly untrue events; thirdly, *wosi*, the various songs, and *vinavina*, ditties, chanted at play or under other special circumstances; and last, not least, *megwa* or *yopa*, the magical spells. All these classes are strictly distinguished from one another by name, function, social setting, and by certain formal characteristics. This brief outline of the Boyowan folk-lore in general must suffice here, as we cannot enter into more details, and the only class which interests us in the present connection is the first one, that called *libogwo*.

This, the 'old talk,' the body of ancient tradition, believed to be true, consists on the one hand of historical tales, such as the deeds of past chiefs, exploits in the Koya, stories of shipwreck, etc. On the other hand, the *libogwo* class also contains what the natives call *lili'u*—myths, narratives, deeply believed by them, held by them in reverence, and exercising an active influence on their conduct and tribal life. Now the natives distinguish definitely between myth and historic account, but this distinction is difficult to formulate, and cannot be stated but in a somewhat deliberate manner.

First of all, it must be borne in mind, that a native would not trouble spontaneously to analyse such distinctions and to put them into words. If an Ethnographer succeeded in making the problem clear to an intelligent informant (and I have tried and succeeded in doing this) the native would simply state:

"We all know that the stories about Tudava, about Kudayuri, about Tokosikuna, are *lili'u*; our fathers, our *kadada* (our maternal uncles) told us so; and we always hear these tales; we know them well; we know that there are no other tales besides them, which are *lili'u*. Thus, whenever we hear a story, we know whether it is a *lili'u* or not."

Indeed, whenever a story is told, any native, even a boy, would be able to say whether this is one of his tribal *lili'u* or not. For the other tales, that is the historical ones, they have no special word, but they would describe the events as happening among 'humans like ourselves.' Thus tradition, from which the store of tales is received, hands them on labelled as *lili'u*, and the definition of a *lili'u*, is that it is a story transmitted with such a label. And even this definition is contained by the facts themselves, and not explicitly stated by the natives in their current stock of expressions.

For us, however, even this is not sufficient, and we have to search further, in order to see whether we cannot find other indices, other characteristic features which differentiate the world of mythical events from that of real ones. A reflection which would naturally present itself would be this: "Surely the natives place their myths in ancient, pre-historic times, while they put historical events into recent ages?" There is some truth in this, in so far as most of the historical events related by the natives are quite recent, have occurred within the community where they are told and can be directly connected with people and conditions existing at present, by memory of living man, by genealogies or other records.

On the other hand, when historical events are told from other districts, and cannot be directly linked with the present, it would be erroneous to imagine that the natives place them into a definite compartment of time different from that of the myth. For it must be realised that these natives do not conceive of a past as of a lengthy duration, unrolling itself in successive stages of time. They have no idea of a long vista of historical occurrences, narrowing down and dimming as they recede towards a distant background of legend and myth, which stands out as something entirely different from the nearer planes. This view, so characteristic of the naive, historical thinking among ourselves, is entirely foreign to the natives. Whenever they speak of some event of the past, they distinguish whether it happened within their own memory or that of their fathers' or not. But, once beyond this line of demarcation, all the past events are placed by them on one plane, and there are no gradations of 'long ago' and 'very long ago.' Any idea of epochs in time is absent from their mind; the past is one vast storehouse of events, and the line of demarcation between myth and history does not coincide with any division into definite and distinct periods of time. Indeed, I have found very often that when they told me some story of the past, for me obviously mythological, they would deem it necessary to emphasise that this did not happen in their fathers' time or in their grand-fathers' time, but long ago, and that it is a *lili'u*.

Again, they have no idea of what could be called the evolution of the world or the evolution of society; that is, they do not look back towards a series of successive changes, which happened in nature or in humanity, as we do. We, in our religious and scientific outlook alike, know that earth ages and that humanity ages, and we think of both in these terms; for them, both are eternally the same, eternally youthful. Thus, in judging the remoteness of traditional events, they cannot use the co-ordinates of a social setting constantly in change and divided into epochs. To give a concrete example, in the myths of Torosipupu and Tolikalaki, we saw them having the same interest and concerns, engaged in the same type of fishing, using the same means of locomotion as the present natives do. The mythical personages of the natives' legends, as we shall presently see, live in the same houses, eat the same food, handle the same weapons and implements as those in use at present. Whereas in any of our historical stories, legends or myths, we have a whole set of changed cultural conditions, which allow us to co-ordinate any event with a certain epoch, and which make us feel that a distant historical event, and still more, a mythological one, is happening in a setting of cultural conditions entirely different from those in which we are living now. In the very telling of the stories of, let us say, Joan of Arc, Solomon, Achilles, King Arthur, we have to mention all sorts of things and conditions long since disappeared from among us, which make even a superficial and an uneducated listener realise that it is a story of a remote and different past.

I have said just now that the mythical personages in the Trobriand tradition are living the same type of life, under the same social and cultural conditions as the present natives. This needs one qualification, and in this we shall find a very remarkable criterion for a distinction between what is legendary and what is historical: in the mythical world, although surrounding conditions were similar, all sorts of events happened which do not happen nowadays, and people were endowed with powers such as present men and their historical ancestors do not possess. In mythical times, human beings come out of the ground, they change into animals, and these become people again; men and women rejuvenate and slough their skins; flying canoes speed through the air, and things are transformed into stone.

Now this line of demarcation between the world of myth and that of actual reality—the simple difference that in the former things happen which never occur nowadays—is undoubtedly felt and realised by the natives, though they themselves could not put it into words. They know quite well that to-day no one emerges from underground; that people do not change into animals, and *vice versa*; nor do they give birth to them; that present-day canoes do not fly. I had the opportunity of grasping their mental attitude towards such things by the following occurrence. The Fijian missionary teacher in Omarakana was telling them about white man's flying machines. They inquired from me, whether this was true, and when I corroborated the Fijian's report and showed them pictures of aeroplanes in an illustrated paper, they asked me whether this happened nowadays or whether it were a *lili'u*. This circumstance made it clear to me then, that the natives would have a tendency, when meeting with an extraordinary and to them supernatural event, either to discard it as untrue, or relegate it into the regions of the *lili'u*. This does not mean, however, that the untrue and the mythical are the same or even similar to them. Certain stories told to them, they insist on treating as *sasopa* (lies), and maintain that they are not *lili'u*. For instance, those opposed to missionary teaching will not accept the view that Biblical stories told to them are a *lili'u*, but they reject them as *sasopa*. Many a time did I hear such a conservative native arguing thus:—

"Our stories about Tudava are true; this is a *lilu'u*. If you go to Laba'i you can see the cave in which Tudava was born, you can see the beach where he played as a boy. You can see his footmark in a stone at a place in the Raybwag. But where are the traces of Yesu Keriso? Who ever saw any signs of the tales told by the misinari? Indeed they are not *lili'u*."

To sum up, the distinction between the *lili'u* and actual or historical reality is drawn firmly, and there is a definite cleavage between the two. *Prima facie*, this distinction is based on the fact that all myth is labelled as such and known to be such to all natives. A further distinctive mark of the world of *lili'u* lies in the super-normal, supernatural character of certain events which happen in it. The supernatural is believed to be true, and this truth is sanctioned by tradition, and by the various signs and traces left behind by mythical events, more especially by the magical powers handed on by the ancestors who lived in times of *lili'u*. This magical inheritance is no doubt the most palpable link between the present and the mythical past. But this past must not be imagined to form a prehistoric, very distant background, something which preceded a long evolution of mankind. It is rather the past, but extremely near reality, very much alive and true to the natives.

As I have just said, there is one point on which the cleavage between myth and present reality, however deep, is bridged over in native ideas. The extraordinary powers which men possess in myths are mostly due to their knowledge of magic. This knowledge is, in many cases, lost, and therefore the powers of doing these marvellous things are either completely gone, or else considerably reduced. If the magic could be recovered, men would fly again in their canoes, they could rejuvenate, defy ogres, and perform the many heroic deeds which they did in ancient times. Thus, magic, and the powers conferred by it, are really the link between mythical tradition and the present day. Myth has crystallised into magical formulæ, and magic in its turn bears testimony to the authenticity of myth. Often the main function of myth is to serve as a foundation for a system of magic, and, wherever magic forms the backbone of an institution, a myth is also to be found at the base of it. In this perhaps, lies the greatest sociological importance of myth, that is, in its action upon institutions through the associated magic. The sociological point of view and the idea of the natives coincide here in a remarkable manner. In this book we see this exemplified in one concrete case, in that of the relation between the mythology, the magic, and the social institution of the Kula.

Thus we can define myth as a narrative of events which are to the native supernatural, in this sense, that he knows well that to-day they do not happen. At the same time he believes deeply that they did happen then. The socially sanctioned narratives of these events; the traces which they left on the surface of the earth; the magic in which they left behind part of their supernatural powers, the social institutions which are associated with the practice of this magic—all this brings about the fact that a myth is for the native a living actuality, though it has happened long ago and in an order of things when people were endowed with supernatural powers.

I have said before that the natives do not possess any historical perspective, that they do not range events—except of course, those of the most recent decades—into any successive stages. They also do not classify their myths into any divisions with regard to their antiquity. But in looking at their myths, it becomes at once obvious that they represent events, some of which must have happened prior to others. For there is a group of stories describing the origin of humanity, the emerging of the various social units from underground. Another group of mythical tales gives accounts of how certain important institutions were introduced and how certain customs crystallised. Again, there are myths referring to small changes in culture, or to the introduction of new details and minor customs. Broadly speaking, the mythical folk-lore of the Trobrianders can be divided into three groups referring to three different strata of events. In order to give a general idea of Trobriand mythology, it will be good to give a short characterisation of each of these groups.

1. *The Oldest Myths*, referring to the origin of human beings; to the sociology of the sub-clans and villages; to the establishment of permanent relations between this world and the next. These myths describe events which took place just at the moment when the earth began to be peopled from underneath. Humanity existed, somewhere underground, since people emerged from there on the surface of Boyowa, in full decoration, equipped with magic, belonging to social divisions, and obeying definite laws and customs. But beyond this we know nothing about what they did underground. There is, however, a series of myths, of which one is attached to every one of the more important sub-clans, about various ancestors coming out of the ground, and almost at once, doing some important deed, which gives a definite character to the sub-clan. Certain mythological versions about the nether world belong also to this series.

2. *Kultur myths.*—Here belong stories about ogres and their conquerors; about human beings who established definite customs and cultural features; about the origin of certain institutions. These myths are different from the foregoing ones, in so far as they refer to a time when humanity was already established on the surface of the earth, and when all the social divisions had already assumed a definite character. The main cycle of myths which belong here, are those of a culture hero, Tudava, who slays an ogre and thus allows people to live in Boyowa again, whence they all had fled in fear of being eaten. A story about the origins of cannibalism belongs here also, and about the origin of garden making.

3. *Myths in which figure only ordinary human beings*, though endowed with extraordinary magical powers. These myths are distinguished from the

foregoing ones, by the fact that no ogres or non-human persons figure in them, and that they refer to the origin, not of whole aspects of culture, such as cannibalism or garden-making, but to definite institutions or definite forms of magic. Here comes the myth about the origins of sorcery, the myth about the origins of love magic, the myth of the flying canoe, and finally the several Kula myths. The line of division between these three categories is, of course, not a rigid one, and many a myth could be placed in two or even three of these classes, according to its several features or episodes. But each myth contains as a rule one main subject, and and if we take only this, there is hardly ever the slightest doubt as to where it should be placed.

A point which might appear contradictory in superficial reading is that before, we stressed the fact that the natives had no idea of change, yet here we spoke of myths about 'origins' of institutions. It is important to realise that, though natives do speak about times when humanity was not upon the earth, of times when there were no gardens, etc., yet all these things arrive ready-made; they do not change or evolve. The first people who came from underground, came up adorned with the same trinkets, carrying their lime-pot and chewing their betel-nut. The event, the emergence from the earth was mythical, that is, such as does not happen now; but the human beings and the country which received them were such as exist to-day.

III

The myths of the Kula are scattered along a section of the present Kula circuit. Beginning with a place in Eastern Woodlark Island, the village of Wamwara, the mythological centres are spread round almost in a semi-circle, right down to the island of Tewara, where we have left for the present our party from Sinaketa.

In Wamwara there lived an individual called Gere'u, who, according to one myth, was the originator of the Kula. In the island of Digumenu, West of Woodlark Island, Tokosikuna, another hero of the Kula, had his early home, though he finished his career in Gumasila, in the Amphletts. Kitava, the westernmost of the Marshall Bennetts, is the centre of canoe magic associated with the Kula. It is also the home of Monikiniki, whose name figures in many formulæ of the Kula magic, though there is no explicit myth about him, except that he was the first man to practice an important system of *mwasila* (Kula magic), probably the most widespread system of the present day. Further West, in Wawela, we are at the other end of the Kasabwaybwayreta myth, which starts in Tewara, and goes over to Wawela in its narrative of events, to return to Tewara again. This mythological narrative touches the island of Boyowa at its southernmost point, the passage Giribwa, which divides it from Vakuta. Almost all myths have one of their incidents laid in a small island between Vakuta and the Amphletts, called Gabuwana. One of the myths leads us to the Amphletts, that of Tokosikuna; another has its beginning and end in Tewara. Such is the geography of the Kula myths on the big sector between Murua and Dobu.

Although I do not know the other half through investigations made on the spot, I have spoken with natives from those districts, and I think that there are no myths localised anywhere on the sector Murua (Woodlark Island), Tubetube, and Dobu. What I am quite certain of, however, is that the whole of the Trobriands, except the two points mentioned before, lie outside the mythological area of the Kula. No Kula stories, associated with any village in the Northern half of Boyowa exist, nor does any of the mythical heroes of the other stories ever come to the Northern or Western provinces of the Trobriands. Such extremely important centres as Sinaketa and Omarakana are never mentioned. This would point, on the surface of it, to the fact that in olden days, the island of Boyowa, except its Southern end and the Eastern settlement of Wawela, either did not enter at all or did not play an important part in the Kula.

I shall give a somewhat abbreviated account of the various stories, and then adduce in extenso the one last mentioned, perhaps the most noteworthy of all the Kula myths, that of Kasabwaybwayreta, as well as the very important canoe myth, that of the flying *waga* of Kudayuri.

The Muruan myth, which I obtained only in a very bald outline, is localised in the village of Wamwara, at the Eastern end of the island. A man called Gere'u, of the Lukuba clan, knew very well the *mwasila* magic, and wherever he went, all the valuables were given to him, so that all the others returned empty-handed. He went to Gawa and Iwa, and as soon as he appeared, *pu-pu* went the conch shells, and everybody gave him the *bagi* necklaces. He returned to his village, full of glory and of Kula spoils. Then he went to Du'a'u, and obtained again an enormous amount of arm-shells. He settled the direction in which the Kula valuables have to move. *Bagi* necklaces have 'to go,' and the arm-shells 'to come.' As this was spoken on Boyowa, 'go' meant to travel from Boyowa to Woodlark, 'come' to travel from Gere'u's village to Sinaketa. The culture hero Gere'u was finally killed, through envy of his success in the Kula.

I obtained two versions about the mythological hero, Tokosikuna of Digumenu. In the first of them, he is represented as a complete cripple, without hands and feet, who has to be carried by his two daughters into the canoe. They sail on a Kula expedition through Iwa, Gawa, through the Straits of Giribwa to Gumasila. Then they put him on a platform, where he takes a meal and goes to sleep. They leave him there and go into a garden which they see on a hill above, in order to gather some food. On coming back, they find him dead. On hearing their wailing, an ogre comes out, marries one of them and adopts the other. As he was very ugly, however, the girls killed him in an obscene manner, and then settled in the island. This obviously mutilated and superficial version does not give us many clues to the native ideas about the Kula.

The other version is much more interesting. Tokosikuna, according to it, is also slightly crippled, lame, very ugly, and with a pitted skin; so ugly indeed that he could not marry. Far North, in the mythical land of Kokopawa, they play a flute so beautifully that the chief of Digumenu, the village of Tokosikuna, hears it. He wishes to obtain the flute. Many men set out, but all fail, and they have to return half way, because it is so far. Tokosikuna goes, and, through a mixture of cunning and daring, he succeeds in getting possession of the flute, and in returning safely to Digumenu. There, through magic which one is led to infer he has acquired on his journey, he changes his appearance, becomes young, smooth-skinned and beautiful. The *guya'u* (chief) who is away in his garden, hears the flute played in his village, and returning there, he sees Tokosikuna sitting on a high platform, playing the flute and looking beautiful. "Well," he says, "all my daughters, all my granddaughters, my nieces and my sisters, you all marry Tokosikuna! Your husbands, you leave behind! You marry Tokosikuna, for he has brought the flute from the distant land!" So Tokosikuna married all the women.

The other men did not take it very well, of course. They decided to get rid of Tokosikuna by stratagem. They said: "The chief would like to eat giant clam-shell, let us go and fish it." "And how shall I catch it?" asks Tokosikuna. "You put your head, where the clam-shell gapes open." (This of course would mean death, as the clam-shell would close, and, if a really big one, would easily cut off his head). Tokosikuna, however, dived and with his two hands, broke a clam-shell open, a deed of superhuman strength. The others were angry, and planned another form of revenge. They arranged a shark-fishing, advising Tokosikuna to catch the fish with his hands. But he simply strangled the big shark, and put it into the canoe. Then, he tears asunder a boar's mouth, bringing them thus to despair. Finally they decide to get rid of him at sea. They try to kill him first by letting the heavy tree, felled for the *waga*, fall on him. But he supports it with his outstretched arms, and does no harm to himself. At the time of lashing, his companions wrap some *wayaugo* (lashing creeper) into a soft pandanus leaf; then they persuade him to use pandanus only for the lashing of his canoe, which he does indeed, deceived by seeing them use what apparently is the same. Then they sail, the other men in good, sea-worthy canoes, he in an entirely unseaworthy one, lashed only with the soft, brittle pandanus leaf.

And here begins the real Kula part of the myth. The expedition arrives at Gawa, where Tokosikuna remains with his canoe on the beach, while the other men go to the village to *kula*. They collect all the smaller arm-shells of the *soulava* type, but the big ones, the *bagi*, remain in the village, for the local men are unwilling to give them. Then Tokosikuna starts for the village after all the others have returned. After a short while, he arrives from the village, carrying all the *bagido'u bagidudu*, and *bagiriku*—that is, all the most valuable types of spondylus necklaces. The same happens in Iwa and Kitava. His companions from the other canoes go first and succeed only in collecting the inferior kinds of valuables. He afterwards enters the village, and easily obtains the high grades of necklace, which had been refused to the others. These become very angry; in Kitava, they inspect the lashings of his canoe, and see that they are rotten. "Oh well, to-morrow, Vakuta! The day after, Gumasila,—he will drown in Pilolu." In Vakuta the same happens as before, and the wrath of his unsuccessful companions increases.

They sail and passing the sandback of Gabula (this is the Trobriand name for Gabuwana, as the Amphlettans pronounce it) Tokosikuna eases his helm; then, as he tries to bring the canoe up to the wind again, his lashings snap, and the canoe sinks. He swims in the waves, carrying the basket-full of valuables in one arm. He calls out to the other canoes: "Come and take your *bagi*! I shall get into your *waga*!" "You married all our women," they answer, "now, sharks will eat you! We shall go to make Kula in Dobu!" Tokosikuna, however, swims safely to the point called Kamsareta, in the island of Domdom. From there he beholds the rock of Selawaya standing out of the jungle on the eastern slope of Gumasila. "This is a big rock, I shall go and live there," and turning towards the Digumenu canoes he utters a curse:

"You will get nothing in Dobu but poor necklaces, *soulava* of the type of *tutumuyuwa* and *tutuyanabwa*. The big *bagido'u* will stop with me." He remains in the Amphletts and does not return to Digumenu. And here ends the myth.

I have given an extensive summary of this myth, including its first part, which has nothing to do with the Kula, because it gives a full character sketch of the hero as a daring sailor and adventurer. It shoes, how Tokosikuna, after his Northern trip, acquired magic which allowed him to change his ugly and weak frame into a powerful body with a beautiful appearance. The first part also contains the reference to his great success with women, an association between Kula magic and love magic, which as we shall see, is not without importance. In this first part, that is, up to the moment when they start on the Kula, Tokosikuna appears as a hero, endowed with extraordinary powers, due to his knowledge of magic.

In this myth, as we see, no events are related through which the natural appearance of the landscape is changed. Therefore this myth is typical of what I have called the most recent stratum of mythology. This is further confirmed by the circumstance that no allusion is made in it to any origins, not even to the origins of the *mwasila* magic. For, as the myth is at present told and commented upon, all the men who go on the Kula expedition with our hero, know a system of Kula magic, the *mwasila* of Monikiniki. Tokosikuna's superiority rests with his special beauty magic; with his capacity to display enormous strength, and to face with impunity great dangers; with his ability to escape from drowning, finally, with his knowledge of the evil magic, *bulubwalata*, with which he prevents his companions from doing successful Kula. This last point was contained in a commentary upon this myth, given to me by the man who narrated it. When I speak about the Kula magic more explicitly further on, the reader will see that the four points of superiority just mentioned correspond to the categories into which we have to group the Kula magic, when it is classified according to its leading ideas, according to the goal towards which it aims.

One magic Tokosikuna does not know. We see from the myth that he is ignorant of the nature of the *wayugo*, the lashing creeper. He is therefore obviously not a canoe-builder, nor acquainted with canoe-building magic. This is the point on which his companions are able to catch him.

Geographically, this myth links Digumenu with the Amphletts, as also did the previous version of the Tokosikuna story. The hero, here as there, settles finally in Gumasila, and the element of migration is contained in both versions. Again, in the last story, Tokosikuna decides to settle in the Amphletts, on seeing the Selawaya rock. If we remember the Gumasilan legend about the origin of Kula magic, it also refers to the same rock. I did not obtain the name of the individual who is believed to have lived on the Selawaya rock, but it obviously is the same myth, only very mutilated in the Gumasilan version.

IV

Moving Westwards from Digumenu, to which the Tokosikuna myth belongs, the next important centre of Kula magic is the island of Kitava. With this place, the magical system of Monikiniki is associated by tradition, though no special story is told about this individual. A very important myth, on the other hand, localised in Kitava, is the one which serves as foundation for canoe magic. I have obtained three independent versions of this myth, and they agree substantially. I shall adduce at length the story as it was told to me by the best informant, and written down in Kiriwinian, and after that, I shall show on what points the other versions vary. I shall not omit from the full account certain tedious repetitions and obviously inessential details, for they are indispensable for imparting to the narrative the characteristic flavour of native folk-lore.

To understand the following account, it is necessary to realise that Kitava is a raised coral island. Its inland part is elevated to a height of about three hundred feet. Behind the flat beach, a steep coral wall rises, and from its summit the land gently falls towards the central declivity. It is in this central part that the villages are situated, and it would be quite impossible to transport a canoe from any village to the beach. Thus, in Kitava, unlike what happens with some of the Lagoon villages of Boyowa, the canoes have to be always dug out and lashed on the beach.

The Myth of the Flying Canoe of Kudayuri.

"Mokatuboda of the Lukuba clan and his younger brother Toweyre'i lived in the village of Kudayuri. With them lived their three sisters Kayguremwo, Na'ukuwakula and Murumweyri'a. They had all come out from underground in the spot called Labikewo, in Kitava. These people were the u'ula (foundation, basis, here: first possessors) of the ligogu and wayugo magic."

"All the men of Kitava decided on a great Kula expedition to the Koya. The men of Kumwageya, Kaybutu, Kabululo and Lalela made their canoes. They scooped out the inside of the waga, they carved the tabuyo and lagim (decorated prow boards), they made the budaka (lateral gunwale planks). They brought the component parts to the beach, in order to make the yowaga (to put and lash them together)."

"The Kudayuri people made their canoe in the village. Mokatuboda, the head man of the Kudayuri village, ordered them to do so. They were angry: 'Very heavy canoe. Who will carry it to the beach?' He said: 'No, not so; it will be well. I shall just lash my waga in the village.' He refused to move the canoe; it remained in the village. The other people pieced their canoe on the beach; he pieced it together in the village. They lashed it with the wayugo creeper on the beach; he lashed his in the village. They caulked their canoes on the sea-shore; he caulked his in the village. They painted their canoes on the beach with black; he blackened his in the village. They made the youlala (painted red and white) on the beach; he made the youlala in the village. They sewed their sail on the beach; he did it in the village. They rigged up the mast and rigging on the beach; he in the village. After that, the men of Kitava made tasasoria (trial run) and kabigidoya (visit of ceremonial presentation), but the Kudayuri canoe did not make either."

"By and by, all the men of Kitava ordered their women to prepare the food. The women one day put all the food, the gugu'a (personal belongings), the *pari* (presents and trade goods) into the canoe. The people of Kudayuri had all these things put into their canoe in the village. The headman of the Kudayuri, Mokatuboda, asked all his younger brothers, all the members of his crew, to bring some of their *pari*, and he performed magic over it, and made a *lilava* (magical bundle) of it."

"The people of other villages went to the beach; each canoe was manned by its *usagelu* (members of the crew). The man of Kudayuri ordered his crew to man his canoe in the village. They of the other villages stepped the mast on the shore; he stepped the mast in the village. They prepared the rigging on the shore; he prepared the rigging in the village. They hoisted the sail on the sea; he spoke 'May our sail be hoisted,' and his companions hoisted the sail. He spoke: 'Sit in your places, every man!' He went into the house, he took his *ligogu* (adze), he took some coco-nut oil, he took a staff. He spoke magic over the adze, over the coco-nut oil. He came out of the house, he approached the canoe. A small dog of his called Tokulubweydoga jumped into the canoe.* He spoke to his crew: 'Pull up the sail higher.' They pulled at the halyard. He rubbed the staff with the coco-nut oil. He knocked the canoe's skids with the staff. Then he struck with his ligogu the *u'ula* of his canoe and the *dobwana* (that is, both ends of the canoe). He jumped into the canoe, sat down, and the canoe flew!"

"A rock stood before it. It pierced the rock in two, and flew through it. He bent down, he looked; his companions (that is, the other canoes of Kitava) sailed on the sea. He spoke to his younger brothers, (that is to his relatives in the canoe): 'Bail out the water, pour it out!' Those who sailed on the earth thought it was rain, this water which they poured out from above."

"They (the other canoes) sailed to Giribwa, they saw a canoe anchored there. They said: 'Is that the canoe from Dobu?' They thought so, they wanted to *lebu* (take by force, but not necessarily as a hostile act) the *buna* (big cowrie) shells of the Dobu people. Then they saw the dog walking on the beach. They said: 'Wi-i-i! This is Tokulubweydoga, the dog of the Lukuba! This canoe they lashed in the village, in the village of Kudayuri. Which way did it come? It was anchored in the jungle!' They approached the people of Kudayuri, they spoke: 'Which way did you come?' 'Oh, I came together with you (the same way).' 'It rained. Did it rain over you?' 'Oh yes, it has rained over me.' "

"Next day, they (the men of the other villages of Kitava), sailed to Vakuta and went ashore. They made their Kula. The next day they sailed, and he (Mokatuboda) remained in Vakuta. When they disappeared on the sea, his canoe flew. He flew from Vakuta. When they (the other crews) arrived in

---

* The reader will note that this is the same name, which another mythical dog bore, also of the Lukuba clan as all dogs are, the one namely from whom the *kayga'u* magic is traced. Cf. Chapter X, Division V.

Gumasila, he was there on the promontory of Lububuyama. They said: 'This canoe is like the canoe of our companions,' and the dog came out. 'This is the dog of the Lukuba clan of Kudayuri.' They asked him again which way he came; he said he came the same way as they. They made the Kula in Gumasila. He said: 'You sail first, I shall sail later on.' They were astonished. 'Which way does he sail?' They slept in Gumasila."

"Next day they sailed to Tewara, they arrived at the beach of Kadimwatu. They saw his canoe anchored there, the dog came out and ran along the beach. They spoke to the Kudayuri men, 'How did you come here?' 'We came with you, the same way we came.' They made Kula in Tewara. Next day, they sailed to Bwayowa (village in Dobu district). He flew, and anchored at the beach Sarubwoyna. They arrived there, they saw: 'Oh, look at the canoe, are these fishermen from Dobu?' The dog came out. They recognised the dog. They asked him (Mokatuboda) which way he came: 'I came with you, I anchored here.' They went to the village of Bwayowa, they made Kula in the village, they loaded their canoes. They received presents from the Dobu people at parting, and the Kitava men sailed on the return journey. They sailed first, and he flew through the air."

On the return journey, at every stage, they see him first, they ask him which way he went, and he gives them some sort of answer as the above ones.

"From Giribwa they sailed to Kitava; he remained in Giribwa; he flew from Giribwa; he went to Kitava, to the beach. His *gugu'a* (personal belongings) were being carried to the village when his companions came paddling along, and saw his canoe anchored and the dog running on the beach. All the other men were very angry, because his canoe flew."

"They remained in Kitava. Next year, they made their gardens, all the men of Kitava. The sun was very strong, there was no rain at all. The sun burned their gardens. This man (the head man of Kudayuri, Mokatuboda) went into the garden. He remained there, he made a *bulubwalata* (evil magic) of the rain. A small cloud came and rained on his garden only, and their gardens the sun burned. They (the other men of Kitava) went and saw their gardens. They arrived there, they saw all was dead, already the sun had burned them. They went to his garden and it was all wet: yams, *taitu*, taro, all was fine. They spoke: 'Let us kill him so that he might die. We shall then speak magic over the clouds, and it will rain over our gardens.' "

"The real, keen magic, the Kudayuri man (i.e. Mokatuboda) did not give to them; he gave them not the magic of the *ligogu* (adze); he gave them not the magic of *kunisalili* (rain magic); he gave them not the magic of the *wayugo* (lashing creeper), of the coco-nut oil and staff. Toweyre'i, his younger brother, thought that he had already received the magic, but he was mistaken. His elder brother gave him only part of the magic, the real one he kept back."

"They came (to Mokatuboda, the head man of Kudayuri), he sat in his village. His brothers and maternal nephews sharpened the spear, they hit him, he died."

"Next year, they decided to make a big Kula expedition, to Dobu. The old *waga*, cut and lashed by Mokatuboda, was no more good, the lashings had perished. Then Toweyre'i, the younger brother, cut a new one to replace the old. The people of Kumwageya and Lalela (the other villages in Kitava) heard that Toweyre'i cuts his *waga*, and they also cut theirs. They pieced and lashed their canoes on the beach. Toweyre'i did it in the village."

Here the native narrative enumerates every detail of canoe making, drawing the contrast between the proceedings on the beach of the other Kitavans, and of Toweyre'i building the canoe in the village of Kudayuri. It is an exact repetition of what was said at the beginning, when Mokatuboda was building his canoe, and I shall not adduce it here. The narrative arrives at the critical moment when all the members of the crew are seated in the canoe ready for the flight.

"Toweyre'i went into the house and made magic over the adze and the coco-nut oil. He came out, smeared a staff with the oil, knocked the skids of the canoe. He then did as his elder brother did. He struck both ends of the canoe with the adze. He jumped into the canoe and sat down; but the *waga* did not fly. Toweyre'i went into the house and cried for his elder brother, whom he had slain; he had killed him without knowing his magic. The people of Kumwageya and Lalela went to Dobu and made their Kula. The people of Kudayuri remained in the village."

"The three sisters were very angry with Toweyre'i, for he killed the elder brother and did not learn his magic. They themselves had learnt the *ligogu*, the *wayugo* magic; they had it already in their *lopoula* (belly). They could fly through the air, they were *yoyova*. In Kitava they lived on the top of Botigale'a hill. They said: 'Let us leave Kitava and fly away.' They flew through the air. One of them, Na'ukuwakula, flew to the West, pierced through the sea-passage Dikuwa'i (somewhere in the Western Trobriands); she arrived at Simsim (one of the Lousançay). There she turned into a stone, she stands in the sea."

"The two others flew first (due West) to the beach of Yalumugwa (on the Eastern shore of Boyowa). There they tried to pierce the coral rock named Yakayba—it was too hard. They went (further South on the Eastern shore) through the sea-passage of Vilasasa and tried to pierce the rock Kuyaluya— they couldn't. They went (further South) and tried to pierce the rock of Kawakari—it was too hard. They went (further South). They tried to pierce the rocks at Giribwa. They succeeded. That is why there is now a sea passage at Giribwa (the straits dividing the main island of Boyowa from the island of Vakuta)."

"They flew (further South) towards Dobu. They came to the island of Tewara. They came to the beach of Kadimwatu and pierced it. This is where
the straits of Kadimwatu are now between the islands of Tewara and Uwama.
They went to Dobu; they travelled further South, to the promontory of Sa-
ramwa (near Dobu island). They spoke: 'Shall we go round the point or
pierce right through?' They went round the point. They met another obsta-
cle and pierced it through, making the Straits of Loma (at the Western end
of Dawson Straits). They came back, they returned and settled near Tewara.
They turned into stones; they stand in the sea. One of them cast her eyes on
Dobu, this is Murumweyri'a; she eats men, and the Dobuans are cannibals.
The other one, Kayguremwo, does not eat men, and her face is turned towards Boyowa. The people at Boyowa do not eat man."

This story is extremely clear in its general outline, and very dramatic,
and all its incidents and developments have a high degree of consistency
and psychological motivation. It is perhaps the most telling of all myths
from this part of the world which came under my notice. It is also a good
example of what has been said before in Division II. Namely that the
identical conditions, sociological and cultural, which obtain at the present
time, are also reflected in mythical narratives. The only exception to this
is the much higher efficiency of magic found in the world of myth. The
tale of Kudayuri, on the one hand, describes minutely the sociological
conditions of the heroes, their occupations and concerns, and all these do
not differ at all from the present ones. On the other hand, it shows the
hero endowed with a truly super-normal power through his magic of canoe building and of rain making. Nor could it be more convincingly
stated than is done in this narrative that the full knowledge of the right
magic was solely responsible for these supernatural powers.

In its enumeration of the various details of tribal life, this myth is truly
a fount of ethnographic information. Its statements, when made complete
and explicit by native comment, contain a good deal of what is to be
known about the sociology, technology and organisation of canoe-making,
sailing, and of the Kula. If followed up into detail, the incidents of this
narrative make us acquainted for instance, with the division into clans;
with the origin and local character of these latter; with ownership of
magic and its association with the totemic group. In almost all mythological narratives of the Trobriands, the clan, the sub-clan and the locality
of the heroes are stated. In the above version, we see that the heroes
have emerged at a certain spot, and that they themselves came from underground; that is, that they are the first representatives of their totemic
sub-clan on the surface of the earth. In the two other versions, this last
point was not explicitly stated, though I think it is implied in the incidents of this myth, for obviously the flying canoe is built for the first

time, as it is for the last. In other versions, I was told that the hole from which this sub-clan emerged is also called Kudayuri, and that the name of their magical system is Viluvayaba.

Passing to the following part of the tale, we find in it a description of canoe-building, and this was given to me in the same detailed manner in all three versions. Here again, if we would substitute for the short sentences a fuller account of what happens, such as could be elicited from any intelligent native informant; if for each word describing the stages of canoe-building we insert a full description of the processes for which these words stand—we would have in this myth an almost complete, ethnographic account of canoe-building. We would see the canoe pieced together, lashed, caulked, painted, rigged out, provided with a sail till it lies ready to be launched. Besides the successive enumeration of technical stages, we have in this myth a clear picture of the rôle played by the headman, who is the nominal owner of the canoe, and who speaks of it as his canoe and at the same time directs its building; overrides the wishes of others, and is responsible for the magic. We have even the mention of the *tasasoria* and *kabigidoya*, and several allusions to the Kula expedition of which the canoe-building in this myth is represented as a preliminary stage. The frequent, tedious repetitions and enumerations of customary sequences of events, interesting as data of folk-lore, are not less valuable as ethnographic documents, and as illustrations of the natives' attitude towards custom. Incidentally, this feature of native mythology shows that the task of serving as ethnographic informant is not so foreign and difficult to a native as might at first appear. He is quite used to recite one after the other the various stages of customary proceedings in his own narratives, and he does it with an almost pedantic accuracy and completeness, and it is an easy task for him to transfer these qualities to the accounts, which he is called upon to make in the service of ethnography.

The dramatic effect of the climax of the story, of the unexpected flight of the canoe is clearly brought out in the narrative, and it was given to me in all its three versions. In all three, the members of the crew are made to pass through the numerous preparatory stages of sailing. And the parallel drawn between the reasonable proceedings of their fellows on the beach, and the absurd manner in which they are made to get ready in the middle of the village, some few hundred feet above the sea, makes the tension more palpable and the sudden *denouement* more effective. In all accounts of this myth, the magic is also performed just before the flight, and its performance is explicitly mentioned and included as an important episode in the story.

The incident of bailing some water out of a canoe which never touched the sea, seems to show some inconsistency. If we remember, however, that water is poured into a canoe, while it is built, in order to prevent its drying and consequently its shrinking, cracking and warping, the inconsistency and flaw in the narrative disappear. I may add that the bailing and rain incident is contained in one of my three versions only.

The episode of the dog is more significant and more important to the natives, and is mentioned in all three versions. The dog is the animal associated with the Lukuba clan; that is, the natives will say that the dog is a Lukuba, as the pig is a Malasi, and the igwana a Lukulabuta. In several stories about the origin and relative rank of the clans, each of them is represented by its totemic animal. Thus the igwana is the first to emerge from underground. Hence the Lukulabuta are the oldest clan. The dog and the pig dispute with one another the priority of rank, the dog basing his claims on his earlier appearance on the earth, for he followed immediately the igwana; the pig, asserting himself in virtue of not eating unclean things. The pig won the day, and therefore the Malasi clan are considered to be the clan of the highest rank, though this is really reached only in one of its sub-clans, that of the Tabalu of Omarakana. The incident of the *lebu* (taking by force) of some ornaments from the Dobuans refers to the custom of using friendly violence in certain Kula transactions (see chapter XIV, Division II).

In the second of the story, we find the hero endowed again with magical powers far superior to those of the present-day wizards. They can make rain, or stay the clouds, it is true, but he is able to create a small cloud which pours copious rain over his own gardens, and leaves the others to be shrivelled up by the sun. This part of the narrative does not touch the canoe problem, and it is of interest to us only in so far as it again shows what appears to the natives the real source of their hero's supernatural powers.

The motives which lead to the killing of Mokatuboda are not stated explicitly in the narrative. No myth as a rule enters very much into the subjective side of its events. But, from the lengthy, indeed wearisome repetition of how the other Kitava men constantly find the Kudayuri canoe outrunning them, how they are astonished and angry, it is clear that his success must have made many enemies to Mokatuboda. What is not so easily explained, is the fact that he is killed, not by the other Kitava men, but by his own kinsmen. One of the versions mentions his brothers and his sister's sons as the slayers. One of them states that the people of Kitava ask Toweyre'i, the younger brother, whether he has already acquired the flying magic and the rain magic, and only after an affirmative is received, is Mokatuboda killed by his younger brother, in connivance with the other people. An interesting variant is added to this version, according to which Toweyre'i kills his elder brother in the garden. He then comes back to the village and instructs and admonishes Mokatuboda's children to take the body, to give it the mortuary attentions, to prepare for the burial. Then he himself arranges the *sagali*, the big mortuary distribution of food. In this we find an interesting document of native custom and ideas. Toweyre'i, in spite of having killed his brother, is still the man who has to arrange the mortuary proceedings, act as master of ceremonies, and pay for the functions performed in them by others. He personally may neither touch the corpse, nor do any act of mourning or burial; nevertheless he, as the nearest of kin of the dead man, is the bereaved one, is the one from whom a limb has been severed, so to speak. A man whose brother has died cannot mourn any more than he could mourn for himself.* To return to the motives of killing, as this was done according to all accounts by Mokatuboda's own kinsmen, with the approval of the other men, envy, ambition, the desire to succeed the headman in his dignity, must have been mixed with spite against him. In fact, we see that Toweyre'i proceeds confidently to perform the magic, and bursts out into wailing only after he has discovered he has been duped.

Now we come to one of the most remarkable incidents of the whole myth, that namely which brings into connection the *yoyova*, or the flying witches, with the flying canoe, and with such speed of a canoe, as is imparted to it by magic. In the spells of swiftness there are frequent allusions to the *yoyova* or *mulukwausi*. This can be clearly seen in the spell of the *wayugo*, already adduced (Chapter V, Division III), and which is still to be analysed linguistically (Chapter XVIII, Divisions II to IV). The *kariyala* (magical portent, cf. Chapter XVII, Division VII) of the *wayugo* spell consists in shooting stars, that is, when a *wayugo* rite is performed at night over the creeper coils, there will be stars falling in the sky. And again, when a magician, knowing this system of magic, dies, shooting stars will be seen. Now, as we have seen (Chapter X, Division I), falling stars are *mulukwausi* in their flight.

In this story of the Kudayuri we see the mythological ground for this association. The same magic which allowed the canoe to sail through the air gives the three sisters of Kudayuri their power of being *mulukwausi*, and of flying. In this myth they are also endowed with the power of cleaving the rocks, a power which they share with the canoe, which cleft a rock immediately after leaving the village. The three sisters cleave rocks and pierce the land in several places. My native commentators assured me that when the canoe first visited Giribwa and Kadimwatu at the beginning of this myth, the land was still joined at these places and there

* Cf. Professor C. G. Seligman, "The Melanesians," Chapter LIV, "Burial and Mourning Ceremonies" (among the natives of the Trobriand Islands, of Woodlark and the Marshall Bennetts).

was a beach at each of them. The *mulukwausi* tried to pierce Boyowa at several spots along the Eastern coast, but succeeded only at Giribwa. The myth thus has the archaic stamp of referring to deep changes in natural features. The two sisters, who fly to the South return from the furthest point and settle near Tewara, in whicih there is some analogy to several other myths in which heroes from the Marshall Bennett Islands settle down somewhere between the Amphletts and Dobu. One of them turns her eyes northwards towards the non-cannibal people of Boyowa and she is said to be averse to cannibalism. Probably this is a sort of mythological explanation of why the Boyowan people do not eat men and the Dobuans do, an explanation to which there is an analogy in another myth shortly to be adduced, that of Atu'a'ine and Aturamo'a, and a better one still in a myth about the origins of cannibalism, which I cannot quote here.

In all these traditions, so far, the heroes belonged to the clan of Lukuba. To it belong Gere'u, Tokosikuna, the Kudayuri family and their dog, and also the dog, Tokulubwaydoga of the myth told in Chapter X, Division V. I may add that, in some legends told about the origin of humanity, this clan emerges first from underground and in some it emerges second in time, but as the clan of highest rank, though in this it has to yield afterwards to the Malasi. The main Kultur-hero of Kiriwina, the ogre-slayer Tudava, belongs, also to the clan of Lukuba. There is even a historic fact, which agrees with this mythological primacy, and subsequent eclipse. The Lukuba were, some six or seven generations ago, the leading clan in Vakuta, and then they had to surrender the chieftainship of this place to the Malasi clan, when the sub-clan of the Tabalu, the Malasi chiefs of the highest rank in Kiriwina, migrated South, and settled down in Vakuta. In the myths quoted here, the Lukuba are leading canoe-builders, sailors, and adventurers, that is with one exception, that of Tokosikuna, who, though excelling in all other resepcts, knows nothing of canoe construction.

V

Let us now proceed to the last named mythological centre, and taking a very big step from the Marshall Bennetts, return to Tewara, and to its myth of the origin of the Kula. I shall tell this myth in a translation, closely following the original account, obtained in Kiriwinian from an informant at Oburaku. I had an opportunity of checking and amending his narrative, by the information obtained from a native of Sanaro'a in pidgin English.

The Story of Kasabwaybwayreta and Gumakarakedakeda

"Kasabwaybwayreta lived in Tewara. He heard the renown of a *soulava* (spondylus necklace) which was lying (kept) in Wawela. Its name was Gumakarakedakeda. He said to his children: 'Let us go to Wawela, make Kula to get this *soulava*.' He put into his canoe unripe coco-nut, undeveloped betel-nut, green bananas."

"They went to Wawela; they anchored in Wawela. His sons went ashore, they went to obtain Gumakarakedakeda. He remained in the canoe. His son made offering of food, they (the Wawela people) refused. Kasabwaybwayreta spoke a charm over the betel-nut: it yellowed (became ripe); he spoke the charm over the coco-nut: its soft kernel swelled; he charmed the bananas: they ripened. He took off his hair, his gray hair; his wrinkled skin, it remained in the canoe. He rose, he went, he gave a *pokala* offering of food, he received the valuable necklace as Kula gift, for he was already a beautiful man. He went, he put it down, he thrust it into his hair. He came to the canoe, he took his covering (the sloughed skin); he donned the wrinkles, the gray hairs, he remained."

"His sons arrived, they took their places in the canoe, they sailed to Giribwa. They cooked their food. He called his grandson; 'Oh, my grandson, come here, look for my lice.' The grandson came there, stepped near him. Kasabwaybwayreta spoke, telling him: 'My grandson, catch my lice in the middle (of my hair).' His grandson parted his hair; he saw the valuable necklace, Gumakarakedakeda remaining there in the hair of Kasabwaybwayreta. 'Ee . . .' he spoke to his father, telling him, 'My father, Kasabwaybwayreta already obtained Gumakarakedakeda.' 'O, no, he did not obtain it! I am a chief, I am beautiful, I have not obtained that valuable. Indeed, would this wrinkled old man have obtained the necklace? No, indeed!' 'Truly, my father, he has obtained it already. I have seen it; already it remains in his hair!' "

"All the water-vessels are empty already; the son went into the canoe, spilled the water so that it ran out, and only the empty vessels (made of coconut shell) remained. Later on they sailed, they went to an island, Gabula (Gabuwana in Amphlettan and in Dobuan). This man, Kasabwaybwayreta wanted water, and spoke to his son. This man picked up the water vessels— no, they were all empty. They went on the beach of Gabula, the *usagelu* (members of the crew) dug out their water-holes (in the beach). This man remained in the canoe and called out: 'O my grandson, bring me here my water, go there and dip out my water!' The grandson said, 'No, come here and dip out (yourself)!' Later on, they dipped out water, they finished, and Kasabwaybwayreta came. They muddied the water, it was muddy. He sat down, he waited."

"They went, they sailed in the canoe. Kasabwaybwayreta called out, 'O, my son, why do you cast me off?' Spoke the son: 'I think you have obtained Gumakarakedakeda!' 'O, by and by, my son, when we arrive in the village, I shall give it to you!' 'O, no! Well, you remain, I shall go!" He takes a stone, a *binabina* one, this man Kasabwaybwayreta, he throws so that he might make a hole in the canoe, and the men might go into the sea. No! they sped away, they went, this stone stands up, it has made an island in the sea. They went, they anchored in Tewara. They (the villagers) asked: 'And where is Kasabwaybwayreta?' 'O, his son got angry with him, already he had obtained Gumakarakedakeda!'"

"Well, then, this man Kasabwaybwayreta remained in the island Gabula. He saw Tokom'mwawa (evening star) approach. He spoke: 'My friend, come here, let me just enter into your canoe!' 'O no, I shall go to another place.' There came Kaylateku (Sirius). He asked him: 'Let me go with you.' He refused. There came Kayyousi (Southern Cross). Kasabwaybwayreta wanted to go with him. He refused. There came Umnakayva'u, (Alpha and Beta Centauri). He wanted a place in his canoe. He refused. There came Kibi (three stars widely distant, forming no constellation in our sky-chart). He also refused to take Kasabwaybwayreta. There came Uluwa (the Pleiades). Kasabwaybwayreta asked him to take him. Uluwa said: 'You wait, you look out, there will come Kaykiyadiga, he will take you." There came Kaykiyadiga (the three central stars in Orion's belt). Kasabwaybwayreta asked him: 'My friend, which way will you go?' 'I shall come down on top of Taryebutu mountain. I shall go down, I shall go away.' 'Oh, my friend, come here, let me just sit down (on you).' 'Oh come,—see on one side there is a *va'i* (sting-aree) on the other side, there is the *lo'u* (a fish with poisonous spikes); you sit in the middle, it will be well! Where is your village?' 'My village is Tewara.' 'What stands in the site of your village?' 'In the site of my village, there stands a *busa* tree!' "

"They went there. Already the village of Kasabwaybwayreta is straight below them. He charmed this *busa* tree, it arose, it went straight up into the skies. Kasabwaybwayreta changed place (from Orion's belt on to the tree), he sat on the *busa* tree. He spoke: 'Oh, my friend, break asunder this necklace. Part of it, I shall give you; part of it, I shall carry to Tewara.' He gave part of it to his companion. This *busa* tree came down to the ground. He was angry because his son left him behind. He went underground inside. He there remained for a long time. The dogs came there, and they dug and dug. They dug him out. He came out on top, he became a *tauva'u* (evil spirit, see Chapter II, Division VII). He hits human beings. That is why in Tewara the village is that of sorcerers and witches, because of Kasabwaybwayreta."

To make this somewhat obscure narrative clearer, a short commentary is necessary. The first part tells of a Kula expedition in which the hero, his son, his grandson, and some other members of the crew take part. His son takes with him good, fresh food, to give as solicitory offering and thus tempt his partners to present him with the famous necklace. The son is a young man and also a chief of renown. The later stages are clearer; by means of magic, the hero changes himself into a young, attractive man, and makes his own unripe, bad fruit into splendid gifts to be offered to his partner. He obtains the prize without difficulty, and hides it in his hair. Then, in a moment of weakness, and for motives which it is impossible to find out from native commentators, he on purpose reveals the necklace to his grandson. Most likely, the motive was vanity. His son, and probably also the other companions, become very angry and set a trap for him. They arrange things so that he has to go for his own water on the beach of Gabula. When they have already got theirs and while he is dipping it out, they sail away, leaving him marooned on the sand-bank. Like Polyphemus after the escaping party of Odysseus, he throws a stone at the treacherous canoe, but it misses its mark, and becomes an outstanding rock in the sea.

The episode of his release by the stars is quite clear. Arrived at the village, he makes a tree rise by his magic, and after he has given the bigger part of his necklace to his rescuer, he descends, with the smaller part. His going underground and subsequent turning into a *tauva'u* shows how bitter he feels towards humanity. As usual, the presence of such a powerful, evil personality in the village, gives its stamp to the whole community, and this latter produces sorcerers and witches. All these additions and comments I obtained in cross-questioning my original informant.

The Dobuan informant from Sanaro'a introduced one or two variants into the second part of the narrative. According to him, Kasabwaybwayreta marries while in the sky, and remains there long enough to beget three male and two female children. After he has made up his mind to descend to earth again, he makes a hole in the heavens, looks down and sees a betel-nut tree in his village. Then he speaks to his child, 'When I go down, you pull at one end of the necklace.' He climbs down by means of the necklace on to the betel palm and pulls at one end of Gumakarakedakeda. It breaks, a big piece remains in the skies, the small one goes with him below. Arrived in the village, he arranges a feast, and invites all the villagers to it. He speaks some magic over the food and after they have eaten it the villagers are turned into birds. This last act is quite in harmony with his profession of *tauva'u*, which he assumed in the previous version of the myth. My Dobuan informant also added, by way of commentary, that the companions of Kasabwaybwayreta were angry with him, because he obtained the necklace in Boyowa, which was not the right direction for a necklace to travel in the Kula. This, however, is obviously a rationalisation of the events of the myth.

Comparing the previously related story of Tokosikuna with this one, we see at once a clear resemblance between them in several features. In both, the heroes start as old, decrepit, and very ugly men. By their magical powers, they rejuvenate in the course of the story, the one permanently, the other just sloughing off his skin for the purpose of a Kula transaction. In both cases, the hero is definitely superior in the Kula, and by this arouses the envy and hatred of his companions. Again, in both stories, the companions decide to punish the hero, and the island or sandbank of Gabuwana is the scene of the punishment. In both, the hero finally settles in the South, only in one case it is his original home, while in the other he has migrated there from one of the Marshall Bennett Islands. An anomaly in the Kasabwaybwayreta myth, namely, that he fetches his necklace from the North, whereas the normal direction for necklaces to travel is from South to North in this region, makes us suspect that perhaps this story is a transformation of a legend about a man who made the Kula from the North. Ill-treated by his companions, he settled in Tewara, and becoming a local Kultur-hero, was afterwards described as belonging to the place. However this might be, and the hypothetical interpretation is mine, and not obtained from the natives, the two stories are so similar that they must be regarded obviously as variants of the same myth, and not as independent traditions.

VI

So much about the ethnographic analysis of these myths. Let us now return to the general, sociological considerations with which we opened this digression into mythology. We are now better able to realise to what extent and in what manner Kula myths influence the native outlook.

The main social force governing all tribal life could be described as the inertia of custom, the love of uniformity of behaviour. The great moral philosopher was wrong when he formulated his *categorical imperative*, which was to serve human beings as a fundamental guiding principle of behaviour. In advising us to act so that our behaviour might be taken as a norm of universal law, he reversed the natural state of things. The real rule guiding human behaviour is this: "what everyone else does, what appears as norm of general conduct, this is right, moral and proper. Let me look over the fence and see what my neighbour does, and take it as a rule for my behaviour." So acts every 'man-in-the-street' in our own society, so has acted the average member of any society through the past ages, and so acts the present-day savage; and the lower his level of cultural development, the greater stickler he will be for good manners, propriety and form, and the more incomprehensive and odious to him will be the non-conforming point of view. Systems of social philosophy have been built to explain and interpret or misinterpret this general principle. Tarde's 'Imitation,' Giddings' 'Consciousness of Kind,' Durkheim's 'Collective Ideas,' and many such conceptions as 'social consciousness,' 'the soul of a nation,' 'group mind' or now-a-days prevalent and highly fashionable ideas about 'suggestibility of the crowd,' 'the instinct of herd,' etc., etc., try to cover this simple empirical truth. Most of these systems, especially those evoking the Phantom of Collective Soul are futile, to my mind, in so far as they try to explain in the terms of a hypothesis that which is most fundamental in sociology, and can therefore be reduced to nothing else, but must be simply recognised and accepted as the basis of our science. To frame verbal definitions and quibble over terms does not seem to bring us much more forward in a new branch of learning, where a knowledge of facts is above all needed.

Whatever might be the case with any theoretical interpretations of this principle, in this place, we must simply emphasise that a strict adherence to custom, to that which is done by everyone else, is the main rule of conduct among our natives in the Trobriands. An important corollary to this rule declares that the past is more important than the present. What has been done by the father—or, as the Trobriander would say, by the maternal uncle—is even more important as norm of behaviour than what is done by the brother. It is to the behaviour of the past generations that the Trobriander instinctively looks for his guidance. Thus the mythical events which relate what has been done, not by the immediate ancestors but by mythical, illustrious forbears, must evidently carry an enormous social weight. The stories of important past events are hallowed because they belong to the great mythical generations and because they are generally accepted as truth, for everybody knows and tells them. They bear the sanction of righteousness and propriety in virtue of these two qualities of preterity and universality.

Thus, through the operation of what might be called the elementary law of sociology, myth possesses the normative power of fixing custom, of sanctioning modes of behaviour, of giving dignity and importance to an institution. The Kula receives from these ancient stories its stamp of extreme importance and value. The rules of commercial honour, of generosity and punctiliousness in all its operations, acquire through this their binding force. This is what we could call the normative influence of myth on custom.

The Kula myth, however, exercises another kind of appeal. In the Kula, we have a type of enterprise where the vast possibilities of success are very much influenced by chance. A man, whether he be rich or poor in partners, may, according to his luck, return with a relatively big or a small haul from an expedition. Thus the imagination of the adventurers, as in all forms of gambling, must be bent towards lucky hits and turns of extraordinarily good chance. The Kula myths feed this imagination on stories of extreme good luck, and at the same time show that it lies in the hands of man to bring this luck on himself, provided he acquires the necessary magical lore.

I have said before that the mythological events are distinct from those happening nowadays, in so far as they are extraordinary and super-normal. This adds both to their authoritative character and to their desirability. It sets them before the native as a specially valuable standard of conduct, and as an ideal towards which their desires must go out.

<h2 style="text-align:center">VII</h2>

But I also said before that, distinct as it is, the mythical world is not separated by an unbridgeable gulf from the present order of events. Indeed, though an ideal must be always beyond what actually exists, yet it must appear just within reach of realisation if it is to be effective at all. Now, after we have become acquainted with their stories, we can see clearly what was meant when it was said, that magic acts as a link between the mythical and the actual realities. In the canoe myth, for instance, the flying, the super-normal achievement of the Kudayuri canoe, is conceived only as the highest degree of the virtue of speed, which is still being imparted nowadays to canoes by magic. The magical heritage of the Kudayuri clan is still there, making the canoes sail fast. Had it been transmitted in its complete form, any present canoe, like the mythical one, could be seen flying. In the Kula myths also, magic is found to give super-normal powers of beauty, strength and immunity from danger. The mythological events demonstrate the truth of the claims of magic. Their validity is established by a sort of retrospective, mythical empiry. But magic, as it is practised nowadays, accomplishes the same effects, only in a smaller degree. Natives believe deeply that the formulæ and rites of *mwasila* magic make those who carry them out attractive, irresistible and safe from dangers (compare next chapter).

Another feature which brings the mythical events into direct connection with the present state of affairs, is the sociology of mythical personages. They all are associated with certain localities, as are the present local groups. They belong to the same system of totemic division into clans and sub-clans as obtains nowadays. Thus, members of a sub-clan, or a local unit, can claim a mythical hero as their direct ancestor, and members of a clan can boast of him as of a clansman. Indeed, myths, like songs and fairy stories, are 'owned' by certain sub-clans. This does not mean that other people would abstain from telling them, but members of the sub-clan are supposed to possess the most intimate knowledge of the mythical events, and to be an authority in interpreting them. And indeed, it is a rule that a myth will be best known in its own locality, that is, known with all the details and free from any adulterations or not quite genuine additions and fusions.

This better knowledge can be easily understood, if we remember that myth is very often connected with magic in the Trobriands, and that this latter is a possession, kept by some members of the local group. Now, to know the magic, and to understand it properly, it is necessary to be well acquainted with the myth. This is the reason why the myth must be better known in the local group with which it is connected. In some cases, the local group has not only to practise the magic associated with the myth, but it has to look after the observance of certain rites, ceremonies and taboos connected with it. In this case, the sociology of the mythical events is intimately bound up with the social divisions as they exist now. But even in such myths as those of the Kula, which have become the property of all clans and local groups within the district, the explicit statement of the hero's clan, sub-clan and of his village gives the whole myth a stamp of actuality and reality. Side by side with magic, the sociological continuity bridges over the gap between the mythical and the actual. And indeed the magical and the sociological bridges run side by side.

I spoke above (beginning of Division II) of the enlivening influence of myth upon landscape. Here it must be noted also that the mythically changed features of the landscape bear testimony in the native's mind to the truth of the myth. The mythical word receives its substance in rock and hill, in the changes in land and sea. The pierced sea-passages, the cleft boulders, the petrified human beings, all these bring the mythological world close to the natives, make it tangible and permanent. On the other hand, the story thus powerfully illustrated, re-acts on the landscape, fills it with dramatic happenings, which, fixed there for ever, give it a definite meaning. With this I shall close these general remarks on mythology though with myth and mythical events we shall constantly meet in further inquiries.

VIII

As we return to our party, who, sailing past the mythical centre of Tewara, make for the island of Sanaro'a, the first thing to be related about them, brings us straight to another mythological story. As the natives enter the district of Siayawawa, they pass a stone or rock, called Sinatemubadiye'i. I have not seen it, but the natives tell me it lies among the mangroves in a tidal creek. Like the stone Gurewaya, mentioned before, this one also enjoys certain privileges, and offerings are given to it.

The natives do not tarry in this unimportant district. Their final goal is now in sight. Beyond the sea, which is here land-locked like a lake, the hills of Dobu, topped by Koyava'u loom before them. In the distance to their right as they sail South, the broad Easterly flank of Koyatabu runs down to the water, forming a deep valley; behind them spreads the wide plain of Sanaro'a, with a few volcanic cones at its Northern end, and far to the left the mountains of Normanby unfold in a long chain. They sail straight South, making for the beach of Sarubwoyna, where they will have to pause for a ritual halt in order to carry out the final preparations and magic. They steer towards two black rocks, which mark the Northern end of Sarubwoyna beach as they stand, one at the base, the other at the end of a narrow, sandy spit. These are the two rocks Atu'a'ine and Aturamo'a, the most important of the tabooed places, at which natives lay offerings when starting or arriving on Kula expeditions. The rock among the mangroves of Siyawawa is connected with these two by a mythical story. The three—two men whom we see now before us in petrified form, and one woman—came to this district from somewhere 'Omuyuwa,' that is, from Woodlark Island or the Marshall Bennetts. This is the story:

Myth of Atu'a'ine, Aturamo'a and Sinatemubadiye'i.

"They were two brothers and a sister. They came first to the creek called Kadawaga in Siyawawa. The woman lost her comb. She spoke to her brethren: 'My brothers, my comb fell down.' They answered her: 'Good, return, take your comb.' She found it and took it, and next day she said: 'Well, I shall remain here already, as Sinatemubadiye'i.' "

"The brothers went on. When they arrived at the shore of the main island, Atu'a'ine said: 'Aturamo'a, how shall we go? Shall we look towards the sea?' Said Aturamo'a: 'O, no, let us look towards the jungle.' Aturamo'a went ahead, deceiving his brother, for he was a cannibal. He wanted to look towards the jungle, so that he might eat men. Thus Aturamo'a went ahead, and his eyes turned towards the jungle. Atu'a'ine turned his eyes, looked over the sea, he spoke: 'Why did you deceive me, Aturamo'a? Whilst I am looking towards the sea, you look towards the jungle.' Aturamo'a later on returned and came towards the sea. He spoke, 'Good, you Atu'a'ine, look towards the sea, I shall look to the jungle!' This man, who sits near the jungle, is a cannibal, the one who sits near the sea is good."

This short version of the myth I obtained in Sinaketa. The story shows us three people migrating for unknown reasons from the North-East to this district. The sister, after having lost her comb, decides to remain in Siyawawa, and turns into the rock Sinatemubadiye'i. The brothers go only a few miles further, to undergo the same transformation at the Northern end of Sarubwoyna beach. There is the characteristic distinction between the cannibal and the non-cannibal. As the story was told to me in Boyowa, that is, in the district where they were not man-eaters, the qualification of 'good' was given to the non-cannibal hero, who became the rock further out to sea. The same distinction is to be found in the previous quoted myth of the Kudayuri sisters who few to Dobu, and it is to be found also in a myth, told about the origins of cannibalism, which I shall not quote here. The association between the jungle and cannibalism on the one hand, and between the sea and abstention from human flesh on the other, is the same as the one in the Kudayuri myth. In that myth, the rock which looks toward the South is cannibal, while the Northern one is not, and for the natives this is the reason why the Dobuans do eat human flesh and the Boyowans do not. The designation of one of these rocks as a man-eater (*tokamlata'u*) has no further meaning, more especially it is not associated with the belief that any special dangers surround the rock.

The importance of these two rocks, Atu'a'ine and Aturamo'a lies, however, not so much in the truncated myth as in the ritual surrounding them. Thus, all three stones receive an offering—*pokala*—consisting of a bit of coco-nut, a stale yam, a piece of sugar cane and banana. As the canoes go past, the offerings are placed on the stone, or thrown towards it, with the words:

> "Old man (or in the case of Sinatemubadiye'i, 'old woman')" here comes your coco-nut, your sugar cane, your bananas, bring me good luck so that I may go and make my Kula quickly in Tu'utauna."

This offering is given by the Boyowan canoes on their way to Dobu, and by the Dobuans as they start on the Kula Northwards, to Boyowa. Besides the offerings, certain taboos and observances are kept at these rocks. Thus, any people passing close to the rock would have to bathe in the sea out of their canoes, and the children in the canoes would be sprinkled with sea-water. This is done to prevent disease. A man who would go for the first time to *kula* in Dobu would not be allowed to eat food in the vicinity of these rocks. A pig, or a green coco-nut would not be placed on the soil in this neighbourhood, but would have to be put on a mat. A novice in the Kula would have to make a point of going and bathing at the foot of Atu'a'ine and Aturamo'a.

The Dobuans *pokala* some other stones, to which the Boyowans do not give any offerings. The previously mentioned Gurewaya rock receives its share from the Dobuans, who believe that if they passed it close by without making a *pokala*, they would become covered with sores and die. Passing Gurewaya, they would not stand up in their canoes, nor would they eat any food when camping on a beach within sight of Gurewaya. If they did so, they would become seasick, fall asleep, and their canoe would drift away into the unknown. I do not know whether there is any myth in Dobu about the Gurewaya stone. There is a belief that a big snake is coiled on the top of this rock, which looks after the observance of the taboos, and in case of breach of any of them would send down sickness on them. Some of the taboos of Gurewaya are also kept by the Boyowans, but I do not exactly know which.

I obtained from a Dobuan informant a series of names of other, similar stones, lying to the East of Dobu, on the route between there and Tubtube. Thus, somewhere in the district of Du'a'u, there is a rock called Kokorakakedakeda. Besides this, near a place called Makaydokodoko there is a stone, Tabudaya. Further East, near Bunama, a small stone called Sinada enjoys some Kula prestige. In a spot Sina'ena, which I cannot place on the map, there is a stone called Taryadabwoyro, with eye, nose, legs and hind-quarters shaped like those of a pig. This stone is called 'the mother of all the pigs,' and the district of Sina'ena is renowned for the abundance of these animals there.

The only mythical fragment about any of these stones which I obtained is the one quoted above. Like the two Kula myths previously adduced, it is a story of a migration from North to South. There is no allusion to the Kula in the narrative, but as the stones are *pokala'd* in the Kula, there is evidently some association between it and them. To understand this association better, it must be realised that similar offerings are given in certain forms of magic to ancestral spirits and to spirits of Kultur-heroes, who have founded the institution in which the magic is practised. This suggests the conclusion that Atu'a'ine and Aturamo'a are heroes of the Kula like Tokosikuna and Kasabwaybwayreta; and that their story is another variant of the fundamental Kula myth.

2

ETHNOLOGY AND THE STUDY OF SOCIETY

EVERY BRANCH of knowledge can be made useful; first, in its direct application to the practical management of the subject; secondly, in opening a wider outlook upon its subject matter, in allowing us to build up a more adequate theory of the phenomenon in question. The study of savage and coloured races possesses practical value, in the first sense, for purposes of colonial administration and the management of the relations between white and coloured people. In the second sense, ethnology may be a most powerful means of widening our outlook on human nature, of allowing us to build up a correct theory of society for the future scientific guidance of human affairs. This latter claim sounds yet, in our present state of things, like a mixture of wild utopia and an anæmic truism, but I think even the most pessimistic will have to admit that to cultivate and spread *true* and *correct* views of human nature and human society, cannot be without its good effects.

Let us say a few words first about the direct application of ethnology to colonial legislation and policy. We must remember that slavery, "dispersing of natives," indiscriminate "punitive expeditions," and the grossest forms of reckless injustice to natives, are things of the very recent past. One has to remember only the opium war on China, the Australian "blackbirding" in the South Seas, the even more recent "transplanting" of the Hereros in German South-West Africa and the Belgian and French atrocities in Africa scarcely a generation ago. With such an attitude prevalent, it was not to be hoped that a *scientific* management of natives or native affairs could become the guiding force in colonial policy. Of course, there existed always exceptionally able and far-sighted administrators who understood that in order to govern, one must know the human material. We owe, indeed, some of our best ethnographic information to men like Sir Everard im Thurn, Sir Richard Temple, Captain Francis Barton and other colonial officials. Also, many missionaries understood well that in order to spread a new creed, it is necessary to study thoroughly the existing religion and morality, which have to be supplanted and ultimately destroyed. But neither the religious nor the civil transformers of savage societies, as a body, took any trouble about a systematic, purposeful study of the material on which they were going to work and about the application of this study to practice. And even now, with the possible exception of Holland, none of the colonial powers in existence to-day seems to be willing to spend much money or effort on summoning the help of science to their difficult task of managing the subject native races.

And yet there are problems of high importance, where no haphazard methods, no rule-of-thumb acquired in a few years' colonial experience can be of any use. The most sinister of these problems is that of the gradual dying out of the majority of native races. The survival of natives—apart from humanitarian, æsthetic or moral considerations—is a matter of vital importance for practical purposes. Are the South Sea colonies to be repeopled by imported yellow or Hindu labour or are they going to be left to waste, since white labour seems absolutely inadequate? The first course creates a serious political danger, the second means ruin. Millions of money—if we overlook the millions of human lives—are at stake and yet no serious effort has been made by the administrators to assess the danger and try to find out a cure for it.

For a field ethnologist, however, there is an overwhelming mass of evidence to prove that remedies for this dreadful danger are within reach. Broadly speaking, the evil is mainly caused by the destruction of all vital interest for the native, by taking away from him of all that was dear and valuable to him, of all that gave him the joy of living. Whole departments of tribal law and morality, of custom and usage, have been senselessly wiped out by a superficial, haphazard legislation, made in the early days often by newcomers unused to native ways and unprepared to face the difficult problem. They applied to the regulation of native life all the prejudices of the uneducated man to anything strange, foreign, unconventional and to him incomprehensible. All that would appear to a convention-bound, parochial, middle-class as "disgusting," "silly," "immoral," was simply destroyed with a stroke of the pen, and, worse, with rifles and bayonets. And yet to a deeper knowledge, based on real human sympathy, and on conscientious scientific research, many of these "savage" customs are revealed as containing the very essence of the tribal life of a people as something indispensable to their existence as a race.

Imagine a board of well-meaning, perhaps, but rigid and conceited Continental bureaucrats, sitting in judgment over British civilization. They would see thousands of youths and men "wasting their time" over "silly" games, like golf, cricket or football, in "immoral" betting, in "disgusting" boxing or fox-hunting. "These forms of sport are *streng verboten*," would be their verdict! For it is a fact that we Eastern or Central Europeans—I, a member of the Polish Intelligencia as well as the average cultured German—feel exactly as I have just written about certain forms of English sport and especially about the great importance and the great amount of time given to it in this country. Yet, anyone looking from an ethnological point of view on this problem would soon see that to wipe out sport, or even to undermine its influence, would be a crime, as it would be an attempt to destroy one of the main features of national life and national enjoyment.

The savage, like anyone else, must have his pastimes and amusements, his sports and pleasures, which give zest and meaning to his life. Some of them are really fine, æsthetic and significant, beneficent, hygienically and psychologically, and devoid of any harm whatever, even from the point of view of European morality. I have watched and taken part, time after time, in Melanesian surf bathing, in yachting on the Lagoon, in open air play, as well as in some of their big tribal festivities, with floral distributions, customary games and exchange of gifts. For weeks and months have I watched native dances, performed in a manner monotonous to us, though beautiful and extremely important to them, and at the same time, of an absolutely Puritanical chastity.

Yet the ignorant and pedantic morality-monger, whether clerical or official, cannot help scenting some sexual mischief, wherever he finds amusement and pleasure. In my experience of almost all tribes, I have found some sort of disapprobation, or actual interference, on the part of missionary or Government authorities with the amusements, and especially with the dancing, of the natives. In the Trobriand Islands in the N.E. of New Guinea, no elements of sex enter at all into their dancing which, in part, consists of conventionalized imitation of animals, but mainly is a performance where athletic, rhythmic and musical skill is exhibited. Strong passions of vanity, ambition and rivalry are displayed, but sexual *libido* is entirely absent. None the less, some missionaries try to eradicate this "evil," though an exceptionally enlightened one—Mr. Gilmour, a Methodist—did all he could to prevent this meddling. On the south coast of New Guinea, in and around Port Moresby, the use of drums has been prohibited for years, half of the public life of the natives being thus completely paralysed. This happened because the Administrator of the colony, entirely ignorant of, and out of touch with, native affairs, but very much under missionary influence, had been persuaded that drums serve immorality![1] In the district of Dobu, in the d'Entrecasteaux Islands, the native flute has been tabooed by a missionary, who was at the same time Government agent, because it had been suspected that love messages were sent by means of certain melodious strains, and there was no guarantee that they could not be used in an ungodly manner— nay, for adulterous purposes!

The tragic humour of all these cases—because for the natives it is a

---

[1] This prohibition was withdrawn after a few years by Captain F. Barton, the new Administrator. It may be said at once that Captain Barton, a friend and collaborator of Professor Seligman, must be counted as a genuine ethnologist.

tragedy to be deprived of half their pleasures—consists in the fact that in one and all of them the scented "evil" did not exist, as I can vouch on the basis of careful ethnographical inquiries. Thus, through mere ignorance, mental laziness and that hypocrisy which shrinks from even touching pitch, a good deal of real mischief has been and is being done, by wanton destruction of certain customs, which, by all standards, even by the most rigid ones of the very destroyers, are perfectly innocent, and which possess at the same time a high biological value to the natives.

I have given these examples to show that, even without deepening their essential outlook on the world, and merely by increasing their knowledge of the natives, and their capacity for ethnographic inquiry, the modern petty inquisitors of primitive life could be saved from committing some of their worst crimes. But it would be much better if ethnographical knowledge could altogether change the average white man's whole outlook on savage morality. For there is no doubt that, taking native life as a whole, the element of sex plays a great part, and that it appears in certain forms which at first sight shock the white man's sense of morality. Although we find, even among the lowest savages, some tribes where strict chastity of girls, fidelity of married women and a monogamous marriage are laid down and enforced by usage and custom, yet in the majority of cases, general laxity, licentious, sometimes grotesque, customs and institutions, and a much greater overt cultivation of crude sexuality obtain. And this seems to show that there must be some biological reasons why primitive mankind lives and thrives under such conditions. To attempt a radical, complete change of all this by a few talks with the natives would seem to anyone with an even mediocre biological and sociological training, absurd from the outset. One might agree with the missionary principle that a change is here necessary, if the natives have to come into contact with large numbers of white men and women. In this case one might agree, thus far at least, that certain of the worst crudities and public obscenities should be eradicated, since they would be intolerable to the white onlookers. Again, that gradually the general licence should be limited, even if it were only to protect the natives from the spread of venereal disease, which the European brings, side by side with his "higher morality." But such gradual and selective change must be done carefully, with a deep knowledge of human nature, as well as of the local customs, that is, under expert guidance from ethnology.

A rapid and indiscriminate suppression of all sexual licence, in the first place never succeeds completely, and in so far as it succeeds partially, produces results which one must assume are not those desired by the reformers. In the Trobriand Islands, where sexual laxity is very great, unnatural vice, perversion or homosexuality and bestiality have been completely unknown. The only cases now on record are three or four of natives who have come under the influence of the white man's morals. These exceptions, which have, of course, been cast forth from the fold as black sheep, and sent back to their villages, are looked down upon with an amused contempt and disgust by the uncontaminated savage. The psychological and physiological mechanism of these cases is obvious. If you take a number of people from a community where an almost daily satisfaction of the sexual instinct is considered an absolutely legitimate and necessary right of a man and woman, and if you then divide the sexes and coop each up into separate compounds, their powerful passions and instincts will turn into wrong channels. This example, as all others which have come under my notice through field work or reading, shows unmistakably how dangerous it is to tamper ignorantly with that most powerful human instinct, sex, and with the various regulations and liberties which a natural biological and social development has built up round it. Another aspect of native life, against which the destructive reform of administrator and missionary alike has to turn at the very outset, is warfare and all forms of fighting and raiding between the tribes. Especially cannibalism, so repugnant to our gastronomical and moral principles, arouses the European's ire and zeal for annihilation. It is quite comprehensible, of course, that the pioneer preacher or magistrate is keen on putting an end to cannibalism before it puts an end to him. Since *"l'appétit vient en mangeant,"* it is better to prohibit consumption of black flesh, or some day a gourmet may feel a craving for a white dish. And, seriously speaking, even the most antiquarian of all ethnologists would not plead for the preservation and fostering by white authorities of cannibalism among the savages.

For similar reasons, it is an invariable rule to stop all hostilities among the natives, and to prohibit the use, and even the possession, of arms. For, with savages bearing arms, there is no knowing when they would turn them against Europeans. For reasons of self-preservation, therefore, the European finds himself compelled to disarm the native, and paralyse the free use of some of their most important activities.

But though one can admit fully the cogency of the white man's case, some ethnological insight shows that it is by no means simple. First of all, it would be good to make it quite clear to ourselves that it is sheer hypocrisy and humbug to pretend that the prohibition of fighting is done for the good of the natives. I may add at once that I am a convinced pacifist, that I believe that modern warfare cannot in any way be shown to be beneficent, that, indeed, ever since the invention of firearms, war has lost all its redeeming features and has remained an unmitigated evil.

But savage warfare is something quite different, the toll in human life and suffering which it takes is as a rule relatively small. On the other hand, it provides a wide field for physical exercise, the development of personal courage, cunning and initiative, and the sort of dramatic and romantic interest, the wide vision of possibilities and ideals, which probably nothing else can replace. I am speaking here, of course, of savages, and all these expressions must be translated into savage values. Also, there is no doubt that in some cases, especially when any more powerful people wages war on its weak and inferior neighbours, as frequently happens, especially in Africa, then war becomes almost as bad as it is between European nations. But in no case is the mental anguish and suffering of a native comparable to that of a civilized man.

In many cases, again, savage warfare is nothing worse than a dangerous sport. In the Trobriand Islands, British New Guinea, in a big war, where a couple of thousand warriors took part, the total casualties might amount to half-a-dozen killed and a dozen wounded—nothing compared to a baseball match! And such a war afforded excellent amusement, exercise and development of personal qualities to large numbers of men for several weeks. Warfare on the south coast of New Guinea, with the wonderful treetop fortresses, with long marches in the jungle, moves and countermoves in difficult country, was perhaps a trifle more severe but not much, and even more romantic. Round the east end of New Guinea, where cannibalism and head-hunting flourish, the natives had the unpleasant habit of making nocturnal raids, and of killing without any necessity, and in an unsportsmanlike manner, women and children as well as combatants. But when investigated more closely and concretely, such raids appear rather as daring and dangerous enterprises, crowned, as a rule, with but small success—half-a-dozen victims or so—rather than as a wholesale slaughter, which indeed they never were. For the weaker communities used to live in inaccessible fastnesses, perched high up above precipitous slopes, and they used to keep good watch over the coast. Now, when European rule has established peace and security, these communities have come down to the sea-coast and to swampy and unhealthy districts, and their numbers have rapidly diminished.

Thus, the establishment of peace and safety is by no means an unmixed blessing, and it is always deeply resented by the natives themselves. And even here where the case for the eradicating and paralysing reformer is the strongest, we can legitimately ask the question, whether the reforms could not have been done with less wholesale destruction. Perhaps while forbidding the more bloody and pernicious types of fighting, some sort of milder forms might have been left so as not to unman the natives completely. Perhaps some sportive imitations of warfare might have been permitted without bloodshed, yet allowing the savages to settle their quarrels and satisfy their ambitions in this manner. These suggestions are not entirely fantastic, because in some cases the natives have themselves tried to provide such substitute activities. In this manner, there would remain the healthy exercise, the means of developing personality, of maintaining tribal rivalry and individual ambition, while all real and imaginary dangers would be entirely obliterated.

But the policy, both of administrator and missionary, has been quite the reverse. To take examples again from my personal field of observation in Eastern New Guinea, all war canoes were destroyed; club-houses and communal sitting places associated with head-hunting and cannibalism, but fulfilling many other functions besides, were made to disappear; social organizations referring primarily to warfare were abolished.

I could still multiply examples from other aspects of native life, besides the two most "shocking" ones, sex and warfare. Thus all savage belief, myth and ritual is evil growth in the eyes of the missionary, to be weeded out and burnt. That, of course, is his business. It is all very well to call everything which a native believes "superstition," and to try to import "true faith" instead. But the fact is that a savage community has obtained its religion as the product through centuries of natural development, and that it suits savage mentality and their social organization perfectly well, whereas European religion cannot be grafted on to an entirely different social, mental and moral soil, and requires an absolute upheaval of all the natives' own civilization before it can be introduced at all.

A series of customs again arouses the indignation of the benevolent hygienist, who pounces especially on burial arrangements, and on some of the practices of mourning. In some tribes, where the burial of the dead in the village is considered the first duty of filial piety, the European has compelled the bereaved family to bury their dead in the bush, upsetting thus the whole aspect of religious ritual and of social organization. Here once more we can question whether the negative good of preventing just here and there an isolated, unhygienic mode of behavior is not outweighed by the positive evil of destroying much that is the mainstay of tribal life.

Everywhere the same fanatical zeal to prune, uproot, make an *auto-da-fé* of all that shocks our own moral, hygienic or parochial susceptibilities, the same ignorant and stupid lack of comprehension of the fact that every item of culture, every custom and belief, represents a value, fulfils a social function, has a positive, biological significance. For tradition is a fabric in which all the strands are so closely woven that the destruction of one unmakes the whole. And tradition is, biologically speaking, a form of collective adaptation of a community to its surroundings. Destroy tradition, and you will deprive the collective organism of its protective shell, and give it over to the slow but inevitable process of dying out.

To draw a moral, I am going to put the case briefly: there is much in native life that has to succumb to the contact with European influence.

There is a good deal which is already undermined by missionary teaching and by indispensable claims of European interests and European prejudices. When, therefore, the legislator and administrator, in a burst of uncalled-for reformatory zeal, further prune and uproot much of the native's tree of life—is there no urgent need to stop and think? To invoke the advice of dispassionate study and scientific expert opinion?

I have only touched on the one, though the most essential point, where scientific study ought to be taken into the councils of colonial administration and legislation, that, namely, of preserving the integrity of tribal life as far as possible, so as to prevent complete extinction. It would be easy to adduce many other very telling instances, if opportunity were offered to go into the matter more deeply and with more detail.

I want, however, to say a few words about the second great chance for ethnology to become really useful in human affairs, that is by serving as one of the most important foundations for a general science of Man in his mental and social nature. Whether we call such a science Sociology or Social Psychology, or Philosophy of History or Politics, is of no great importance as long as we agree that it must be based on a purely empirical basis and that it must aim at real utility in the conduct of affairs.

Although the present political atmosphere seems hardly conducive to optimism, there is no doubt that a better knowledge of the social mechanism would lead to a better appreciation of their *real* interests by the various conflicting groups and classes. In the present endless strife of group egoisms—national interests, class interests, racial interests—the introduction of the scientific spirit of dispassionate research would necessarily lead to a broader and more conciliatory attitude. A sober and heart-searching inquiry as to "What are we fighting for? What can we hope for from the defeat of our antagonists?"—might lead us to understand that co-operation and constructive work are more beneficial to both parties than hatred and opposition. Perhaps, even, not only to understand this truism, but even to act on it! Such an attitude in itself, apart from the more concrete and detailed counsels afforded from social study, would be a powerful gain to true progress and would, therefore, be an achievement of real practical value. A systematic exposition of this attitude—based on all available material scientifically formulated—will be the Sociology of the Future—The New Humanism—and, indeed, much of the Sociology of to-day has already fully justified the hopes and anticipations in this direction.[2]

---

[2] To mention only efforts on British soil, there are the excellent works of Professor Hobhouse, Mr. and Mrs. Sidney Webb, Dr. Westermarck, Professor Graham Wallas, Sir William Beveridge, and others: in fact, all the theoretical work carried on in Sociology, Economics and Politics at the London School of Economics. Also we might class here the many valuable attempts at Social Reform based on scientific research.

Now if this New Humanism is to have sufficient force to shape human ideals and even to influence policies, it must be based on a *really scientific* knowledge of human nature. This knowledge must, therefore, be empirical. But how and whence is the sociologist to draw empirical material? Where can he obtain observations of changes occurring through variation in conditions? The ready answer to this is: there is history which teaches us the fate of humanity throughout the moving ages and changing conditions. Here, however, it is necessary to consider a point of extreme importance, though of almost philosophic subtlety. The only knowledge of past history we possess, we owe to the testimony of chroniclers and historians of past ages, whose views on social matters and human nature widely differ from our own. They were entirely unfit to act as our vicarious observers, except in certain aspects of history, aspects which the most modern historian tends to consider as rather superficial. Aristotle was a great genius and had an encyclopædic knowledge of contemporaneous science. Yet the modern physicist would not rest content in founding his theory of electricity on Aristotle's observations! Great men though they often were, the chroniclers of the past can give us poor stuff only as foundation for the less obvious problems of sociology.

Social theory, as well as natural science, constantly opens up new vistas, discloses new ranges of facts, and on these the documents of past ages, as a rule, say nothing or very little and that indirectly. To the chronicler—who as often as not was a courtier—the court gossip, the often inglorious exploits of the monarch, of his ministers and mistresses, were more important than an obscure economic change slowly working its way among the peasants or artisans. Only after a social phenomenon flared up in the form of a civil war, revolt or other dramatic and sensational event, would the average chronicler take stock of it. To the exponents of the modern tendency in history—popularly and brilliantly set forth in Mr. H. G. Wells' recent work on history—it is just the fundamental forces of human society, the forms of social constitution, the types of economic organization, the great moral, religious and philosophic tendencies of an age that matter above all. The great men and the great masses alike make history, in mutual interplay or co-operation. To speak of leaders and forget the led is an error of method.

This new tendency in history meets insurmountable obstacles in the inadequacy of the historical chronicles. There are, of course, the indirect sources, deeds, legal documents, account books and such like, but how meagre and oblique is their testimony! How often a historian must dream of being transported into the period of his researches, of becoming his own source and vindicating his conclusions by direct observation!

But what never can be vouchsafed to a historian, is given in a full measure to the field ethnologist. What *time* has hidden from us for ever, *space* keeps preserved for a while, and under the modern conditions of travel reveals easily to an ethnographic explorer. In the various parts of our globe, there exist phases of civilization as far removed from ours as the Middle Ages or Classical Antiquity, as the Homeric Epoch or the Neolithic times. To the old-fashioned historian who hunts after kings, great men, heroes and sensational events only, the study of the various non-European cultures will not reveal much of interest. To the modern sociologist-historian, the records of a scientific field ethnologist will be very stimulating.

The field ethnologist, who studies the various types of civilization under varied conditions, is the only sociologist who can, on a large scale, do anything comparable to an experiment in social matters. He can observe the differences in human mental constitution and human social behaviour under the various forms of physical and mental environment, as divergent as physical and mental nature will allow.

The opening up of a new vista of forgotten civilization gave the first great impulse to Humanism: that of the Renaissance. In the eighteenth century the work of Lessing and Winckelmann threw a new light on the classical cultures, and especially on the relative value of the Greek and Latin contributions, and there came again a new revival of humanistic studies. Humanism was broadened again in its scope and subject matter by the inclusion of Sanskrit linguistics and literature and the comparative study of Indo-European cultures and languages. The most important final step was taken when modern anthropology became a science in the achievements of Tylor, Robertson Smith, the *Völkerpsychologen*, Bastian, Morgan and Lubbock, and in its most modern development with the great works of Sir James Frazer. This new development, the placing of sociological and historical theory on the broadest basis of comprehensive comparison of all civilization, including those of the savage races, may be called without too much pretension the New Humanism.

This New Humanism has, however, its obligations and duties, as well as its claims and privileges. So far, ethnological research, whether at home or in the field, has shown too much of a tendency towards the sensational and singular, towards isolating customs and beliefs of an outstanding, striking character and towards treating them as a collector treats savage "curios." There was a tendency with the travellers among native races to skim the surface of tribal life in search of queer and quaint peculiarities. Barbarous mutilations of body, as well as distorted, incongruous beliefs, have been recorded very much as scandals or monstrosities are reported in the yellow press to satisfy our craving for the sensational and strange. We have excellent accounts of the dreadful rites of subincision in Australia and infibulation in the Sudan, of "survivals of primitive promiscuity" in Fiji and "group marriage" among the Dieri.

Not that all these subjects are not of the greatest importance: but they are not the only facts worth study. These sensational plums stick in a very ordinary cake of the drab, commonplace tribal life, in which the native does and lives through many phases very much resembling our own conditions. And it is the *need of studying all the phases of native life* that I am urging here, attractive and ugly, sensational and commonplace alike.

This, of course, is not an entirely new outlook, because it is to be found in the works of Sir James Frazer, Prof. Hobhouse, Dr. Marett, Prof. Westermarck, and all those who attempt to reach the deeper layers of magic, religion, social organization, and primitive social order. All these problems cannot be solved, except by a deeper analysis of big complexes of cultural phenomenon, of whole aspects of human civilization. Again, in ethnographic field work the research done by trained men of science— inaugurated by the memorable Cambridge Expedition to the South Seas, by Haddon, Ray, Rivers, Seligman and others—has, or ought to have, put once for all an end to mere curio-hunting in ethnology.[3]

But although the tendency to shift the main weight of scientific attention from isolated details and striking curiosities to comprehensive groups of fundamental ideas is fully acknowledged by the best modern writers—by the late Dr. W. H. R. Rivers, of Cambridge, more consistently and explicitly than by anyone else—this tendency must be followed up further yet. Thus, for instance, there are still whole aspects of tribal life to which hardly any deeper attention has been paid. Even in our best monographs on native races, the *economic* aspect is almost without exception completely neglected. That is, no doubt, due on the one hand to the preconceived idea, which we all tend to have, of the extreme simplicity of primitive economics; on the other hand, it is just this aspect which presents to the observer the least sensational, the most obvious appearance, which promises no surprises or thrills of any sort. Yet this very aspect is of such great importance and of such an obvious one that a whole school of philosophers attribute to the economic organization the rôle of primary cause in all social change. The materialistic view of history, as it is called, is no doubt a metaphysical exaggeration of an important truth, but the neglect of the economic in ethnological field work is an interesting symptom of the need to reform its method still more thoroughly in the direction of a *comprehensive treatment of all aspects of tribal life and their correlation.*

This postulate, if carried through, will do away to a great extent with

[3] Recently the generous endowment by Sir Peter Mackie, of the Mackie Expedition to Central Africa, organized and directed by Sir James Frazer and carried out by the Rev. J. Roscoe, and the financing by Mr. Robert Mond of the Mond Expedition to New Guinea, are hopeful symptoms that funds and initiative will be forthcoming to foster ethnological field work, carried out by competent observers with academic training.

the sensational character of much of our ethnographic knowledge. A belief, which appears crude and senseless in isolation, a practice which seems queer and "immoral," becomes often clear and even clean if understood as a part of a system of thought and practice. From this point of view, it is all important for the field ethnologist to try and assimilate thoroughly the ideas and ways of one single tribe and spend a good deal of time over it, rather than skim through a considerable number of tribes, though this latter is from some points of view an indispensable supplement of the first type of work. To borrow the terminology of Dr. Rivers and his opinion: in the present state of ethnography *intensive* field work is even more urgently needed than *survey* work.

The future development of ethnology lies in its rôle of first handmaiden to a general theory of human society, a theory trying to achieve a deeper grasp of human nature and of human history. Such a theory would give us, within limits, the power to foresee the course of events, and in a dim future, when this power is universally recognized, it might improve and influence those in authority. It would also—and this is of no lesser value—be useful in creating a saner attitude, finer and wider ideals in the minds of men. For the destinies of mankind are shaped not only by the policy from above, but also by the slow, invisible changes which are always at work in all the individuals of a community.

From this point of view there can be no doubt about the *practical value* of a New Humanism, a broad philosophic view of the laws of human society and human nature, based on a strictly scientific study of the widest range of facts at our disposal. And it is not so far-fetched an idea as might at first seem, to appeal to the savages for some light to be shed on our own nature. For nothing stimulates research and understanding as much as contrast and comparison, reached through the widest possible empiric survey of facts. Just as the psychology of normal human beings has received much help and stimulus from the study of mental disorder, so the social science of modern man and of the historical periods can look for much inspiration and assistance from ethnological researches.

PART TWO

PSYCHOANALYSIS AND SOCIETIES

3

PSYCHOANALYSIS AND ANTHROPOLOGY

THE INFECTION by psycho-analysis of the neighbouring fields of science—notably that of anthropology, folklore, and sociology—has been a very rapid and somewhat inflammatory process. The votaries of Freud, or some among them, have displayed in their missionary zeal an amount of dogmatism and of aggressiveness not calculated to allay the prejudice and suspicion which usually greet every new extension of their theories. Some of their critics, on the other hand, go so far as to dismiss all anthropological contributions of Freud and his school as "utterly preposterous" and "obviously futile," as "an intrigue with Ethnology which threatens disaster to both parties," as "a striking demonstration of *reductio ad absurdum*."[1] This is a harsh judgment and it carries much weight, coming from one by no means hostile to psychoanalysis and thoroughly well acquainted with anthropological problems, especially those discussed by Freud and his school. This seems the right moment to consider impartially, without enthusiasm or prejudice, the scope, importance, and value of Freud's contribution to anthropology.

Through the initiative and under the direction of Prof. [C. G.] Seligman, who at that time was engaged in practical psycho-analysis of war neuroses, I have been able to apply some of Freud's conclusions directly to savage psychology and customs, while actually engaged in field-work among the natives of Eastern New Guinea.

Freud's fundamental conception of the Oedipus complex contains a sociological as well as a psychological theory. The psychological theory declares that much, if not all of human mental life has its root in infantile tendencies of a "libidinous" character, repressed later on in childhood by the paternal authority and the atmosphere of the patriarchal family life. Thus there is formed a "complex" in the unconscious mind of a parricidal and "matrogamic" nature. The sociological implications of this theory indicate that throughout the development of humanity there must have existed the institution of individual family and marriage, with the father as a severe, nay, ferocious patriarch, and with the mother representing the principles of affection and kindness. Freud's anthropological views stand and fall with Westermarck's theory of the antiquity and perma-

This Letter to the Editor appeared in Nature, *November 3, 1923 (Vol. 112, No. 2818), pp. 650–51, and is reprinted by permission.*

[1] Prof. G. Elliot Smith, in River's *Psychology and Politics*, 1923, pp. 141–45.

nence of individual and monogamous marriage. Freud himself assumes the existence, at the outset of human development, of a patriarchal family with a tyrannical and ferocious father who repressed all the claims of the younger men.[2] With the hypothesis of a primitive promiscuity or group marriage, Freud's theories are thoroughly incompatible, and in this they have the support, not only of Westermarck's classical researches, but also of the most recent contributions to our knowledge of primitive sexual life.

When we come to examine in detail the original constitution of the human family—not in any hypothetical primeval form, but as we find it in actual observation among present-day savages—some difficulties emerge. We find, for example, that there is a form of matriarchal family in which the relations between children and progenitors do not exist in the typical form as required by Freud's hypothesis of the Oedipus complex. Taking as an example the family as found in the coral archipelagoes of Eastern New Guinea, where I have studied it, the mother and her brother possess in it all the legal *potestas*. The mother's brother is the "ferocious matriarch," the father is the affectionate friend and helper of his children. He has to win for himself the friendship of his sons and daughters, and is frequently their amicable ally against the principle of authority represented by the maternal uncle. In fact, none of the domestic conditions required for the sociological fulfilment of the Oedipus complex, with its repressions, exist in the Melanesian family of Eastern New Guinea, as I shall show fully in a book shortly to be published on the sexual life and family organisation of these natives.

Again, the sexual repression within the family, the taboo on incest, is mainly directed towards the separation of brother and sister, although it also divides mother and son sexually. Thus we have a pattern of family life in which the two elements decisive for psycho-analysis, the repressive authority and the severing taboo, are "displaced," distributed in a manner different from that found in the patriarchal family. If Freud's general theory is correct, there ought to be also a change in the thwarted desires; the repressed wish formation ought to receive a shape different from the Oedipus complex.

This is as a matter of fact what happens. The examination of dreams, myths, and of the prevalent sexual obsessions reveals indeed a most remarkable confirmation of Freudian theories. The most important type of sexual mythology centres round stories of brother-sister incest. The mythical cycle which explains the origin of love and love magic attributes its existence to an act of incest between brother and sister. There is a notable absence of the parricidal motive in their myth. On the other hand

---

[2] Cf. *Totem and Taboo*, 1918, Chap. IV, 5, and *Massen Psychologie and Ich-Analyze* [*Group Psychology and the Analysis of the Ego*, 1922], Chap. X.

the motive of castration comes in, and it is carried out not on the father but on the maternal uncle. He also appears in other legendary cycles as a villainous, dangerous, and oppressive foe.

In general I have found in the area of my studies an unmistakable correlation between the nature of family and kinship on one hand and the prevalent "complex" on the other, a complex which can be traced in many manifestations of the folklore, customs, and institutions of these natives.

To sum up, the study of savage life and some reflection on Freud's theories and their application to anthropology have led me to the conviction that a great deal of these theories requires modification and in its present form will not stand the test of evidence—notably the theory of *libido*, the exaggeration of infantile sexuality, and the manner in which "sexual symbolisation" is dealt with. The character of the argumentation and the manner and mannerisms of exposition moreover often contain such glaring surface absurdities and show such lack of anthropological insight that one cannot wonder at the impatience of a specialist, such as expressed in the remarks of Prof. Elliot Smith quoted above. But with all this, Freud's contribution to anthropology is of the greatest importance and seems to me to strike a very rich vein which must be followed up. For Freud has given us the first concrete theory about the relation between instinctive life and social institutions. His doctrine of repression due to social influence allows us to explain certain typical latent wishes or "complexes," found in folklore, by reference to the organisation of a given society. Inversely it allows us also to trace the pattern on instinctive and emotional tendencies in the texture of the social fabric. By making the theories somewhat more elastic, the anthropologist can not only apply them to the interpretation of certain phenomena, but also in the field he can be inspired by them in the exploration of the difficult borderland between social tradition and social organisation. How fruitful Freud's theories are in this respect I hope to demonstrate clearly in the pending publication previously mentioned.

4

OBSCENITY AND MYTH

W E NOW PROCEED to the discussion of folk-lore in relation to the typical sentiments of the matrilineal family, and with this we enter the best cultivated plot on the boundary of psycho-analysis and anthropology. It has long been recognized that for one reason or another the stories related seriously about ancestral times and the narratives told for amusement correspond to the desires of those among whom they are current. The school of Freud maintain, moreover, that folklore is especially concerned with the satisfaction of repressed wishes by means of fairy tales and legends; and that this is the case also with proverbs, typical jokes and sayings and stereotyped modes of abuse.

Let us begin with these last. Their relation to the unconscious must not be interpreted in the sense that they satisfy the repressed cravings of the person abused, or even of the abuser. For instance, the expression widely current among oriental races and many savages, 'eat excrement,' as well as in a slightly modified form among the Latins, satisfies directly the wish of neither. Indirectly it is only meant to debase and disgust the person thus addressed. Every form of abuse or bad language contains certain propositions fraught with strong emotional possibilities. Some bring into play emotions of disgust and shame; others again draw attention to, or impute, certain actions which are considered abominable in a given society, and thus wound the feelings of the listener. Here belongs blasphemy, which in European culture reaches its zenith of perfection and complexity in the innumerable variations of *'Me cago en Dios!'* pullulating wherever the sonorous Spanish is spoken. Here, also, belong all the various abuses by reference to social position, despised or degraded occupations, criminal habits, and the like, all of them very interesting sociologically, for they indicate what is considered the lowest depth of degradation in that culture.

The incestuous type of swearing, in which the person addressed is invited to have connection with a forbidden relative, usually the mother, is in Europe the speciality of the Slavonic nations, among whom the Russians easily take the lead, with the numerous combinations of 'Yob twayu mat' ('Have connection with thy mother'). This type of swearing interests us most, because of its subject, and because it plays an important part in the Trobriands. The natives there have three incestuous expressions: *'Kwoy inam'*—'Cohabit with thy mother'; *'Kwoy lumuta'*—'cohabit with thy sister'; and *'Kwou um' kwava'*—'cohabit with thy wife.' The combination of the three sayings is curious in itself, for we see, side by side, the most lawful and the most illicit types of intercourse used for the same purpose of offending and hurting. The gradation of intensity is still more remarkable. For while the invitation to maternal incest is but a mild term used in chaff or as a joke, as we might say, 'Oh, go to Jericho', the mention of sister incest in abuse is a most serious offence, and one used only when real anger is aroused. But the worst insult, one which I have known to be seriously used at the most twice, and once, indeed, it was among the causes of the incident of fratricide described above, is the imperative to have connection with the wife. This expression is so bad that I learnt of its existence only after a long sojourn in the Trobriands, and no native would pronounce it but in whispers, or consent to make any jokes about that incongruous mode of abuse.

What is the psychology of this gradation? It is obvious that it stands in no distinct relation to the enormity or unpleasantness of the act. The maternal incest is absolutely and completely out of the question, yet it is the mildest abuse. Nor can the criminality of the action be the reason for the various strengths of the swearing, for the least criminal, in fact the lawful connection, is the most offensive when imputed. The real cause is the plausibility and the reality of the act, and the feeling of shame, anger, and social degradation at the barriers of etiquette being pulled down and the naked reality brought to light. For the sexual intimacy between husband and wife is masked by a most rigid etiquette, not so strict of course as that between brother and sister, but directly aiming at the elimination of any suggestive modes of behaviour. Sexual jokes and indecencies must not be pronounced in the company of the two consorts. And to drag out the personal, dirext sexuality of the relation in coarse language is a mortal offence to the sensitiveness of the Trobrianders. This psychology is extremely interesting, just because it discloses that one of the main forces of abuse lies in the relation between the reality and plausibility of a desire or action and its conventional repressions.

The relation between the abuse by mother and by sister incest is made clear by the same psychology. Its strength is measured mainly by the likelihood of reality corresponding to the imputation. The idea of mother incest is as repugnant to the native as sister incest, probably even more. But just because, as we saw, the whole development of the relationship and of sexual life makes incestuous temptations of the mother almost absent, while the taboo against the sister is imposed with great brutality and kept up with rigid strength, the real inclination to break the strong taboo is much more actual. Hence this abuse wounds to the quick.

There is nothing to be said about proverbs in the Trobriands, for they do not exist. As to the typical sayings and other linguistic uses, I shall mention here the important fact of the word *luguta*, my sister, being used in magic as a word which signifies incompatibility and mutual repulsion.

We pass now to myth and legend, that is, to the stories told with a serious purpose in explanation of things, institutions, and customs. To make the survey of this very extensive and rich material clear yet rapid, we shall classify these stories into three categories: (1) Myths of the origin of man, and of the general order of society, and especially totemic divisions and social ranks; (2) Myths of cultural change and achievements which contain stories about heroic deeds, about the establishment of customs, cultural features and social institutions; (3) Myths associated with definite forms of magic.[1]

The matrilineal character of the culture meets us at once in the first class, that is, in the myths about the origins of man, of the social order, especially chieftainship and totemic divisions, and of the various clans and sub-clans. These myths, which are numerous, for every locality has its own legends or variations, form a sort of connected style. They all agree that human beings have emerged from underground through holes in the earth. Every sub-clan has its own place of emergence, and the events which happened on this momentous occasion determined sometimes the privileges or disabilities of the sub-clan. What interests us most in them is that the first ancestral groups whose appearance is mentioned in the myth consist always of a woman, sometimes accompanied by her brother, sometimes by the totemic animal, but never by a husband. In some of the myths the mode of propagating of the first ancestress is explicitly described. She starts the line of her descendants by imprudent exposure to the rain or, lying in a grotto, is pierced by the dripping of the stalactites; or bathing she is bitten by a fish. She is 'opened up' in this way, and a spirit child enters her womb and she becomes pregnant.[2] Thus instead of the creative force of a father, the myths reveal the spontaneous procreative powers of the ancestral mother.

Nor is there any other rôle in which the father appears. In fact, he is never mentioned, and does not exist in any part of the mythological world. Most of these local myths have come down in very rudimentary form, some containing only one incident or an affirmation of right and

---

[1] Cf. the chapter on Mythology in *Argonauts of the Western Pacific*, especially pp. 304 sqq.

[2] Freudians will be interested in the psychology of symbolism underlying these myths. It must be noted that the natives have no idea whatever of the fertilizing influence of the male semen, but they know that a virgin cannot conceive, and that to become a mother a woman has to be 'opened up' as they express it. This in the everyday life of the village is done at an early age by the appropriate organ. In the myth of the primeval ancestress, where the husband or any sexually eligible male companion is excluded, some natural object is selected, such as a fish or a stalactite. Cf. for further material on this subject my article in *Psyche*, Oct., 1923, reprinted as *The Father in Primitive Psychology*, 1927.

privilege. Those of them which contain a conflict or a dramatic incident, elements essential in ungarbled myth, depict invariably a matrilineal family and the drama happening within it. There is a quarrel between two brothers which makes them separate, each taking his sister. Or, again, in another myth, two sisters set out, disagree, separate and found two different communities.

In a myth which might perhaps be classed in this group, and which accounts for the loss of immortality, or, to put it more correctly, of perpetual youth by human beings, it is the quarrel between grandmother and granddaughter which brings about the catastrophe. Matriliny—in the fact that descent is reckoned by the female—mother-right—in the great importance of the part played by women, the matriarchal configuration of kinship, in the dissensions of brothers—in short, the pattern of the matrilineal family, is evident in the structure of myths of this category. There is not a single myth of origins in which a husband or a father plays any part, or even makes his appearance. That the matrilineal nature of the mythological drama is closely associated with the matrilineal repressions within the family should need no further argument to convince a psycho-analyst.

Let us now turn to the second class of myths, those referring to certain big cultural achievements brought about by heroic deeds and important adventures. This class of myths is less rudimentary, consists of long cycles, and develops pronouncedly dramatic incidents. The most important cycle of this category is the myth of Tudava, a hero born of a virgin who was pierced by the action of stalactite water. The deeds of this hero are celebrated in a number of myths, which differ slightly according to the district in which they are found, and which ascribe to him the introduction of agriculture and the institution of a number of customs and moral rules, though his own moral character is very weakly developed. The main deed of this hero, however, the one known all over the district, and forming the bedrock of all the myths, is the slaying of an ogre. The story runs as follows:—

Humanity led a happy existence in the Trobriand Archipelago. Suddenly a dreadful ogre called Dokonikan made his appearance in the eastern part of the islands. He fed on human flesh and gradually consumed one community after another. At the north-western end of the island in the village of Laba'i there lived at that time a family consisting of a sister and her brothers. When Dokonikan ranged nearer and nearer to Laba'i the family decided to fly. The sister, however, at that moment wounded her foot and was unable to move. She was therefore abandoned by her brothers, who left her with her little son in a grotto on the beach of Laba'i, and sailed away in a canoe to the south-west. The boy was brought up by his mother, who taught him first the choice of proper wood for a strong spear, then instructed him in the *Kwoygapani* magic which steals away a man's understanding. The hero sallied forth, and after having bewitched Dokonikan with the *Kwoygapani* magic, killed him and cut off his head. After that he and his mother prepared a taro pudding, in which they hid and baked the head of the ogre. With this gruesome dish Tudava sailed away in search of his mother's brother. When he found him he gave him the pudding, in which the uncle with horror and dismay found the head of Dokonikan. Seized with fear and remorse, the mother's brother offered his nephew all sorts of gifts in atonement for having abandoned him and his mother to the ogre. The hero refused everything, and was only appeased after he had received his uncle's daughter in marriage. After that he set out again and performed a number of cultural deeds, which do not interest us further in this context.

In this myth there are two conflicts which set the drama in motion: first the cannibalistic appetite of the ogre, and second the abandonment of mother and son by the maternal uncle. The second is a typical matrilineal drama, and corresponds distinctly to the natural tendency, repressed by tribal morals and custom, as we have found it in our analysis of the matrilineal family in the Trobriands. For the mother's brother is the appointed guardian of her and her family. Yet this is a duty which both weighs heavily upon him, and is not always gratefully and pleasantly received by his wards. Thus it is characteristic that the opening of the most important heroic drama in mythology should be associated with a capital sin of the matriarch's neglect of his duty.

But this second matriarchal conflict is not altogether independent of the first. When Dokonikan is killed his head is presented in a dish of wood to the maternal uncle. If it were only to frighten him by the sight of the monster, there would be no point in disguising the head in the taro pudding. Moreover, since Dokonikan was the general enemy of humanity, the sight of his head should have filled the uncle with joy. The whole setting of this incident and the emotion which underlies it, receive meaning only if we assume that there is some sort of association or connivance between the ogre and the uncle. In that case, to give one cannibal's head to be eaten by the other is just the right sort of punishment, and the story contains then in reality one villain and one conflict distributed over two stages and duplicated into two persons. Thus we see that the legend of Tudava contains a typical matrilineal drama which forms its core, and which it brought to a logical conclusion. I shall remain satisfied, therefore, with having pointed out those features which are indisputable, and are clearly contained in the facts themselves, and I shall not enter in detail into further interpretations of this myth, which would necessitate certain historical and mythological hypotheses. But I wish to suggest that the figure of Dokonikan is not altogether explained by his association with the matriarch, that he may be a figure handed from a patriarchal culture into a matriarchal one, in which case he might represent the father and husband. If this be so, the present legend would be extremely interesting in showing how the prevalent cast of a culture moulds and transforms persons and situations to fit them into its own sociological context.

Another incident in this myth which I shall only indicate here, is the marriage at the end of the story of the hero to his maternal cross-cousin. This, in the present kinship system of the natives, is considered distinctly an improper thing, though not actually incestuous.

Passing to another legendary cycle, we have the story of two brothers who quarrel over a garden plot—as so often happens in real life—and in this quarrel the elder kills the younger. Thy myth does not relate any compunction for this act. It describes, instead, in detail the culinary anticlimax of the drama; the elder brother digs a hole in the ground, brings stones, leaves and firewood, and, as if he had just killed a pig or hauled out a big fish, he proceeds to bake his brother in an earthen oven. Then he hawks the baked flesh about from one village to another, rebaking it from time to time when his olfactory sense indicates the necessity of such a procedure. Those communities which decline his offer remain non-cannibalistic; those which accept become flesh-eaters ever afterwards. Thus here cannibalism is traced to a fraticidal act, and to preference or dislike for a food thus criminally and sinfully obtained. Needless to say, this is the myth of the non-cannibalistic tribes only. The same difference between cannibalism and its absence is explained by the man-eating natives of Dobu and the other cannibalistic districts of the d'Entercasteaux Islands by a story in which cannibalism is certainly not branded as anything unpleasant. This story also, however, consists in a difference, if not in an actual quarrel between two brothers and two sisters.[3] What mainly interests us in these myths is the matrilineal imprint which they possess in the quarrel between elder and younger brother.

The myth about the origins of fire, which also contains a brief mention of the origins of sun and moon, describes dissension between two sisters. It may be added that fire in this myth is described as originating in a woman's sexual organs.

The reader accustomed to psycho-analytic interpretations of myth and to psychological and anthropological writings on the subject in general, will find all my remarks singularly simple and unsophisticated. All that is said here is clearly written on the surface of the myth, and I have hardly attempted any complicated or symbolic interpretation. This, however, I

[3] These myths have already been given in *Argonauts of the Western Pacific*, Chapter on 'Mythology', pp. 321, 331, 332.

refrained from doing on purpose. For the thesis here developed that in a matriarchal society myth will contain conflicts of a specially matrilineal nature is better served if supported only by unquestionable arguments. Moreover, if I am right, and if our sociological point of view brings us really one step nearer towards the correct interpretation of myth, then it is clear that we need not rely so much on roundabout or symbolic rein-terpretations of facts, but can confidently let the facts speak for them-selves. It will be obvious to any attentive reader that many of the situa-tions which we understand as direct results of the matrilineal complex could, by artificial and symbolic rehandling, be made to correspond to a patriarchal outlook. The conflict between mother's brother and nephew, who should be natural protectors and always keep common cause, but who often in reality regard each other as one ogre might another, the fight and cannibalistic violence between two brothers, who in tribal law form one body, all this corresponds roughly to analogous conflicts within a patriarchal family. And it is just the difference in the actors, in the cast of the play, which distinguishes the matriarchal from the patriarchal myth. It is the sociological point of view of the tragedy which differs. The foundations of the psycho-analytic explanations of myth we have in no way shaken. We have merely corrected the sociology of this interpreta-tion. That this correction, however, is of extreme importance, and even bears upon fundamental psychological problems, has, I trust, been made sufficiently clear.

Let us pass now to the third class of myth, that which we find at the basis of cultural achievement and magic. Magic plays an extremely im-portant part in everything which these natives do. Whenever they ap-proach any subject which is of vital importance to them and in which they cannot rely solely on their own forces, they summon magic to their aid. To master wind and weather, to ward off dangers in sailing, to secure success in love, ceremonial trading or dancing, the natives perform magic. Black magic and magic of health play a very great rôle in their social life, and in the important economic activities and enterprises, such as gardening, fishing, and the construction of canoes, magic enters as an intrinsic and important element. Now between magic and myth there exists an intimate connexion. Most of the super-normal power displayed by the heroes in myth is due to their knowledge of magic. Present hu-manity differs from the great mythical heroes of the past in that nowadays the most effective types of magic have been lost. Could the strong spells and the powerful rites be recovered, men could fly through the air, re-juvenate and thus retain their life for ever, kill people and bring them to life again, be always beautiful, successful, loved and praised.

But it is not only myth which draws its power from magic. Magic is also dependent upon myth. Almost every type of spell and rite has its mythological foundation. The natives tell a story of the past which explains how this magic came into man's possession, and which serves as a warrant of its efficiency. In this lies perhaps the main sociological influence of myth. For myth lives in magic, and since magic shapes and maintains many social institutions, myth exercises its influence upon them.

Let us now pass to a few concrete examples of such myths of magic. It will be best to discuss the question of one detailed case first, and for this I shall choose the myth of the flying canoe already published *in extenso*.[4] This myth is narrated in connexion with the ship-building magic used by the natives. A long story is told about a time when there existed magic which, performed during the construction of a canoe, could make it fly through the air. The hero of this story, the man who was the last—and as it seems also the first—to perform it, is depicted in his rôle of ship-builder and magician. We are told how under his direction a canoe is built; how, on an overseas expedition to the south, it outruns all others, flying through the air while they have to sail; how its owner obtains an overwhelming success in the expedition. This is the happy beginning of the story. Now comes the tragedy. All the men in the community are jealous and full of hatred against the hero. Another incident occurs. He is in possession also of a successful garden magic, and of one by which he can also damage his neighbours. In a general drought his garden alone survives. Then all the men of his community determine that he must die. The younger brother of the hero had received from him the canoe magic and the garden magic. So no one thought that by killing the elder brother they would also lose the magic. The criminal deed is performed, and it is done not by any strangers, but by the younger brother of the hero. In one of the versions he and the hero's maternal nephews kill him in a joint attack. In another version again, the story proceeds to tell how, after he has killed his elder brother, he then proceeds to organize the mortuary festivities for him. The point of the story remains in the fact that after the deed was done, and the younger brother tried to apply the magic to a canoe, he found out with dismay that he was not in possession of the full magic, but only of its weaker part. Thus humanity lost the flying magic for ever.

In this myth the matrilineal complex comes powerfully to the fore. The hero, whose duty it is according to tribal law to share the magic with his younger brother and maternal nephew, cheats them, to put it in plain terms, by pretending that he has handed them over all the spells and rites while in reality he only gave up an insignificant fraction. The younger man, on the other hand, whose duty it would be to protect his

---

[4] *Op. cit.*, pp. 421 sqq.

brother, to avenge his death, to share all his interests, we find at the head of the conspiracy, red-handed with fratricidal murder.

If we compare this mythical situation with the sociological reality we find a strange correspondence. It is the duty of every man to hand over to his maternal nephew or younger brother the hereditary possessions of the family, such as family myth, family magic and family songs; as well as the titles to certain material possessions and economic rites. The handing over of magic has obviously to be done during the life-time of the elder man. The cession of property rights and privileges is also frequently done before his death. It is interesting that such lawful acquisition by a man of the goods which are due to him by inheritance from his maternal uncle or elder brother has always to be done against a type of payment called *pokala*, which frequently is very substantial indeed. It is still more important to note that when a father gives certain properties to his son he always does it for nothing, out of sheer affection. In actual life, the mythological swindle of the younger by the elder brother is also very often paralleled. There is always a feeling of uncertainty, always a mutual suspicion between the two people who in tribal law should be at one in common interests and reciprocal duties as well as in affection. Ever so often when obtaining magic from a man, I became aware that he was himself doubtful whether he had not been cheated out of some of it in receiving it from his uncle or elder brother. Such a doubt was never in the mind of a man who had received his magic as a gift from the father. Surveying the people now in possession of important systems of magic, I find also that more than half of the outstanding younger magicians have obtained their powers by paternal gift and not by maternal inheritance.

Thus in real life, as well as in myth, we see that the situation corresponds to a complex, to a repressed sentiment, and is at cross variance with tribal law and conventional tribal ideals. According to law and morals, two brothers or a maternal uncle and his nephew are friends, allies, and have all feelings and interests in common. In real life to a certain degree and quite openly in myth, they are enemies, cheat each other, murder each other, and suspicion and hostility obtain rather than love and union.

One more feature in the canoe myth deserves our attention: in an epilogue to the myth we are told that the three sisters of the hero are angry with the younger brother because he has killed the elder one without learning the magic. They had already learnt it, however, and, though, being women, they could not build or sail flying canoes, they were able to fly through the air as flying witches. After the crime had been committed they flew away, each of them settling in a different district. In this episode we see the characteristic matrilineal position of woman, who learns magic first before man has acquired it. The sisters also appear as moral guardians of the clan, but their wrath is directed not against the crime, but against the mutilation of clan property. Had the younger brother known the magic before killing the elder, the three sisters would have lived on happily with him for ever after.

Another fragmentary myth already published deserves our attention,[5] the myth about the origins of salvage magic, in cases of shipwreck. There were two brothers, the elder a man, the younger a dog. One day the senior goes on a fishing expedition, but he refuses to take the younger one with him. The dog, who has acquired the magic of safe swimming from the mother, follows the elder one, diving under water. In the fishing the dog is more successful. In retaliation for the ill-treatment received from the elder brother, the dog changes his clan and bequeaths the magic to his adopted kinsmen. The drama of this myth consists first of all in the favouring by the mother of the second son, a distinctly matrilineal feature, in that the mother here distributes her favours directly, and does not need to cheat the father like her better-known colleague in the Bible, the mother of Esau and Jacob. There is also the typical matrilineal quarrel, the wronging of the younger brother by the elder, and retaliation.

One more important story has to be given here: the legend about the origin of love magic, which forms the most telling piece of evidence with regard to the influence of the matrilineal complex. Among these amorous people the arts of seduction, of pleasing, of impressing the other sex, lead to the display of beauty, of prowess, and of artistic abilities. The fame of a good dancer, of a good singer, of a warrior, has its sexual side, and though ambition has a powerful sway for its own sake, some of it is always sacrificed on the altar of love. But above all the other means of seduction the prosaic and crude art of magic is extensively used, and it commands the supreme respect of the natives. The tribal Don Juan will boast about his magic rather than any personal qualities. The less successful swain will sigh for magic: "If I only knew the real *Kayroiwo*" is the burden of the broken heart. The natives will point to old, ugly, and crippled men who yet have been always successful in love by means of their magic.

This magic is not simple. There is a series of acts, each consisting of a special formula and its rite, which have to be carried out one after the other in order to exercise an increasing charm upon the desired lover. It may be added at once that the magic is carried out by girls to capture an admirer as well as by youths to subdue a sweetheart.

The initial formula is associated with the ritual bathe in the sea. A formula is uttered over the spongy leaves which are used by the natives as a bathing towel to dry and rub the skin. The bather rubs his skin with

5 *Op. cit.*, pp. 262–64.

the bewitched leaves, then throws them into the waves. As the leaves heave up and down so shall the inside of the beloved one be moved by passion. Sometimes this formula is sufficient; if not, the spurned lover will resort to a stronger one. The second formula is chanted over betel-nut, which the lover then chews and spits out in the direction of his be-loved. If even this should prove unavailing, a third formula, stronger than the two preceding ones, is recited over some dainty, such as betel-nut or tobacco, and the morsel is given to the desired one to eat, chew, and smoke. An even more drastic measure is to utter the magic into the open palms and attempt to press them against the bosom of the beloved.

The last and most powerful method might, without pushing the simile too far, be described as psycho-analytic. In fact, long before Freud had discovered the predominately erotic nature of dreams, similar theories were in vogue among the brown-skinned savages of north-west Melane-sia. According to their view, certain forms of magic can produce dreams. The wish engendered in such dreams penetrates into waking life and thus the dream-wish becomes realized. This is Freudianism turned upside-down; but which theory is correct and which is erroneous I shall not try definitely to settle. As regards love magic, there is a method of brewing certain aromatic herbs in coconut oil and uttering a formula over them, which gives them a powerful dream-inducing property. If the magic-maker be successful in making the smell of this brew enter the nostrils of his beloved, she will be sure to dream of him. In this dream she may have visions and undergo experiences which she will inevitably attempt to translate into deeds in actual life.

Among the several forms of love magic that of the *sulumwoya* is by far the most important. A great potency is ascribed to it, and it commands a considerable price if a native wants to purchase the formula and the rite, or if he wants it to be performed on his behalf. This magic is localized in two centres. One of them lies on the eastern shore of the main island. A fine beach of clean coral sand overlooks the open sea towards the west, where beyond the white breakers on the fringing reef there may be seen on a clear day silhouettes of distant raised coral rocks. Among them is the island of Iwa, the second centre of love magic. The spot on the main island, which is the bathing and boating beach of the village of Kumilab-waga, is to the natives almost like a holy shrine of love. There, in the white limestone beyond the fringe of luxuriant vegetation is the grotto where the primeval tragedy was consummated; there on both sides of the grotto are the two springs which still possess the power of inspiring love by ritual.

A beautiful myth of magic and love connects these two spots facing each other across the sea. One of the most interesting aspects of this myth is that it accounts for the existence of love-magic by what to the natives is a horrible and tragic event, an act of incest between brother and sister. In this the story shows some affinity to the legends of Tristan and Isolde, Lancelot and Guinevere, Sigmund and Sigelinde, as well as to a number of similar tales in savage communities.

There lived in the village of Kumilabwaga a woman of the Malasi clan who had a son and a daughter. One day while the mother was cutting out her fibre-petticoat, the son made some magic over herbs. This he did to gain the love of a certain woman. He placed some of the pungent *kway-awaga* leaves and some of the sweet-scented *sulumwoya* (mint) into clarified coconut oil and boiled the mixture, reciting the spell over it. Then he poured it into a receptacle made of toughened banana-leaves and placed it in the thatch. He then went to the sea to bathe. His sister in the meantime had made ready to go to the water hole to fill the coconut bottles with water. As she passed under the spot where the magical oil had been put, she brushed against the receptacle with her hair and some of the oil dropped down over her. She brushed it off with her fingers, and then sniffed at them. When she returned with the water she asked her mother, "Where is the man, where is my brother?" This according to native moral ideas was a dreadful thing to do, for no girl should inquire about her brother, nor should she speak of him as a man. The mother guessed what had happened. She said to herself: "Alas, my children have lost their minds."

The sister ran after her brother. She found him on the beach where he was bathing. He was without his pubic leaf. She loosened her fibre shirt and naked she tried to approach him. Horrified by this dreadful sight the man ran away along the beach till he was barred by the precipitous rock which on the north cuts off the Bokaraywata beach. He turned and ran back to the other rock which stands up steep and inaccessible at the southern end. Thus they ran three times along the beach under the shade of the big overhanging trees till the man, exhausted and overcome, allowed his sister to catch hold of him, and the two fell down, embracing in the shallow water of the caressing waves. Then, ashamed and remorseful, but with the fire of their love not quenched, they went to the grotto of Bokaraywata where they remained without food, without drink, and without sleep. There also they died, clasped in one another's arms, and through their linked bodies there grew the sweet-smelling plant of the native mint (*sulumwoya*).

A man in the island of Iwa dreamt the *kirisala*, the magical dream of this tragic event. He saw the vision before him. He woke, and said: "The two are dead in the grotto of Bokaraywata and the *sulumwoya* is growing out of their bodies. I must go." He took his canoe; he sailed across the sea between his island and that of Kitava. Then from Kitava he went to the main island, till he alighted on the tragic beach. There he saw the reef-heron hovering over the grotto. He went in and saw the *sulumwoya* plant growing out of the lovers' chests. He then went to the village. The mother avowed the shame which had fallen on her family. She gave him the magical formula, which he learned by heart. He took part of the spell over to Iwa and left part of it in Kumilabwaga. At the grotto he plucked off some of the mint, and took it with him. He returned to Iwa, to his island. He said: "I have brought here the tip of the magic; its roots remain in Kumilabwaga. There it will stay, connected with the bathing passage of Kadiusawasa and with the water of Bokaraywata. In one spring the men must bathe, in the other the women." The man of Iwa then imposed the taboos of the magic, he prescribed exactly the ritual and he stipulated that a substantial payment should be made to the people of Iwa and Kumilabwaga, when they allowed others to use their magic or to use their sacred spots. There is also a traditional miracle or at least an augury to those who perform the magic on the beach. In the myth this is represented as laid down by the man of Iwa; when the magic is performed and good results can be foreseen two small fish will be seen playing together in the shallow water of the beach.

I have but summarized here this last part of the myth, for its literal form contains sociological claims which are wearisome and degenerate into boastings; the account of the miraculous element usually leads into reminiscences from the immediate past; the ritual details develop into technicalities and the list of taboos into prescriptive homilies. But to the native narrator this last part of practical, pragmatic, and often of personal interest, is perhaps more important than the rest, and the anthropologist has more to learn from it than from the preceding dramatic tale. The sociological claims are contained in the myth, since the magic to which it refers is personal property. It has to be handed over from a fully entitled possessor to one who lawfully acquires it from him. All the force of magic consists in correct tradition. The fact of direct filiation by which the present officiator is linked to the original source is of paramount relevance. In certain magical formulæ the names of all its wielders are enumerated. In all rites and spells the conviction that they are absolutely in conformity with the original pattern is essential. And myth figures as the ultimate source, as the last pattern of this retrogressive series. It is again the charter of magical succession, the starting-point of the pedigree.

In connection with this a few words must be said about the social setting of magic and myth. Some forms of magic are not localized. Here belong sorcery, love magic, beauty magic, and the magic of *Kula*. In these forms filiation is none the less important, although it is not filiation by kinship. Other forms of magic are associated with a given territory, with the local industries of a community, with certain paramount and exclusive claims, vested in a chief and in his capital village. All garden magic belongs here—the magic which must be born of the soil, on which it can only thus be efficacious. Here belongs the magic of the shark and other fishing of a local character. Here also belong certain forms of canoe magic, that of the red shell used for ornaments, and, above all, *waygigi*, the supreme magic of rain and sunshine, the exclusive privilege of the paramounts chiefs of Omarakana.

In these types of local magic the esoteric power of words is as much chained to the locality as the group who inhabit the village and wield the magic. The magic thus is not merely local but exclusive and hereditary in a matrilineal kinship group. In these cases the myth of magic must be placed side by side with the myth of local origins as an essentially sociological force welding the group together, supplying its quota to the sentiment of unity, endowing the group with a common cultural value.

The other element conspicuous in the end of the above story and present also in most other magic-myths is the enumeration of portents, auguries, and miracles. It might be said that as the local myth establishes the claims of the group by precedent, so the magical myth vindicates them by miracle. Magic is based upon the belief in a specific power, residing always in man, derived always from tradition.[6] The efficiency of this power is vouched for by the myth, but it has to be confirmed also by the only thing which man ever accepts as final proof, namely practical results. "By their fruits ye shall know them." Primitive man is not less eager than the modern man of science to confirm his convictions by empirical fact. The empiricism of faith, whether savage or civilized, consists in miracles. And living belief will always generate miracles. There is no civilized religion without its saints and devils, without its illuminations and tokens, without the spirit of God descending upon the community of the faithful. There is no new-fangled creed, no new religion, whether it be a form of Spiritism, Theosophy, or Christian Science, which cannot prove its legitimacy by the solid fact of supernatural manifestation. The savage has also his thaumatology, and in the Trobriands, where magic dominates all supernaturalism, it is a thaumatology of magic. Round each form of magic there is a continuous trickle of small miracles, at times swelling into bigger, more conspicuously supernatural proofs, then again, running in a smaller stream, but never absent.

In love magic, for instance, from the continuous boasting about its success, through certain remarkable cases in which very ugly men arouse the passion of famous beauties, it has reached the climax of its miracle-working power in the recent notorious case of incest mentioned above. This crime is often accounted for by an accident similar to that which

---

[6] *Op. cit.*, chapters on "Magic" and "Power of Words in Magic", cf. also Ogden and Richards' *The Meaning of Meaning*, chap. ii.

befell the mythical lovers, the brother and sister of Kumilabwaga. Myth thus forms the background of all present-day miracles; it remains their pattern and standard. I might quote from other stories a similar relation between the original miracle narrated by myth and its repetition in the current miracles of living faith. The readers of *The Argonauts of the Western Pacific* will remember how the mythology of ceremonial trading casts its shadow on modern custom and practice. In the magic of rain and weather, of gardening and of fishing, there is a strong tendency to see the original miracle repeated in an attenuated form in outstanding miraculous confirmations of magical power.

Finally, the element of prescriptive injunction, the laying down of ritual, taboos, and social regulations crops up towards the end of most mythical narratives. When the myth of a certain magic is told by a wielder of the magic, he naturally will state his own functions as the outcome of the story. He believes himself to be at one with the original founder of the magic. In the love myth, as we have seen, the locality in which the primeval tragedy happened, with its grotto, its beach, and its springs, becomes an important shrine infused with the power of magic. To the local people, who no longer have the exclusive monopoly of magic, certain prerogatives still associated with the spot are of the greatest value. That part of the ritual which still remains bound to the locality naturally occupies their attention. In the magic of rain and sunshine of Omarakana, which is one of the corner-stones of the chief's power, the myth revolves round one or two local features which also figure in present day ritual.

All sexual attraction, all power of seduction, is believed to reside in the magic of love.

In the fishing of shark and of the *kalala*, specific elements of the locality figure also. But even in these stories which do not wed magic to locality, long prescriptions of ritual are either told as an integral part of the narrative or else are put in the mouth of one of the dramatis personæ. The prescriptive character of myth shows its essentially pragmatic function, its close association with ritual, with belief, with living culture. Myth has often been described by writers of psycho-analysis as "the secular dream of the race." This formula, even as a rough approximation, is incorrect in view of the practical and pragmatic nature of myth just established. It has been necessary barely to touch upon this subject here, for it is treated more fully in another place.[7]

In this work I trace the influence of a matrilineal complex upon one culture only, studied by myself at first-hand in intensive field work. But

[7] "Myth in Primitive Psychology," *Psyche Miniatures*, 1926.

the results obtained have a much wider application. For myths of incest between brother and sister are of frequent occurrence among matrilineal peoples, especially in the Pacific, and hatred and rivalry between elder and younger brother, or between nephew and maternal uncle, is a characteristic feature of the world's folk-lore.

PART THREE

MYTH IN PRIMITIVE PSYCHOLOGY

5

MYTH IN PRIMITIVE PSYCHOLOGY

Dedication
To Sir James Frazer

I F I had the power of evoking the past, I should like to lead you back some twenty years to an old Slavonic university town—I mean the town of Cracow, the ancient capital of Poland and the seat of the oldest university in eastern Europe. I could then show you a student leaving the medieval college buildings, obviously in some distress of mind, hugging, however, under his arm, as the only solace of his troubles, three green volumes with the well-known golden imprint, a beautiful conventionalized design of mistletoe—the symbol of 'The Golden Bough'.

I had just then been ordered to abandon for a time my physical and chemical research because of ill-health, but I was allowed to follow up a favorite side-line of study, and I decided to make my first attempt to read an English masterpiece in the original. Perhaps my mental distress would have been lessened, had I been allowed to look into the future and to foresee the present occasion, on which I have the great privilege of delivering an address in honor of Sir James Frazer to a distinguished audience, in the language of 'The Golden Bough' itself.

For no sooner had I begun to read this great work, than I became immersed in it and enslaved by it. I realized then that anthropology, as presented by Sir James Frazer, is a great science, worthy of as much devotion as any of her elder and more exact sister-studies, and I became bound to the service of Frazerian anthropology.

We are gathered here to celebrate the annual totemic festival of 'The Golden Bough'; to revive and strengthen the bonds of anthropological union; to commune with the source and symbol of our anthropological interest and affection. I am but your humble spokesman, in expressing our joint admiration to the great writer and his classical works; 'The Golden Bough', 'Totemism and Exogamy', 'Folklore in the Old Testament', 'Pysche's Task', and 'The Belief in Immortality'. As a true officiat-

[The above formed the opening passages of an address delivered in honor of Sir James Frazer at the University of Liverpool, in November, 1925.]

ing magician in a savage tribe would have to do, I have to recite the whole list, so that the spirit of the works (their 'mana') may dwell among us.

In all this, my task is pleasant and in a way easy, for implicit in whatever I may say is a tribute to him, whom I have always regarded as the 'Master'. On the other hand this very circumstance also makes my task difficult, for having received so much, I feat I may not have enough to show in return. I have therefore decided to keep my peace even while I am addressing you—to let another one speak through my mouth, another one who has been to Sir James Frazer an inspiration and a lifelong friend, as Sir James has been to us. This other one, I need hardly tell you, is the modern representative of primitive man, the contemporary savage, whose thoughts, whose feelings, whose very life-breath pervades all that Frazer has written.

In other words, I shall not try to serve up any theories of my own, but instead I shall lay before you some results of my anthropological field-work, carried out in northwest Melanesia. I shall restrict myself, moreover, to a subject upon which Sir James Frazer has not directly concentrated his attention, but in which, as I shall try to show you, his influence is as fruitful as in those many subjects that he has made his own.

I
The Role of Myth in Life

By the examination of a typical Melanesian culture and by a survey of the opinions, traditions, and behavior of these natives, I propose to show how deeply the sacred tradition, the myth, enters into their pursuits, and how strongly it controls their moral and social behavior. In other words, the thesis of the present work is that an intimate connection exists between the word, the mythos, the sacred tales of a tribe, on the one hand, and their ritual acts, their moral deeds, their social organization, and even their practical activities, on the other.

In order to gain a background for our description of the Melanesian facts, I shall briefly summarize the present state of the science of mythology. Even a superficial survey of the literature would reveal that there is no monotony to complain of as regards the variety of opinions or the acrimony of polemics. To take only the recent up-to-date theories advanced in explanation of the nature of myth, legend, and fairy-tale, we should have to head the list, at least as regards output and self-assertion, by the so called school of Nature-mythology which flourishes mainly in Germany. (The writers of this school maintain that primitive man is highly interested in natural phenomena, and that his interest is predominantly of a theoretical, contemplative, and poetical character.) In trying to express and interpret the phases of the moon, or the regular and yet changing path of the sun across the skies, primitive man constructs symbolic personified rhapsodies. To writers of this school every myth possesses as its kernel or ultimate reality some natural phenomenon or other, elaborately woven into a tale to an extent which sometimes almost masks and obliterates it. There is not much agreement among these students as to what type of natural phenomenon lies at the bottom of most mythological productions. There are extreme lunar mythologists so completely moonstruck with their idea that they will not admit that any other phenomenon could lend itself to a savage rhapsodic interpretation except that of earth's nocturnal satellite. The Society for the Comparative Study of Myth, founded in Berlin in 1906, and counting among its supporters such famous scholars as Ehrenreich, Siecke, Winckler, and many others, carried on their business under the sign of the moon. Others, like Frobenius for instance, regard the sun as the only subject around which primitive man has spun his symbolic tales. Then there is the school of meteorological interpreters who regard wind, weather, and colors of the skies as the essence of myth. To this belonged such well-known writers of the older generation as Max Müller and Kuhn. Some of these departmental mythologists fight fiercely for their heavenly body or principle; others have a more catholic taste, and prepare to agree that primeval man has made his mythological brew from all the heavenly bodies taken together.

I have tried to state fairly and plausibly this naturalistic interpretation of myths, but as a matter of fact this theory seems to me to be one of the most extravagant views ever advanced by an anthropologist or humanist—and that means a great deal. It has received an absolutely destructive criticism from the great psychologist Wundt, and appears absolutely untenable in the light of any of Sir James Frazer's writings. From my own study of living myths among savages, I should say that primitive man has to a very limited extent the purely artistic or scientific interest in nature; there is but little room for symbolism in his ideas and tales; and myth, in fact, is not an idle rhapsody, not an aimless outpouring of vain imaginings, but a hard-working, extremely important cultural force. Besides ignoring the cultural function of myth, this theory imputes to primitive man a number of imaginary interests, and it confuses several clearly distinguishable types of story, the fairy tale, the legend, the saga, and the sacred tale or myth.

In strong contrast to this theory which makes myth naturalistic, symbolic, and imaginary, stands the theory which regards a sacred tale as a true historical record of the past. This view, recently supported by the so-called Historical School in Germany and America, and represented in England by Dr. Rivers, covers but part of the truth. There is no denying that history, as well as natural environment, must have left a profound imprint on all cultural achievements, hence also on myths. But to take all mythology as mere chronicle is as incorrect as to regard it as the primitive naturalist's musings. It also endows primitive man with a sort of scientific impulse and desire for knowledge. Although the savage has something of the antiquarian as well as of the naturalist in his composition, he is, above all, actively engaged in a number of practical pursuits, and has to struggle with various difficulties; all his interests are tuned up to this general pragmatic outlook. Mythology, the sacred lore of the tribe, is, as we shall see, a powerful means of assisting primitive man, of allowing him to make the two ends of his cultural patrimony meet. We shall see, moreover, that the immense services to primitive culture performed by myth are done in connection with religious ritual, moral influence, and sociological principle. Now religion and morals draw only to a very limited extent upon an interest in science or in past history, and myth is thus based upon an entirely different mental attitude.

The close connection between religion and myth which has been overlooked by many students has been recognized by others. Psychologists like Wundt, sociologists like Durkheim, Hubert, and Mauss, anthropologists like Crawley, classical scholars like Miss Jane Harrison have all understood the intimate association between myth and ritual, between sacred tradition and the norms of social structure. All of these writers have been to a greater or lesser extent influenced by the work of Sir James Frazer. In spite of the fact that the great British anthropologist, as well as most of his followers, have a clear vision of the sociological and ritual importance of myth, the facts which I shall present will allow us to clarify and formulate more precisely the main principles of a sociological theory of myth.

I might present an even more extensive survey of the opinions, divisions, and controversies of learned mythologists. The science of mythology has been the meeting-point of various scholarships: the classical humanist must decide for himself whether Zeus is the moon, or the sun, or a strictly historical personality; and whether his ox-eyed spouse is the morning star, or a cow, or a personification of the wind—the loquacity of wives being proverbial. Then all these questions have to be re-discussed upon the stage of mythology by the various tribes of archaeologists, Chaldean and Egyptian, Indian and Chinese, Peruvian and Mayan. The historian and the sociologist, the student of literature, the grammarian, the Germanist and the Romanist, the Celtic scholar and the Slavist discuss, each little crowd among themselves. Nor is mythology quite safe from logicians and psychologists, from the metaphysician and the epistemologist—to say nothing of such visitors as the theosophist, the modern astrologist, and the Christian Scientist. Finally, we have the psychoanalyst who has come at last to teach us that the myth is a day-dream of the race, and that we can only explain it by turning our back upon nature, history, and culture, and diving deep into the dark pools of the sub-conscious, where at the bottom there lie the usual paraphernalia and symbols of psychoanalytic exegesis. So that when at last the poor anthropologist and student of folk-lore come to the feast, there are hardly any crumbs left for them!

If I have conveyed an impression of chaos and confusion, if I have inspired a sinking feeling towards the incredible mythological controversy with all the dust and din which it raises, I have achieved exactly what I wanted. For I shall invite my readers to step outside the closed study of the theorist into the open air of the anthropological field, and to follow me in my mental flight back to the years which I spent among a Melanesian tribe of New Guinea. There, paddling on the lagoon, watching the natives under the blazing sun at their garden-work, following them through the patches of jungle, and on the winding beaches and reefs, we shall learn about their life. And again, observing their ceremonies in the cool of the afternoon or in the shadows of the evening, sharing their meals round their fires, we shall be able to listen to their stories.

For the anthropologist—one and only among the many participants in the mythological contest—has the unique advantage of being able to step back behind the savage whenever he feels that his theories become involved and the flow of his argumentative eloquence runs dry. The anthropologist is not bound to the scanty remnants of culture, broken tablets, tarnished texts, or fragmentary inscriptions. He need not fill out immense gaps with voluminous, but conjectural, comments. The anthropologist has the myth-maker at his elbow. Not only can he take down as full a text as exists, with all its variations, and control it over and over; he has also a host of authentic commentators to draw upon; still more he has the fulness of life itself from which the myth has been born. And as we shall see, in this live context there is as much to be learned about the myth as in the narrative itself.

Myth as it exists in a savage community, that is, in its living primitive form, is not merely a story told but a reality lived. It is not of the nature of fiction, such as we read today in a novel, but it is a living reality, believed to have once happened in primeval times, and continuing ever since to influence the world and human destinies. This myth is to the savage what, to a fully believing Christian, is the Biblical story of Creation, of the Fall, of the Redemption by Christ's Sacrifice on the Cross. As our sacred story lives in our ritual, in our morality, as it governs our faith and controls our conduct, even so does his myth for the savage.

The limitation of the study of myth to the mere examination of texts has been fatal to a proper understanding of its nature. The forms of myth which come to us from classical antiquity and from the ancient sacred books of the East and other similar sources have come down to us without the context of living faith, without the possibly of obtaining comments from true believers, without the concomitant knowledge of their social organization, their practised morals, and their popular customs—at least without the full information which the modern field-worker can easily obtain. Moreover, there is no doubt that in their present literary form these tales have suffered a very considerable transformation at the hands of scribes, commentators, learned priests, and theologians. It is necessary to go back to primitive mythology in order to learn the secret of its life in the study of a myth which is still alive—before, mummified in priestly wisdom, it has been enshrined in the indestructible but lifeless repository of dead religions.

Studied alive, myth, as we shall see, is not symbolic, but a direct expression of its subject-matter; it is not an explanation in satisfaction of a science interest, but a narrative resurrection of a primeval reality, told in satisfaction of deep religious wants, moral cravings, social submissions, assertions, even practical requirements. Myth fulfills in primitive culture an indispensable function: it expresses, enhances, and codifies belief; it safeguards and enforces morality; it vouches for the efficiency of ritual and contains practical rules for the guidance of man. Myth is thus a vital ingredient of human civilization; it is not an idle tale, but a hard-worked active force; it is not an intellectual explanation or an artistic imagery, but a pragmatic charter of primitive faith and moral wisdom.

I shall try to prove all these contentions by the study of various myths; but to make our analysis conclusive it will first be necessary to give an account not merely of myth, but also of fairy tale, legend, and historical record.

Let us then float over in spirit to the shores of a Trobriand[1] lagoon, and penetrate into the life of the natives—see them at work, see them at play, and listen to their stories. Late in November the wet weather is setting in. There is little to do in the gardens, the fishing season is not in full

---

[1] The Trobriand Islands are a coral archipelago lying to the northeast of New Guinea. The natives belong to the Papuo-Melanesian race, and in their physical appearance, mental equipment, and social organization they show a combination of the Oceanic characteristics mixed with some features of the more backward Papuan culture from the mainland of New Guinea.

For a full account of the Northern Massim, of which the Trobrianders form a section, see the classical treatise of Professor C. G. Seligman, *Melanesians of British New Guinea* (Cambridge, 1910). This book shows also the relation of the Trobrianders to the other races and cultures on and around New Guinea. A short account will also be found in *Argonauts of the Western Pacific, by the present author* (London, 1922).

swing as yet, overseas sailing looms ahead in the future, while the festive mood still lingers after the harvest dancing and feasting. Sociability is in the air, time lies on their hands, while bad weather keeps them often at home. Let us step through the twilight of the approaching evening into one of their villages and sit at the fireside, where the flickering light draws more and more people as the evening falls and the conversation brightens. Sooner or later a man will be asked to tell a story, for this is the season of *fairy tales*. If he is a good reciter, he will soon provoke laughter, rejoinders, and interruptions, and his tale will develop into a regular performance.

At this time of the year folk-tales of a special type called *kukwanebu* are habitually recited in the villages. There is a vague belief, not very seriously taken, that their recital has a beneficial influence on the new crops recently planted in the gardens. In order to produce this effect, a short ditty in which an allusion is made to some very fertile wild plants, the *kasiyena*, must always be recited at the end.

Every story is 'owned' by a member of the community. Each story, though known by many, may be recited only by the 'owner'; he may, however, present it to someone else by teaching that person and authorizing him to retell it. But not all the 'owners' know how to thrill and to raise a hearty laugh, which is one of the main ends of such stories. A good raconteur has to change his voice in the dialogue, chant the ditties with due temperament, gesticulate, and in general play to the gallery. Some of these tales are certainly 'smoking-room' stories, of others I will give one or two examples.

Thus there is the maiden in distress and the heroic rescue. Two women go out in search of birds' eggs. One discovers a nest under a tree, the other warns her: "These are eggs of a snake, don't touch them." "Oh, no! They are eggs of a bird," she replies and carries them away. The mother snake comes back, and finding the nest empty starts in search of the eggs. She enters the nearest village and sings a ditty:—

> "I wend my way as I wriggle along,
> The eggs of a bird it is licit to eat;
> The eggs of a friend are forbidden to touch."

This journey lasts long, for the snake is traced from one village to the other and everywhere has to sing her ditty. Finally, entering the village of the two women, she sees the culprit roasting the eggs, coils around her, and enters her body. The victim is laid down helpless and ailing. But the hero is nigh; a man from a neighboring village dreams of the dramatic situation, arrives on the spot, pulls out the snake, cuts it to pieces, and marries both women, thus carrying off a double prize for his prowess.

In another story we learn of a happy family, a father and two daughters, who sail from their home in the northern coral archipelagoes, and run to the southwest till they come to the wild steep slopes of the rock island Gumasila. The father lies down on a platform and falls asleep. An ogre comes out of the jungle, eats the father, captures and ravishes one of the daughters, while the other succeeds in escaping. The sister from the woods supplies the captive one with a piece of lawyer-cane, and when the ogre lies down and falls asleep they cut him in half and escape.

A woman lives in the village of Okopukopu at the head of a creek with her five children. A monstrously big stingaree paddles up the creek, flops across the village, enters the hut, and to the tune of a ditty cuts off the woman's finger. One son tries to kill the monster and fails. Every day the same performance is repeated till on the fifth day the youngest son succeeds in killing the giant fish.

A louse and a butterfly embark on a bit of aviation, the louse as a passenger, the butterfly as aeroplane and pilot. In the middle of the performance, while flying over-seas just between the beach of Wawela and the island of Kitava, the louse emits a loud shriek, the butterfly is shaken, and the louse falls off and is drowned.

A man whose mother-in-law is a cannibal is sufficiently careless to go away and leave her in charge of his three children. Naturally she tries to eat them; they escape in time, however, climb a palm, and keep her (through a somewhat lengthy story) at bay, until the father arrives and kills her. There is another story about a visit to the Sun, another about an ogre devastating gardens, another about a woman who was so greedy that she stole all the food at funeral distributions, and many similar ones.

In this place, however, we are not so much concentrating our attention on the text of the narratives, as on their sociological reference. The text, of course, is extremely important, but without the context it remains lifeless. As we have seen, the interest of the story is vastly enhanced and it is given its proper character by the manner in which it is told. The whole nature of the performance, the voice and the mimicry, the stimulus and the response of the audience mean as much to the natives as the text; and the sociologist should take his cue from the natives. The performance, again, has to be placed in its proper time-setting—the hour of the day, and the season, with the background of the sprouting gardens awaiting future work, and slightly influenced by the magic of the fairy tales. We must also bear in mind the sociological context of private ownership, the sociable function and the cultural role of amusing fiction. All these elements are equally relevant; all must be studied as well as the text. The stories live in native life and not on paper, and when a scholar jots them down without being able to evoke the atmosphere in which they flourish he has given us but a mutilated bit of reality.

I pass now to another class of stories. These have no special season, there is no stereotyped way of telling them, and the recital has not the character of a performance, nor has it any magical effect. And yet these tales are more important than the foregoing class; for they are believed to be true, and the information which they contain is both more valuable and more relevant than that of the *kukwanebu*. When a party goes on a distant visit or sails on an expedition, the younger members, keenly interested in the landscape, in new communities, in new people, and perhaps even new customs, will express their wonder and make inquiries. The older and more experienced will supply them with information and comment, and this always takes the form of a concrete narrative. An old man will perhaps tell his own experiences about fights and expeditions, about famous magic and extraordinary economic achievements. With this he may mix the reminiscences of his father, hearsay tales and legends, which have passed through many generations. Thus memories of great droughts and devastating famines are conserved for many years, together with the descriptions of the hardships, struggles, and crimes of the exasperated population.

A number of stories about sailors driven out of their course and landing among cannibals and hostile tribes are remembered, some of them set to song, others formed into historic legends. A famous subject for song and story is the charm, skill, and performance of famous dancers. There are tales about distant volcanic islands; about hot springs in which once a party of unwary bathers were boiled to death; about mysterious countries inhabited by entirely different men or women; about strange adventures which have happened to sailors in distant seas; monstrous fish and octopi, jumping rocks and disguised sorcerers. Stories again are told, some recent, some ancient, about seers and visitors to the land of the dead, enumerating their most famous and significant exploits. There are also stories associated with natural phenomena; a petrified canoe, a man changed into a rock, and a red patch on the coral rock left by a party who ate too much betel nut.

We have here a variety of tales which might be subdivided into *historical accounts* directly witnessed by the narrator, or at least vouched for by someone within living memory; *legends*, in which the continuity of testimony is broken, but which fall within the range of things ordinarily experienced by the tribesmen; and *hearsay tales* about distant countries and ancient happenings of a time which falls outside the range of present-day culture. To the natives, however, all these classes imperceptibly shade into each other; they are designated by the same name, *libwogwo*; they are all regarded as true; they are not recited as a performance, nor told for amusement at a special season. Their subject-matter also shows a substantial unity. They all refer to subjects intensely stimulating to the natives; they all are connected with activities such as economic pursuits, warfare, adventure, success in dancing and in ceremonial exchange. Moreover, since they record singularly great achievements in all such pursuits, they redound to the credit of some individual and his descendants or of a whole community; and hence they are kept alive by the ambition of those whose ancestry they glorify. The stories told in explanation of peculiarities of features of the landscape frequently have a sociological context, that is, they enumerate whose clan or family performed the deed. When this is not the case, they are isolated fragmentary comments upon some natural feature, clinging to it as an obvious survival.

In all this it is once more clear that we can neither fully grasp the meaning of the text, nor the sociological nature of the story, nor the natives' attitude towards it and interest in it, if we study the narrative on paper. These tales live in the memory of man, in the way in which they are told, and even more in the complex interest which keeps them alive, which makes the narrator recite with pride or regret, which makes the listener follow eagerly, wistfully, with hopes and ambitions roused. Thus the essence of a *legend*, even more than that of a *fairy tale*, is not to be found in a mere perusal of the story, but in the combined study of the narrative and its context in the social and cultural life of the natives.

But it is only when we pass to the third and most important class of tales, the *sacred tales* or *myths*, and contrast them with the legends, that the nature of all three classes comes into relief. This third class is called by the natives *liliu*, and I want to emphasize that I am reproducing prima facie the natives' own classification and nomenclature, and limiting myself to a few comments on its accuracy. The third class of stories stands very much apart from the other two. If the first are told for amusement, the second to make a serious statement and satisfy social ambition, the third are regarded, not merely as true, but as venerable and sacred, and they play a highly important cultural part. The *folk-tale*, as we know, is a seasonal performance and an act of sociability. The *legend*, provoked by contact with unusual reality, opens up past historical vistas. The *myth* comes into play when rite, ceremony, or a social or moral rule demands justification, warrant of antiquity, reality, and sanctity.

In the subsequent chapters of this book we will examine a number of myths in detail, but for the moment let us glance at the subjects of some typical myths. Take, for instance, the annual feast of the return of the dead. Elaborate arrangements are made for it, especially an enormous display of food. When this feast approaches, tales are told of how death began to chastise man, and how the power of eternal rejuvenation was lost. It is told why the spirits have to leave the village and do not remain at the fireside, finally why they return once in a year. Again, at certain seasons in preparation for an overseas expedition, canoes are overhauled and new ones built to the accompaniment of a special magic. In this there are mythological allusions in the spells, and even the sacred acts contain elements which are only comprehensible when the story of the flying canoe, its ritual, and its magic are told. In connection with ceremonial trading, the rules, the magic, even the geographical routes are associated with corresponding mythology. There is no important magic, no ceremony, no ritual without belief; and the belief is spun out into accounts of concrete precedent. The union is very intimate, for myth is not only looked upon as a commentary of additional information, but it is a warrant, a charter, and often even a practical guide to the activities with which it is connected. On the other hand the rituals, ceremonies, and social organization contain at times direct references to myth, and they are regarded as the results of mythical event. The cultural fact is a monument in which the myth is embodied; while the myth is believed to be the real cause which has brought about the moral rule, the social grouping, the rite, or the custom. Thus these stories form an integral part of culture. Their existence and influence not merely transcend the act of telling the narrative, not only do they draw their substance from life and its interests—they govern and control many cultural features, they form the dogmatic backbone of primitive civilization.

This is perhaps the most important point of the thesis which I am urging: I maintain that there exists a special class of stories, regarded as sacred, embodied in ritual, morals, and social organization, and which form an integral and active part of primitive culture. These stories live not by idle interest, not as fictitious or even as true narratives; but are to the natives a statement of a primeval, greater, and more relevant reality, by which the present life, fates, and activities of mankind are determined, the knowledge of which supplies man with the motive for ritual and moral actions, as well as with indications as to how to perform them.

In order to make the point at issue quite clear, let us once more compare our conclusions with the current views of modern anthropology, not in order idly to criticize other opinions, but so that we may link our results to the present state of knowledge, give due acknowledgement for what we have received, and state where we have to differ clearly and precisely.

It will be best to quote a condensed and authoritative statement, and I shall choose for this purpose of definition and analysis given in *Notes and Queries on Anthropology*, by the late Miss C. S. Burne and Professor J. L. Myres. Under the heading "Stories, Sayings, and Songs", we are informed that "this section includes many *intellectual* efforts of peoples. . . ." which "represent the earliest attempts to exercise reason, imagination, and memory." With some apprehension we ask where is left the emotion, the interest, and ambition, the social role of all the stories, and the deep connection with cultural values of the more serious ones? After a brief classification of stories in the usual manner we read about the sacred tales: "*Myths* are stories which, however marvelous and improbable to us, are nevertheless related in all good faith, because they are intended, or believed by the teller, to explain by means of something concrete and intelligible an abstract idea or such vague and difficult conceptions as Creation, Death, distinctions of race or animal species, the different occupations of men and women; the origins of rites and customs, or striking natural objects or prehistoric monuments; the meaning of the names of persons or places. Such stories are sometimes described as *etiological*, because their purpose is to explain why something exists or happens."[2]

Here we have in a nutshell all that modern science at its best has to say upon the subject. Would our Melanesians agree, however, with this opinion? Certainly not. They do not want to 'explain', to make 'intelligible' anything which happens in their myths—above all not an abstract idea. Of that there can be found to my knowledge no instance either in Melanesia or in any other savage community. The few abstract ideas which the natives possess carry their concrete commentary in the very word which expresses them. When being is described by verbs to lie, to sit, to stand, when cause and effect are expressed by words signifying foundation and the past standing upon it, when various concrete nouns tend towards the meaning of space, the word and the relation to concrete reality make the abstract idea sufficiently 'intelligible'. Nor would a Trobriander or any other native agree with the view that "Creation, Death distinctions of race or animal species, the different occupations of men and women" are "vague and difficult conceptions". Nothing is more familiar to the native than the different occupations of the male and female sex; there is nothing to be *explained* about it. But though familiar, such differences are at times irksome, unpleasant, or at least limiting, and there is the need to justify them, to vouch for their antiquity and reality, in short to buttress their validity. Death, alas, is not vague, or abstract, or difficult to grasp for any human being. It is only too hauntingly real, too concrete, to easy to comprehend for anyone who has had an experience affecting his near relatives or a personal foreboding. If it were vague or unreal, man would have no desire so much as to mention it; but the idea of death is fraught with horror, with a desire to remove its threat, with the vague hope that it may be, not explained, but rather explained away, made unreal, and actually denied. Myth, warranting the belief in

[2] Quoted from *Notes and Queries on Anthropology*, pp. 210 and 211.

immortality, in eternal youth, in a life beyond the grave, is not an intellectual reaction upon a puzzle, but an explicit act of faith born from the innermost instinctive and emotional reaction to the most formidable and haunting idea. Nor are the stories about "the origins of rites and customs" told in mere explanation of them. They never explain in any sense of the word; they always state a precedent which constitutes an ideal and a warrant for its continuance, and sometimes practical directions for the procedures.

We have, therefore, to disagree on every point with this excellent though concise statement of present-day mythological opinion. This definition would create an imaginary, non-existent class of narrative, the etiological myth, corresponding to a non-existent desire to explain, leading a futile existence as an 'intellectual effort', and remaining outside native culture and social organization with their pragmatic interests. The whole treatment appears to us faulty, because myths are treated as mere stories, because they are regarded as a primitive intellectual arm-chair occupation, because they are torn out of their life-context, and studied from what they look like on paper, and not from what they do in life. Such a definition would make it impossible either to see clearly the nature of myth or to reach a satisfactory classification of folk-tales. In fact we would also have to disagree with the definition of legend and of fairy tale given subsequently by the writers in *Notes and Queries on Anthropology*.

But above all, this point of view would be fatal to efficient field-work, for it would make the observer satisfied with the mere writing down of narratives. The intellectual nature of a story is exhausted with its text, but the functional, cultural, and pragamatic aspect of any native tale is manifested as much in its enactment, embodiment, and contextual relations as in the text. It is easier to write down the story than to observe the diffuse, complex ways in which it enters into life, or to study its function by the observation of the vast social and cultural realities into which it enters. And this is the reason why we have so many texts and why we know so little about the very nature of myth.

We may, therefore, learn an important lesson from the Trobrianders, and to them let us now return. We will survey some of their myths in detail, so that we can confirm our conclusions inductively, yet precisely.

II
Myths of Origin

We may best start with the beginning of things, and examine some of the myths of origin. The world, say the natives, was originally peopled from underground. Humanity had there led an existence similar in all respects to the present life on earth. Underground, men were organized in villages, clans, districts; they had distinctions of rank, they knew privileges and had claims, they owned property, and were versed in magic lore. Endowed with all this, they emerged, establishing by this very act certain rights in land and citizenship prerogative and magical pursuit. They brought with them all their culture to continue it upon this earth.

There are a number of special spots—grottoes, clumps of trees, stone heaps, coral outcrops, springs, heads of creeks—called 'holes' or 'houses' by the natives. From such 'holes' the first couples (a sister as the head of the family and the brother as her guardian) came and took possession of the lands, and gave the totemic, industrial, magical, and sociological character to the communities thus begun.

The problem of rank which plays a great role in their sociology was settled by the emergence from one special hole, called Obukula, near the village of Laba'i. This event was notable in that, contrary to the usual course (which is: one original 'hole', one lineage), from this hole of Laba'i there emerged representatives of the four main clans one after the other. Their arrival, moreover, was followed by an apparently trivial but, in mythical reality, a most important event. First there came the *Kaylavasi* (iguana), the animal of the Lukulabuta clan, which scratched its way through the earth as iguanas do, then climbed a tree, and remained there as a mere onlooker, following subsequent events. Soon there came out the Dog, totem of the Lukuba clan, who originally had the highest rank. As a third came the Pig, representative of the Malasi clan, which now holds the highest rank. Last came the Lukwasisiga totem, represented in some versions by the Crocodile, in others by the Snake, in others by the Opossum, and sometimes completely ignored. The Dog and Pig ran round, and the Dog, seeing the fruit of the *noku* plant, nosed it, then ate it. Said the Pig: "Thou eatest *noku*, thou eatest dirt; thou art a low-bred, a commoner; the chief, the *guya'u*, shall be I." And ever since, the highest sub-clan of the Malasi clan, the Tabalu, have been the real chiefs.

In order to understand this myth, it is not enough to follow the dialogue between the Dog and the Pig which might appear pointless or even trivial. Once you know the native sociology, the extreme importance of rank, the fact that food and it limitations (the taboos of rank and clan) are the main index of man's social nature, and finally the psychology of totemic identification—you begin to understand how this incident, happening as it did when humanity was *in statu nascendi*, settled once for all the relation between the two rival clans. To understand this myth you must have a good knowledge of their sociology, religion, customs, and outlook. Then, and only then, can you appreciate what this story means to the natives and how it can live in their life. If you stayed among them and learned the language you would constantly find it active in discussion and squabbles in reference to the relative superiority of the various clans, and in the discussions about the various food taboos which frequently raise fine questions of casuistry. Above all, if you were brought into contact with communities where the historical process of the spread of influence of the Malasi clan is still in evolution, you would be brought face to face with this myth as an active force.

Remarkably enough the first and last animals to come out, the iguana and the Lukwasisiga totem, have been from the beginning left in the cold: thus the numerical principle and the logic of events is not very strictly observed in the reasoning of the myth.

If the main myth of Laba'i about the relative superiority of the four clans is very often alluded to throughout the tribe, the minor local myths are not less alive and active, each in its own community. When a party arrives at some distant village they will be told not only the legendary historical tales, but above all the mythological charter of that community, its magical proficiencies, its occupational character, its rank and place in totemic organization. Should there arise land-quarrels, encroachment in magical matters, fishing rights, or other privileges the testimony of myth would be referred to.

Let me show concretely the way in which a typical myth of local origins would be retailed in the normal run of native life. Let us watch a party of visitors arriving in one or the other of the Trobriand villages. They would seat themselves in front of the headman's house, in the central place of the locality. As likely as not the spot of origins is near by, marked by a coral outcrop or a heap of stones. This spot would be pointed out, the names of the brother and sister ancestors mentioned, and perhaps it would be said that the man built his house on the spot of the present headman's dwelling. The native listeners would know, of course, that the sister lived in a different house near by, for she could never reside within the same walls as her brother.

As additional information, the visitors might be told that the ancestors had brought with them the substances and paraphernalia and methods of local industry. In the village of Yalaka, for instance, it would be the processes for burning lime from shells. In Okobobo, Obweria, and Obowada the ancestors brought the knowledge and the implements for polishing hard stone. In Bwoytalu the carver's tool, the hafted shark tooth, and the knowledge of the art came out from underground with the original ancestors. In most places the economic monopolies are thus traced to the autochthonous emergence. In villages of higher rank the insignia of hereditary dignity were brought; in others some animal associated with the local sub-clan came out. Some communities started on their political career of standing hostility to one another from the very beginning. The most important gift to this world carried from the one below is always magic; but this will have to be treated later on and more fully.

If a European bystander were there and heard nothing but the information given from one native to the other, it would mean very little to him. In fact, it might lead him into serious misunderstandings. Thus the simultaneous emergence of brother and sister might make him suspicious either of a mythological allusion to incest, or else would make him look for the original matrimonial pair and inquire about the sister's husband. The first suspicion would be entirely erroneous, and would shed a false light over the specific relation between brother and sister, in which the former is the indispensable guardian, and the second, equally indispensable, is responsible for the transmission of the line. Only a full knowledge of the matrilineal ideas and institutions gives body and meaning to the bare mention of the two ancestral names, so significant to a native listener. If the European were to inquire who was the sister's husband and how she came to have children, he would soon find himself once more confronted by an entirely foreign set of ideas—the sociological irrelevance of the father, the absence of any ideas about physiological procreation, and the strange and complicated system of marriage, matrilineal and patrilocal at the same time.[3]

The sociological relevance of these accounts of origins would become clear only to a European inquirer who had grasped the native legal ideas about local citizenship and the hereditary rights to territory, fishing grounds, and local pursuits. For according to the legal principles of the tribe all such rights are the monopolies of the local community, and only people descendent in the female line from the original ancestress are entitled to them. If the European were told further that, besides the first place of emergence, there are several other 'holes' in the same village, he would become still more baffled until, by a careful study of concrete details and the principles of native sociology, he became acquainted with the idea of compound village communities, i.e., communities in which several sub-clans have merged.

It is clear, then, that the myth conveys much more to the native than is contained in the mere story; that the story gives only the really relevant concrete local differences; that the real meaning, in fact the full account, is contained in the traditional foundations of social organization; and that this the native learns, not by listening to the fragmentary mythical stories, but by living within the social texture of his tribe. In other

---

[3] For a full statement of the psychology and sociology of kinship and descent see articles on "The Psychology of Sex and the Foundations of Kinship in Primitive Societies," "Psychoanalysis and Anthropology," "Complex and Myth in Mother Right," all three in the psychological journal, *Psyche*, Oct. 1923, April, 1924, and Jan. 1925. The first article is included in *The Father in Primitive Psychology* (Psyche Miniature, 1926).

words, it is the context of social life, it is the gradual realization by the native of how everything which he is told to do has its precedent and pattern in bygone times, which brings home to him the full account and the full meaning of his myths of origin.

For an observer, therefore, it is necessary to become fully acquainted with the social organization of the natives if he wants really to grasp its traditional aspect. The short accounts, such as those which are given about local origins, will then become perfectly plain to him. He will also clearly see that each of them is only a part, and a rather insignificant one, of a much bigger story, which cannot be read except from native life. What really matters about such a story is its social function. It conveys, expresses, and strengthens the fundamental fact of the local unity and of the kinship unity of the group of people descendent from a common ancestress. Combined with the conviction that only common descent and emergence from the soil give full rights to it, the story of origin literally contains the legal charter of the community. Thus, even when the people of a vanquished community were driven from their grounds by a hostile neighbor their territory always remained intact for them; and they were always, after a lapse of time and when their peace ceremony had been concluded, allowed to return to the original site, rebuild their village, and cultivate their gardens once more.[4] The traditional feeling of a real and intimate connection with the land; the concrete reality of seeing the actual spot of emergence in the middle of the scenes of daily life; the historical continuity of privileges, occupations, and distinctive characters running back into the mythological first beginnings—all this obviously makes for cohesion, for local patriotism, for a feeling of union and kinship in the community. But although the narrative of original emergence integrates and welds together the historical tradition, the legal principles, and the various customs, it must also be clearly kept in mind that the original myth is but a small part of the whole complex of traditional ideas. Thus on the one hand the reality of myth lies in it social function; on the other hand, once we begin to study the social function of myth, and so to reconstruct its full meaning, we are gradually led to build up the full theory of native social organization.

One of the most interesting phenomena connected with traditional precedent and charter is the adjustment of myth and mythological principle to cases in which they very foundation of such mythology is flagrantly violated. This violation always takes place when the local claims of an autochthonous clan, i.e., a clan which has emerged on the spot, are

---

[4] Cf. the account given of these facts in the article on "War and Weapons among the Trobriand Islanders," *Man*, Jan. 1918; and in Professor Seligman's *Melanesians*, pp. 663–68.

over-ridden by an immigrant clan. Then a conflict of principles is created, for obviously the principle that land and authority belong to those who are literally born out of it does not leave room for any newcomers. On the other hand, members of a sub-clan of high rank who choose to settle down in a new locality cannot very well be resisted by the autochthons—using this word again in the literal native mythological sense. The result is that there come into existence a special class of mythological stories which justify and account for the anomalous state of affairs. The strength of the various mythological and legal principles is manifested in that the myths of justification still contain the antagonistic and logically irreconcilable facts and points of view, and only try to cover them by facile reconciliatory incident, obviously manufactured *ad hoc.* The study of such stories is extremely interesting, both because it gives us a deep insight into the native psychology of tradition, and because it tempts us to reconstruct the past history of the tribe, though we must yield to the temptation with due caution and scepticism.

In the Trobriands we find that the higher the rank of a totemic sub-clan, the greater its power of expansion. Let us first state the facts and then proceed to their interpretation. The sub-clan of the highest rank, the Tabalu sub-clan of the Malasi clan, are found now ruling over a number of villages: Omarakana, their main capital; Kasanayi, the twin village of the capital; and Olivilevi, a village founded some three 'reigns' ago after a defeat of the capital. Two villages, Omlamwaluwa, now extinct, and Dayagila, no longer ruled by the Tabalu, also once belonged to them. The same sub-clan, bearing the same name and claiming the same descent, but not keeping all the taboos of distinction and not entitled to all the insignia, is found ruling in the villages of Oyweyowa, Gumilababa, Kavataria, and Kadawaga, all in the western part of the archipelago, the last mentioned on the small island Kayleula. The village of Tukwa'ukwa was but recently taken over by the Tabalu some five 'reigns' ago. Finally, a sub-clan of the same name and claiming affinity rules over the two big and powerful communities of the South, Sinaketa and Vakuta.

The second fact of importance referring to these villages and their rulers is that the ruling clan does not pretend to have emerged locally in any of those communities in which its members own territory, carry on local magic, and wield power. They all claim to have emerged, accompanied by the original pig, from the historical hole of Obukula on the northwestern shore of the island near the village of Laba'i. From there they have, according to their tradition, spread all over the district.[5]

[5] The reader who wants to grasp these historical and geographical details should consult the map facing p. 51 of the writer's *Argonauts of the Western Pacific.*

In the traditions of this clan there are certain definitely historical facts which must be clearly disentangled and registered; the foundation of the village of Olivilevi three 'reigns' ago, the settlement of the Tabula in Tukwa'ukwa five 'reigns' ago, the taking over of Vakuta some seven or eight 'reigns' ago. By 'reign' I mean the life-rule of one individual chief. Since in the Trobriands, as no doubt in most matrilineal tribes, a man is succeeded by his younger brother, the average 'reign' is obviously much shorter than the span of a generation and also much less reliable as a measure of time, since in many cases it need not be shorter. These particular historical tales, giving a full account of how, when, by whom, and in what manner the settlement was effected, are sober matter-of-fact statements. Thus it is possible to obtain from independent informants the detailed account of how, in the time of their fathers or grandfathers respectively, the chief Bugwabwaga of Omarakana, after an unsuccessful war, had to flee with all his community far south, to the usual spot where a temporary village was erected. After a couple of years he returned to perform the peace-making ceremony and to rebuild Omarakana. His younger brother, however, did not return with him, but erected a permanent village, Olivilevi, and remained there. The account, which can be confirmed in the minutest detail from any intelligent adult native in the district, is obviously as reliable an historical statement as one can obtain in any savage community. The data about Tukwa'ukwa, Vakuta, and so on are of similar nature.

What lifts the trustworthiness of such accounts above any suspicion is their sociological foundation. The flight after defeat is a general rule of tribal usage; and the manner in which the other villages become the seat of the highest rank people, i.e., intermarriage between Tabalu women and head men of other villages, is also characteristic of their social life. The technique of this proceeding is of considerable importance and must be described in detail. Marriage is patrilocal in the Trobriands, so that the woman always moves to her husband's community. Economically, marriage entails the standing exchange of food given by the wife's family for valuables supplied by the husband. Food is especially plentiful in the central plains of Kiriwina, ruled over by the chiefs of highest rank from Omarakana. The valuable shell ornaments, coveted by the chiefs, are produced in the coastal districts to the west and south. Economically, therefore, the tendency always has been, and still is, for women of high rank to marry influential headmen in such villages as Gumilababa, Kavataria, Tukwa'ukwa, Sinaketa, and Vakuta.

So far everything happens according to the strict letter of tribal law. But once a Tabalu woman has settled in her husband's village, she overshadows him by rank and very often by influence. If she has a son or sons these are, until puberty, legal members of their father's community.

They are the most important males in it. The father, as things are in the Trobriands, always wishes to keep them even after puberty for reasons of personal affection; the community feels that their whole status is being raised thereby. The majority desire it; and the minority, the rightful heirs to the headmen, his brothers and his sisters' sons, do not dare to oppose. If, therefore, the sons of high rank have no special reasons for returning to their rightful village, that of their mother, they remain in the father's community and rule it. If they have sisters these may also remain, marry within the village, and thus start a new dynasty. Gradually, though perhaps not at once, they succeed to all the privileges, dignities, and functions vested till then in the local headman. They are styled 'masters' of the village and of its lands, they preside over the formal councils, they decide upon all communal matters where a decision is needed, and above all they take over the control of local monopolies and local magic.

All the facts I have just reviewed are strictly empirical observations; let us now look at the legends adduced to cover them. According to one story two sisters, Botabalu and Bonumakala, came out of the original hole near Laba'i. They went at once to the central district of Kiriwina, and both settled in Omarakana. Here they were welcomed by the local lady in charge of magic and all the rights, and thus the mythological sanction of their claims to the capital was established. (To this point we shall have to return again.) After a time they had a quarrel about some banana leaves pertaining to the beautiful fibre petticoats used for dress. The elder sister then ordered the younger to go, which among the natives is a great insult. She said: "I shall remain here and keep all the strict taboos. You go and eat bush-pig, *katakayluva* fish." This is the reason why the chiefs in the coastal district, though in reality they have the same rank, do not keep the same taboos. The same story is told by natives of the coastal villages with the difference, however, that it is the younger sister who orders her senior to remain in Omarakana and keep all the taboos, while she herself goes to the west.

According to a Sinaketan version, there were three original women of the Tabalu sub-clan, the eldest remained in Kiriwina, the second settled in Kuboma, the youngest came to to Sinaketa and brought with her the *Kaloma* shell discs, which started the local industry.

All these observations refer only to one sub-clan of the Malasi clan. The other sub-clans of this clan, of which I have some dozen on record, are all of low rank; are all local, that is have not immigrated into their present territory; and some of them, those of Bwoytalu, belong to what might be called the pariah or specially despised category of people. Although they all bear the same generic name, have the same common totem, and on ceremonial occasions would range themselves side by side with the people of the highest rank, they are regarded by the natives as belonging to an entirely different class.

Before I pass to the re-interpretation or historical reconstruction of these facts, I shall present the facts referring to the other clans. The Lukuba clan is perhaps the next in importance. They count among their sub-clans two or three which immediately follow in rank the Tabalu of Omarakana. The ancestors of these sub-clans are called Mwauri, Mulobwaima, and Tudava; and they all three came out from the same main hole near Laba'i, out of which the four totemic animals emerged. They moved afterwards to certain important centers in Kiriwina and in the neighboring islands of Kitava and Vakuta. As we have seen, according to the main myth of emergence, the Lukuba clan had the highest rank at first, before the dog and pig incident reversed the order. Moreover, most mythological personalities or animals belong to the Lukuba clan. The great mythological culture hero Tudava, reckoned also as ancestor by the sub-clan of that name, is a Lukuba. The majority of the mythical heroes in connection with the inter-tribal relations and the ceremonial forms of trading belong also to the same clan.[6] Most of the economic magic of the tribe also belongs to people of this clan. In Vakuta, where they have been recently overshadowed, if not displaced, by the Tabalu, they are still able to assert themselves; they have still retained the monopoly in magic; and, taking their stand upon mythological tradition, the Lukuba still affirm their real superiority to the usurpers. There are far fewer sub-clans of low rank among them than among the Malasi.

About the third large totemic division, the Lukwasisiga, there is much less to be said as regards mythology and cultural or historic role. In the main emergence myth they are either completely left out, or else their ancestral animal or person is made to play an entirely insignificant part. They do not own any specially important forms of magic and are conspicuously absent from any mythological reference. The only important part which they play is in the great Tudava cycle in which the ogre Dokonikan is made to belong to the Lukwasisiga totem. To this clan belongs the headman of the village Kabwaku, who is also the chief of the district of Tilataula. The district was always in a relation of potential hostility to the district of Kiriwina proper, and the chiefs of Tilataula were the political rivals of the Tabalu, the people of the highest rank. From time to time the two would wage war. No matter which side was defeated and had to fly, peace was always restored by a ceremonial reconciliation, and the same relative status once more obtained between the two provinces. The chiefs of Omarakana always retained superiority of rank and a sort of general control over the hostile district, even after this had been victorious.

---

[6] Cf. *Argonauts of the Western Pacific*, p. 321.

The chiefs of Kabwaku were to a certain extend bound to execute their orders; and more especially if a direct capital punishment had to be meted out in olden days the chief of Omarakana would delegate his potential foe to carry it out. The real superiority of the chiefs of Omarakana was due to their rank. But to a great extent their power and the fear with which they inspired all the other natives was derived from the important sun and rain magic which they wielded. Thus members of a sub-clan of the Lukwasisiga were the potential foes and the executive vassals, but in war the equals, of the highest chiefs. For, as in peace times the supremacy of the Tabalu would remain unchallenged, so in war the Toliwaga of Kabwaku were considered generally the more efficient and redoubtable. The Lukwasisiga clan were also on the whole regarded as land-lubbers (*Kulita'odila*). One or two other sub-clans of this clan were of rather high rank and intermarried rather frequently with the Tabalu of Omarakana.

The fourth clan, the Lukulabuta, includes only sub-clans of low rank among its numbers. They are the least numerous clan, and the only magic with which they are associated is sorcery.

When we come to the historical interpretation of these myths a fundamental question meets us at the outset: must we regard the sub-clans which figure in legend and myth as representing merely the local branches of a homogeneous culture, or can we ascribe to them a more ambitious significance and regard them as standing for representatives of various cultures, that is as units of different migration waves. If the first alternative is accepted then all the myths, historical data, and sociological facts refer simply to small internal movements and changes, and there is nothing to be added to them except what we have said.

In support of the more ambitious hypothesis, however, it might be urged that the main legend of emergence places the origins of the four clans in a very suggestive spot. Laba'i lies on the northwestern beach, the only place open to sailors who would have come from the direction of the prevailing monsoon winds. Moreover, in all the myths the drift of a migration, the trend of cultural influence, the travels of culture heroes, take place from north to south and generally, though less uniformly, from west to east. This is the direction which obtains in the great cycle of Tudava stories; this is the direction which we have found in the migration myths; this is the direction which obtains in the majority of the Kula legends. Thus the assumption is plausible that a cultural influence has been spreading from the northern shores of the archipelago, an influence which can be traced as far east as Woodlark Island, and as far south as the D'Entrecasteaux Archipelago. This hypothesis is suggested by the conflict element in some of the myths, such as that between the dog and the pig, between Tudava and Dokonikan, and between the cannibal and non-cannibal brother. If we then accept this hypothesis for what it is worth, the following scheme emerges. The oldest layer would be represented by the Lukwasisiga and Lukulabuta clans. The latter is the first to emerge mythologically; while both are relatively autochthonous in that they are not sailors, their communities usually lie inland, and their occupation is mainly agriculture. The generally hostile attitude of the main Lukwasisiga sub-clan, the Toliwaga, to what would be obviously the latest immigrants, the Tabalu, might also be made to fit into this hypothesis. It is again plausible that the cannibal monster who is fought by the innovator and cultural hero, Tudava, belongs to the Lukwasisiga clan.

I have expressly stated that the sub-clans and not the clans must be regarded as migration units. For it is an incontrovertible fact that the big clan, which comprises a number of sub-clans, is but a loose social unit, split by important cultural rifts. The Malasi clan, for instance, includes the highest sub-clan, the Tabalu, as well as the most despised sub-clans, Wabu'a and Gumsosopa of Bwoytalu. The historical hypothesis of migratory units would still have to explain the relation between sub-clans and clan. It seems to me that the minor sub-clans must also have been of a previous arrival, and that their totemic assimilation is a by-product of a general process of sociological reorganization which took place after the strong and influential immigrants of the Tudava and Tabalu type had arrived.

The historical reconstruction requires, therefore, a number of auxiliary hypotheses, each of which must be regarded as plausible, but must remain arbitrary; while each assumption adds a considerable element of uncertainty. The whole reconstruction is a mental game, attractive and absorbing, often spontaneously obtruding itself upon a field-worker, but always remaining outside the field of observation and sound conclusion—that is, if the field-worker keeps his powers of observation and his sense of reality under control. The scheme which I have here developed is the one into which the facts of Trobriand sociology, myth, and custom naturally arrange themselves. Nevertheless, I do not attach any serious importance to it, and I do not believe that even a very exhaustive knowledge of a district entitles the ethnographer to anything but tentative and cautious reconstructions. Perhaps a much wider collation of such schemes might show their value, or else prove their utter futility. It is only perhaps as working hypotheses, stimulating to more careful and minute collection of legend, of all tradition, and of sociological difference, that such schemes possess any important whatever.

As far as the sociological theory of these legends goes the historical reconstruction is irrelevant. Whatever the hidden reality of their unrecorded past may be, myths serve to cover certain inconsistencies created by historical events, rather than to record these events exactly. The myths associated with the spread of the powerful sub-clans show on certain points a fidelity to life in that they record facts inconsistent with one another. The incidents by which this inconsistency is obliterated, if not hidden, are most likely fictitious; we have seen certain myths vary according to the locality in which they are told. In other cases the incidents bolster up non-existent claims and rights.

The historical consideration of myth is interesting, therefore, in that it shows that myth, taken as a whole, cannot be sober dispassionate history, since it is always made *ad hoc* to fulfil a certain sociological function, to glorify a certain group, or to justify an anomalous status. These considerations show us also that to the native mind immediate history, semi-historic legend, and unmixed myth flow into one another, form a continuous sequence, and fulfil really the same sociological function.

And this brings us once more to our original contention that the really important thing about the myth is its character of a retrospective, ever-present, live actuality. It is to a native neither a fictitious story, nor an acount of a dead past; it is a statement of a bigger reality still partially alive. It is alive in that its precedent, its law, its moral, still rule the social life of the natives. It is clear that myth functions especially where there is a sociological strain, such as in matters of great difference in rank and power, matters of precedence and subordination, and unquestionably where profound historical changes have taken place. So much can be asserted as a fact, though it must always remain doubtful how far we can carry out historical reconstruction from the myth.

We can certainly discard all explanatory as well as all symbolic interpretations of these myths of origin. The personages and beings which we find in them are what they appear to be on the surface, and not symbols of hidden realities. As to any explanatory function of these myths, there is no problem which they cover, no curiosity which they satisfy, no theory which they contain.

III
Myths of Death and of the Recurrent Cycle of Life

In certain versions of origin myths the existence of humanity underground is compared to the existence of human spirits after death in the present-day spirit-world. Thus a mythological rapprochement is made between the primeval past and the immediate destiny of each man, another of those links with life which we find so important in the understanding of the psychology and the cultural value of myth.

The parallel between primeval and spiritual existence can be drawn even further. The ghosts of the deceased move after death to the island of Tuma. There they enter the earth through a special hole—a sort of reversed proceeding to the original emergence. Even more important is the fact that after a span of spiritual existence in Tuma, the nether world, an individual grows old, grey, and wrinkled; and that then he has to rejuvenate by sloughing his skin. Even so did human beings in the old primeval times, when they lived underground. When they first came to the surface they had not yet lost this ability; men and women could live eternally young.

They lost the faculty, however, by an apparently trivial, yet important and fateful event. Once upon a time there lived in the village of Bwadela an old woman who dwelt with her daughter and grand-daughter; three generations of genuine matrilineal descent. The grandmother and grand-daughter went out one day to bathe in the tidal creek. The girl remained on the shore, while the woman went away some distance out of sight. She took off her skin, which carried by the tidal current, floated along the creek until it stuck on a bush. Transformed into a young girl, she came back to her grand-daughter. The latter did not recognize her; she was afraid of her, and bade her begone. The old woman, mortified and angry, went back to her bathing place, searched for her old skin, put it on again, and returned to her grand-daughter. The time she was recognized and thus greeted: "A young girl came here; I was afraid; I chased her away." Said the grandmother: "No, you didn't want to recognize me. Well, you will become old—I shall die." They went home to where the daughter was preparing the meal. The old woman spoke to her daughter: "I went to bathe; the tide carried by skin away; your daughter did not recognize me; she chased me away. I shall not slough my skin. We shall all become old. We shall all die."

After that men lost the power of changing their skin and of remaining youthful. The only animals who have retained the power of changing the skin are the 'animals of the below'—snakes, crabs, iguanas, and lizards: this is because men also once lived under the ground. These animals come out of the ground and they still can change their skin. Had men lived above, the 'animals of the above'—birds, flying-foxes, and insects—would also be to change their skins and renew their youth.

Here ends the myth as it is usually told. Sometimes the natives will add other comments drawing parallels between spirits and primitive humanity; sometimes they will emphasize the regeneration motive of the reptiles; sometimes tell only the bare incident of the lost skin. The story is, in itself, trivial and unimportant; and it would appear so to anyone who did not study it against the background of the various ideas, customs, and rites associated with death and future life. The myth is obviously but a developed and dramatized belief in the previous human power of rejuvenation and in its subsequent loss.

Thus, through the conflict between grand-daughter and grandmother, human beings, one and all, had to submit to the process of decay and debility brought on by old age. This, however, did not involve the full incidence of the inexorable fate which is the present lot of man; for old age, bodily decay, and debility do not spell death to the natives. In order to understand the full cycle of their beliefs it is necessary to study the factors of illness, decay, and death. The native of the Trobriands is definitely an optimist in his attitude to health and illness. Strength, vigor, and bodily perfection are to him the natural status which can only be affected or upset by an accident or by a supernatural cause. Small accidents such as excessive fatigue, over-eating, or exposure may cause minor and temporary ailments. By a spear in battle, by poison, by a fall from a rock or a tree a man may be maimed or killed. Whether these accidents and others, such as drowning and the attack of a crocodile or a shark, are entirely free from sorcery is ever a debatable question to a native. But there is no doubt whatever to him that all serious and especially all fatal illnesses are due to various forms and agencies of witchcraft. The most prevalent of these is the ordinary sorcery practised by wizards, who can produce by their spells and rites a number of ailments covering well nigh the whole domain of ordinary pathology, with the exception of very rapid fulminating diseases and epidemics.

The source of witchcraft is always sought in some influence coming from the south. There are two points in the Trobriand Archipelago at which sorcery is said to have originated, or rather to have been brought over from the D'Entrecasteaux Archipelago. One of these is the grove of Lawaywo between the villages of Ba'u and Bwoytalu, and the other is the southern island of Vakuta. Both these districts are still considered the most redoubtable centers of witchcraft.

The district of Bwoytalu occupies a specially low social position in the island, inhabited as it is by the best wood-carvers, the most expert fibre-plaiters, and the eaters of such abominations as stingaree and bush-pig. These natives have been endogamous for a long time, and they probably represent the oldest layer of indigenous culture in the island. To them sorcery was brought from the southern archipelago by a crab. This animal is either depicted as emerging out of a hole in the Lawaywo grove, or else as travelling by the air and dropping from above at the same place. About the time of its arrival a man and a dog went out. The crab was red, for it had the sorcery within it. The dog saw it and tried to bite it. Then the crab killed the dog, and having done this, proceeded to kill the man. But looking at him the crab became sorry, 'its belly was moved', and it brought him back to life. The man then offered his murderer and saviour a large payment, a *pokala*, and asked the crustacean to give him the magic. This was done. The man immediately made use of his sorcery to kill his benefactor, the crab. He then proceeded to kill, according to a rule observed or believed to have been observed until now, a near maternal relative. After that he was in full possession of witchcraft. The crabs at present are black, for sorcery has left them; they are, however, slow to die for once they were the masters of life and of death.

A similar type of myth is told in the southern island of Vatuka. They tell how a malicious being of human shape, but not human nature, went into a piece of bamboo somewhere on the northern shore of Normanby Island. The piece of bamboo drifted northwards till it was washed ashore near the promontory of Yayvau or Vatuka. A man from the neighboring village of Kwadagila heard a voice in the bamboo and opened it. The demon came out and taught him sorcery. This, according to the informants in the south, is the real starting point of black magic. It went to the district of Ba'u in Bwoytalu from Vakuta and not directly from the southern archipelagos. Another version of the Vakuta tradition maintains that the *tauva'u* came to Vakuta not in a bamboo but by a grander arrangement. At Sewatupa on the northern shore of Normanby Island there stood a big tree in which many of the malignant beings used to reside. It was felled, and it tumbled right across the sea, so that while its base remained on Normanby Island the trunk and the branches came across the sea and the top touched Vakuta. Hence sorcery is most rampant in the southern archipelago; the intervening sea is full of fish who live in the branches and boughs of the tree; and the place whence sorcery came to the Trobriands is the southern beach of Vakuta. For in the top of the tree there were three malignant beings, two males and a female, and they gave some magic to the inhabitants of the island.

In these mythical stories we have but one link in the chain of beliefs which surround the final destiny of human beings. The mythical incidents can be understood and their importance realized only in connection with the full beliefs in the power and nature of witchcraft, and with the feelings and apprehensions regarding it. The explicit stories about the advent of sorcery do not quite exhaust or account for all the supernatural dangers. Rapid and sudden disease and death are, in native belief, brought about, not by the male sorcerers, but by flying witches who act act differently and possess altogether a more supernatural character. I was unable to find any initial myth about the origin of this type of witchcraft. On the other hand, the nature and the whole proceedings of these witches are surrounded by a cycle of beliefs which form what might be called a standing or current myth. I shall not repeat them with detail, for I have given a full account in my book, the *Argonauts of the Western Pacific*.[7] But it is important to realize that the halo of supernatural powers surrounding individuals who are believed to be witches gives rise to a

[7] Chap. X, *passim*: especially pp. 236–48, also pp. 320, 321, 393.

continuous flow of stories. Such stories can be regarded as minor myths generated by the strong belief in the supernatural powers. Similar stories are also told about the male sorcerers, the *bwaga'u*.

Epidemics, finally, are ascribed to the direct action of the malignant spirits, the *tauva'u*, who, as we saw, are mythologically often regarded as the source of all witchcraft. These malignant beings have a permanent abode in the south. Occasionally, they will move to the Trobriand Archipelago, and, invisible to ordinary human beings, they walk at night through the villages rattling their lime-gourds and clanking their wooden sword clubs. Wherever this is heard fear falls upon the inhabitants, for those whom the *tauva'u* strike with their wooden weapons die, and such an invasion is always associated with death in masses. *Leria*, epidemic disease, obtains then in the villages. The malignant spirits can sometimes change into reptiles and then become visible to human eyes. It is not always easy to distinguish such a reptile from an ordinary one, but it is very important to do so, for a *tauva'u*, injured or ill-treated, revenges itself by death.

Here, again, around this standing myth, around this domestic tale of a happening which is not placed in the past but still occurs, there cluster innumerable concrete stories. Some of them even occurred while I was in the Trobriands; there was a severe dysentery once, and the first outbreak of what probably was Spanish influenza in 1918. Many natives reported having heard the *tauva'u*. A giant lizard was seen in Wawela; the man who killed it died soon after, and the epidemic broke out in the village. While I was in Oburaku, and sickness was rife in the village, a real *tauva'u* was seen by the crew of the boat in which I was being paddled; a large multi-colored snake appeared on a mangrove, but vanished mysteriously as we came near. It was only through my short-sightedness, and perhaps also my ignorance of how to look for a *tauva'u* that I failed to observe this miracle myself. Such and similar stories can be obtained by the score from natives in all localities. A reptile of this type should be put on a high platform and valuables placed in front of it; and I have been assured by natives who have actually witnessed it that this is not infrequently done, though I never have seen this myself. Again, a number of women witches are said to have had intercourse with *tauva'u*, and of one living at present this is positively affirmed.

In the case of this belief we see how minor myths are constantly generated by the big schematic story. Thus with regard to all the agencies of disease and death the belief, and the explicit narratives which cover part of it, the small concrete supernatural events constantly registered by the natives, form one organic whole. These beliefs are obviously not a theory or explanation. On the one hand, they are the whole complex of cultural practices, for sorcery is not only believed to be practised, but actually is practised, at least in its male form. On the other hand, the complex under discussion covers the whole pragmatic reaction of man towards disease and death; it expresses his emotions, his forebodings; it influences his behavior. The nature of myth again appears to us as something very far removed from a mere intellectual explanation.

We are now in full possession of the native ideas about the factors which in the past cut short man's power of rejuvenation, and which at present cut short his very existence. The connection, by the way, between the two losses is only indirect. The natives believe that although any form of sorcery can reach the child, the youth, or the man in the prime of life, as well as the aged, yet old people are more easily stricken. Thus the loss of rejuvenation at least prepared the ground for sorcery.

But although there was a time when people grew old and died, and thus became spirits, they yet remained in the villages with the survivors—even as now they stay around the dwellings when they return to their village during the annual feast of the *milamala*. But one day an old woman-spirit who was living with her people in the house crouched on the floor under one of the bedstead platforms. Her daughter, who was distributing food to the members of the family, spilled some broth out of the cocoanut cup and burnt the spirit, who expostulated and reprimanded her daughter. The latter replied: "I thought you had gone away; I thought you were only coming back at one time in the year during the *milamala*." The spirit's feelings were hurt. She replied: "I shall go to Tuma and live underneath." She then took up a cocoanut, cut it in half, kept the half with the three eyes, and gave her daughter the other. "I am giving you the half which is blind, and therefore you will not see me. I am taking the half with the eyes, and I shall see you when I come back with other spirits." This is the reason why the spirits are invisible, though they themselves can see human beings.

This myth contains a reference to the seasonal feast of *milamala*, the period at which the spirits return to their villages while festive celebrations take place. A more explicit myth gives an account of how the *milamala* was instituted. A woman of Kitava died leaving a pregnant daughter behind her. A son was born, but his mother had not enough milk to feed him. As a man of a neighboring island was dying, she asked him to take a message to her own mother in the land of spirits, to the effect that the departed one should bring food to her grandson. The spirit-woman filled her basket with spirit-food and came back wailing as follows: "Whose food am I carrying? That of my grandson to whom I am going to give it; I am going to give him his food." She arrived on Bomagema beach in the island of Kitava and put down the food. She spoke to her daughter: "I bring the food; the man told me I should bring it. But I am weak; I fear that people may take me for a witch." She then roasted one of the yams and gave it to her grandson. She went into the bush and made a garden for her daughter. When she came back, however, her daughter received a fright for the spirit looked like a sorceress. She ordered her to go away saying: "Return to Tuma, to the spirit-land; people will say that you are a witch." The spirit-mother complained: "Why do you chase me away? I thought I would stay with you and make gardens for my grandchild." The daughter only replied: "Go away, return to Tuma" The old woman then took up a cocoanut, split it in half, gave the blind half to her daughter, and kept the half with the eyes. She told her that once a year, she and other spirits would come back during the *milamala* and look at the people in the villages, but remain invisible to them. And this is how the annual feast came to be what it is.

In order to understand these mythological stories, it is indispensable to collate them with native beliefs about the spiritworld, with the practices during the *milamala* season, and with the relations between the world of the living and the world of the dead, such as exist in native forms of spiritism.[8] After death every spirit goes to the nether world in Tuma. He has to pass at the entrance Topileta, the guardian of the spirit world. The new-comer offers some valuable gift, the spiritual part of the valuables with which he had been bedecked at the time of dying. When he arrives among the spirits he is received by his friends and relatives who have previously died, and he brings the news from the upper world. He then settles down to spirit-life, which is similar to earthly existence, though sometimes its description is colored by hopes and desires and made into a sort of real Paradise. But even those natives who describe it thus never show any eagerness to reach it.

Communication between spirits and the living is carried out in several ways. Many people have seen spirits of their deceased relatives or friends, especially in or near the island of Tuma. Again, there are now, and seem to have been from time immemorial, men and women who in trances, or sometimes in sleep, go on long expeditions to the nether world. They take part in the life of the spirits, and carry back and forth news, items of information, and important messages. Above all they are always ready to convey gifts of food and valuables from the living to the spirits. These people bring home to other men and women the reality of the spirit world. They also give a great deal of comfort to the survivors who are ever eager to receive news from their dear departed.

To the annual feast of the *milamala*, the spirits return from Tuma to

---

[8] An account of these facts has been already given in an article on "Baloma: Spirits of the Dead in the Trobriand Islands" in the *Journal of the Royal Anthropological Institute*, 1916.

their villages. A special high platform is erected for them to sit upon, from which they can look down upon the doings and amusements of their brethren. Food is displayed in big quantities to gladden their hearts, as well as those of the living citizens of the community. During the day valuables are placed on mats in front of the headman's hut and the huts of important and wealthy people. A number of taboos are observed in the village to safeguard the invisible spirits from injury. Hot fluids must not be spilled, as the spirits might be burned like the old woman in the myth. No native may sit, cut wood within the village, play about with spears or sticks, or throw missiles, for fear of injuring a *Baloma*, a spirit. The spirits, moreover, manifest their presence by pleasant and unpleasant signs, and express their satisfaction or the reverse. Slight annoyance is sometimes shown by unpleasant smells, more serious ill-humor is displayed in bad weather, accidents, and damage to property. On such occasions—as well as when an important medium goes into a trance, or someone is near to death—the spirit-world seems very near and real to the natives. It is clear that myth fits into these beliefs as an integral part of them. There is a close and direct parallel between, on the one hand, the relations of man to spirit, as expressed in present-day religious beliefs and experiences, and, on the other hand, the various incidents of the myth. Here again the myth can be regarded as constituting the furthest background of a continuous perspective which ranges from an individual's personal concerns, fears, and sorrows as the one end, through the customary setting of belief, through the many concrete cases told from personal experience and memory of past generations, right back into the epoch where a similar fact is imagined to have occurred for the first time.

I have presented the facts and told the myths in a manner which implies the existence of an extensive and coherent scheme of beliefs. This scheme does not exist, of course, in any explicit form in the native folklore. But it does correspond to a definite cultural reality, for all the concrete manifestations of the natives' beliefs, feelings, and forebodings with reference to death and after-life hang together and form a great organic unit. The various stories and ideas just summarized shade into one another, and the natives spontaneously point out the parallels and bring out the connections between them. Myths, religious beliefs, and experiences in connection with spirits and the supernatural are really all parts of the same subject; the corresponding pragmatic attitude is expressed in conduct by the attempts to commune with the nether world. The myths are but a part of the organic whole; they are an explicit development into narrative of certain crucial points in native belief. When we examine the subjects which are thus spun into stories we find that they all refer to what might be called the specially unpleasant or negative truths; the loss of rejuvenation, the onset of disease, the loss of life by sorcery, the withdrawal of the spirits from permanent contact with men, and finally the partial communication re-established with them. We see also that the myths of this cycle are more dramatic, they also form a more consecutive, yet complex, account than was the case with the myths of origins. Without laboring the point, I think that this is due to a deeper metaphysical reference, in other words, to a stronger emotional appeal in stories which deal with human destiny, as compared with sociological statements or charters.

In any case we see that the point where myth enters in these subjects is not to be explained by any greater amount of curiosity or any more problematic character, but rather by emotional coloring and pragmatic importance. We have found that the ideas elaborated by myth and spun out into narrative are especially painful. In one of the stories, that of the institution of the *milamala* and the periodical return of the spirits, it is the ceremonial behavior of man, and the taboos observed with regard to the spirits, which are in question. The subjects developed in these myths are clear enough in themselves; there is no need to 'explain' them, and the myth does not even partially perform this function. What it actually does is to transform an emotionally overwhelming foreboding, behind which, even for a native, there lurks the idea of an inevitable and ruthless fatality. Myth presents, first of all, a clear realization of this idea. In the second place, it brings down a vague but great apprehension to the compass of a trivial, domestic reality. The longed-for power of eternal youth and the faculty of rejuvenation which gives immunity from decay and age, have been lost by a small accident which it would have been in the power of a child and a woman to prevent. The separation from the beloved ones after death is conceived as due to the careless handling of a cocoanut cup and to a small altercation. Disease, again, is conceived as something which came out of a small animal, and originated through an accidental meeting of a man, a dog, and a crab. Elements of human error, of guilt, and of mischance assume great proportions. Elements of fate, of destiny, and of the inevitable are, on the other hand, brought down to the dimension of human mistakes.

In order to understand this, it is perhaps well to realize that in his actual emotional attitude towards death, whether his own or that of his loved ones, the native is not completely guided by his belief and his mythological ideas. His intense fear of death, his strong desire to postpone it, and his deep sorrow at the departure of beloved relatives belie the optimistic creed and the easy reach of the beyond which is inherent in native customs, ideas, and ritual. After death had occurred, or at a time when death is threatening, there is no mistaking the dim division of shaking faith. In long conversations with several seriously ill natives, and especially with my consumptive friend Bagido'u, I felt, half-expressed and roughly formulated, but still unmistakable in them all, the same melancholy sorrow at the transience of life and all its good things, the same dread of the inevitable end, and the same questioning as to whether it could be staved off indefinitely or at least postponed for some little time. But again, the same people would clutch at the hope given to them by their beliefs. They would screen, with the vivid texture of their myths, stories, and beliefs about the spirit world, the vast emotional void gaping beyond them.

IV
Myths of Magic

Let me discuss in more detail another class of mythical stories, those connected with magic. Magic, from many points of view, is the most important and the most mysterious aspect of primitive man's pragmatic attitude towards reality. It is one of the problems which are engaging at present the most vivid and most controversial interests of anthropologists. The foundations of this study have been laid by Sir James Frazer who has also erected a magnificent edifice thereon in his famous theory of magic.

Magic plays such a great part in northwest Melanesia that even a superficial observer must soon realize its enormous sway. Its incidence, however, is not very clear at first sight. Although it seems to crop up everywhere, there are certain highly important and vital activities from which magic is conspicuously absent.

No native would ever make a yam or taro garden without magic. Yet certain important types of planting, such as the raising of the cocoanut, the cultivation of the banana, of the mango, and of the bread-fruit, are devoid of magic. Fishing, the economic activity only second in importance to agriculture, has in some of its forms a highly developed magic. Thus the dangerous fishing of the shark, the pursuit of the uncertain *kalala* or of the *to'ulam* are smothered in magic. The equally vital, but easy and reliable method of fishing by poison has no magic whatever. In the construction of the canoe—an enterprise surrounded with technical difficulties, requiring organized labor, and leading to an ever-dangerous pursuit—the ritual is complex, deeply associated with the work, and regarded as absolutely indispensable. In the construction of houses, technically quite as difficult a pursuit, but involving neither danger, nor chance, nor yet such complex forms of co-operation as the canoe, there is no magic whatever associated with the work. Wood-carving, an industrial activity of the greatest importance, is carried on in certain communities as a universal trade, learnt in childhood, and practised by everyone. In these communities there is no magic of carving at all. A different

type of artistic sculpture in ebony and hardwood, practised only by people of special technical and artistic ability all over the district, has, on the
other hand, its magic, which is considered as the main source of skill and
inspiration. In trade, a ceremonial form of exchange known as the *Kula*
is surrounded by important magical ritual; while on the other hand, certain minor forms of barter of a purely commercial nature are without any
magic at all. Pursuits such as war and love, as well as certain forces of
destiny and nature such as disease, wind, and weather are in native belief
almost completely governed by magical forces.

Even this rapid survey leads us to an important generalization which
will serve as a convenient starting-point. We find magic wherever the
elements of chance and accident, and the emotional play between hope
and fear have a wide and extensive range. We do not find magic wherever
the pursuit is certain, reliable, and well under the control of rational
methods and technological processes. Further, we find magic where the
element of danger is conspicuous. We do not find it wherever absolute
safety eliminates any elements of foreboding. This is the psychological
factor. But magic also fulfils another and highly important sociological
function. As I have tried to show elsewhere, magic is an active element
in the organization of labor and in its systematic arrangement. It also
provides the main controlling power in the pursuit of game. The integral
cultural function of magic, therefore, consists in the bridging-over of gaps
and inadequacies in highly important activities not yet completely mas-
tered by man. In order to achieve this end, magic supplies primitive man
with a firm belief in his power of succeeding; it provides him also with a
definite mental and pragmatic technique wherever his ordinary means
fail him. It thus enables man to carry out with confidence his most vital
tasks, and to maintain his poise and his mental integrity under circumstances which, without the help of magic, would demoralize him by despair and anxiety, by fear and hatred, by unrequited love and impotent
hate.

Magic is thus akin to science in that it always has a definite aim intimately associated with human instincts, needs, and pursuits. The magic
art is directed towards the attainment of practical ends; like any other art
of craft it is also governed by theory, and by a system of principles which
dictate the manner in which the act has to be performed in order to be
effective. Thus magic and science show a number of similarities, and with
Sir James Frazer, we can appropriately call magic a pseudo-science.

Let us look more closely at the nature of the magic art. Magic, in all
its forms, is composed of three essential ingredients. In its performance
there always enter certain words, spoken or chanted; certain ceremonial
actions are always carried out; and there is always an officiating minister
of the ceremony. In analyzing, therefore, the nature of magic, we have

to distinguish the formula, the rite, and the condition of the performer. It may be said at once that in the part of Melanesia with which we are concerned, the spell is by far the most important constituent of magic. To the natives, knowledge of magic means the knowledge of the spell; and in any act of witchcraft the ritual centers round the utterance of the spell. The rite and the competence of the performer are merely conditioning factors which serve for the proper preservation and launching of the spell. This is very important from the point of view of our present discussion, for the magical spell stands in close relation to traditional lore and more especially to mythology.[9]

In the case of almost all types of magic we find some story accounting for its existence. Such a story tells when and where that particular magical formula entered the possession of man, how it became the property of a local group, how it passed from one to another. But such a story is not the story of magical origins. Magic never 'originated'; it never was created or invented. All magic simply *was* from the beginning, as an essential adjunct to all those things and processes which vitally interest man and yet elude his normal rational efforts. The spell, the rite, and the object which they govern are coeval.

Thus the essence of all magic is its traditional integrity. Magic can only be efficient if it has been transmitted without loss and without flaw from one generation to the other, till it has come down from primeval times to the present performer. Magic, therefore, requires a pedigree, a sort of traditional passport in its travel across time. This is supplied by the myth of magic. The manner in which myth endows the performance of magic with worth and validity, in which myth blends with the belief in magical efficiency, will be best illustrated by a concrete example.

As we know, love and the attractions of the other sex play an important role in the life of these Melanesians. Like many races of the South Seas they are very free and easy in their conduct, especially before marriage. Adultery, however, is a punishable offense, and relations with the same totemic clan are strictly forbidden. But the greatest crime in the eyes of the natives is any form of incest. Even the bare idea of such a trespass between brother and sister fills them with violent horror. Brother and sister, united by the nearest bond of kinship in this matriarchal society, may not even converse freely, must never joke or smile at one another, and any allusion to one of them in the presence of the other is considered extremely bad taste. Outside the clan, however, freedom is great, and the pursuit of love assumes a variety of interesting and even attractive forms.

[9] Cf. *Argonauts of the Western Pacific*, in this volume pp. 35–36.

All sexual attraction and all power of seduction are believed to reside in the magic of love. This magic the natives regard as founded in a dramatic occurrence of the past, told in a strange, tragic myth of brother and sister incest, to which I can only refer briefly here.[10] The two young people lived in a village with their mother, and by an accident the girl inhaled a strong love decoction, prepared by her brother for someone else. Mad with passion, she chased him and seduced him on a lonely beach. Overcome by shame and remorse, they forsook food and drink, and died together in a grotto. An aromatic herb grew through their inlaced skeletons, and this herb forms the most powerful ingredient in the substances compounded together and used in love magic.

It can be said that the myth of magic, even more than the other types of savage myth, justifies the sociological claims of the wielder, shapes the ritual, and vouches for the truth of the belief in supplying the pattern of the subsequent miraculous confirmation.

Our discovery of this cultural function of magical myth fully endorses the brilliant theory of the origins of power and kingship developed by Sir James Frazer in the early parts of his *Golden Bough*. According to Sir James, the beginnings of social supremacy are due primarily to magic. By showing how the efficacy of magic is associated with local claims, sociological affiliation, and direct descent, we have been able to forge another link in the chain of causes which connect tradition, magic, and social power.

V

Conclusion

Throughout this book I have attempted to prove that myth is above all a cultural force; but it is not only that. It is obviously also a narrative, and thus it has its literary aspect—an aspect which has been unduly emphasized by most scholars, but which, nevertheless, should not be completely neglected. Myth contains germs of the future epic, romance, and tragedy; and it has been used in them by the creative genius of peoples and by the conscious art of civilization. We have seen that some myths are but dry and succinct statements with scarcely any nexus and no dramatic incident; others, like the myth of love or the myth of canoe magic and of overseas sailing, are eminently dramatic stories. Did space permit, I could repeat a long and elaborate saga of the culture hero Tudava, who slays an ogre, avenges his mother, and carries out a number of cultural

[10] For the complete account of this myth see the author's *Sex and Repression in Primitive Society* (1926), where its full sociological bearings are discussed.

tasks.[11] Comparing such stories, it might be possible to show why myth lends itself in certain of its forms to subsequent literary elaboration, and why certain other of its forms remain artistically sterile. Mere sociological precedence, legal title, and vindication of lineage and local claims do not lead far into the realm of human emotions, and therefore lack the elements of literary value. Belief, on the other hand, whether in magic or in religion, is clearly associated with the deepest desires of man, with his fears and hopes, with his passions and sentiments. Myths of love and of death, stories of the loss of immortality, of the passing of the Golden Age, and of the banishment from Paradise, myths of incest and of sorcery play with the very elements which enter into the artistic forms of tragedy, of lyric, and of romantic narrative. Our theory, the theory of the cultural function of myth, accounting as it does for its intimate relation to belief and showing the close connection between ritual and tradition, could help us to deepen our understanding of the literary possibilities of savage story. But this subject, however fascinating, cannot be further elaborated here.

In our opening remarks, two current theories of myth were discredited and discarded: the view that myth is a rhapsodic rendering of natural phenomena, and Andrew Lang's doctrine that myth is essentially an explanation, a sort of primitive science. Our treatment has shown that neither of these mental attitudes is dominant in primitive culture; that neither can explain the form of primitive sacred stories, their sociological context, or their cultural function. But once we have realized that myth serves principally to establish a sociological charter, or a retrospective moral pattern of behavior, or the primeval supreme miracle of magic—it becomes clear that elements both of explanation and of interest in nature must be found in sacred legends. For a precedent accounts for subsequent cases, though it does so through an order of ideas entirely different from the scientific relation of cause and effect, of motive and consequence. The interest in nature, again, is obvious if we realize how important is the mythology of magic, and how definitely magic clings to the economic concerns of man. In this, however, mythology is very far from a disinterested and contemplative rhapsody about natural phenomena. Between myth and nature two links must be interpolated: man's pragmatic interest in certain aspects of the outer world, and his need of supplementing rational and empirical control of certain phenomena by magic.

Let me state once more that I have dealt in this book with savage myth, and not with the myth of culture. I believe that the study of my-

[11] For one of the main episodes of the myth of Tudava, see pp. 209–10 of the author's "Complex and Myth in Mother Right" in *Psyche*, Vol. V, Jan. 1925.

thology as it functions and works in primitive societies should anticipate the conclusions drawn from the material of higher civilizations. Some of this material has come down to us only in isolated literary texts, without its setting in actual life, without its social context. Such is the mythology of the ancient classical peoples and of the dead civilizations of the Orient. In the study of myth the classical scholar must learn from the anthropologist.

The science of myth in living higher cultures, such as the present civilization of India, Japan, China, and last but not least, our own, might well be inspired by the comparative study of primitive folk-lore; and in its turn civilized culture could furnish important additions and explanations to savage mythology. This subject is very much beyond the scope of the present study. I do, however, want to emphasize the fact that anthropology should be not only the study of savage custom in the light of our mentality and our culture, but also the study of our own mentality in the distant perspective borrowed from Stone Age man. By dwelling mentally for some time among people of a much simpler culture than our own, we may be able to see ourselves from a distance, we may be able to gain a new sense of proportion with regard to our own institutions, beliefs, and customs. If anthropology could thus inspire us with some sense of proportion, and supply us with a finer sense of humor, it might justly claim to be a very great science.

I have now completed the survey of facts and the range of conclusions; it only remains to summarize them briefly. I have tried to show that folklore, these stories handed on in a native community, live in the cultural context of tribal life and not merely in narrative. By this I mean that the ideas, emotions, and desires associated with a given story are experienced not only when the story is told, but also when in certain customs, morals rules, or ritual proceedings, the counterpart of the story is enacted. And here a considerable difference is discovered between the several types of story. While in the mere fireside *tale* the sociological context is narrow, the *legend* enters much more deeply into the tribal life of the community, and the *myth* plays a most important function. Myth, as a statement of primeval reality which still lives in present-day life as a justification by precedent, supplies a retrospective pattern of moral values, sociological order, and magical belief. It is, therefore, neither a mere narrative, nor a form of science, nor a branch of art or history, nor an explanatory tale. It fulfils a function *sui generis* closely connected with the nature of tradition, and the continuity of culture, with the relation between age and youth, and with the human attitude towards the past. The function of myth, briefly, is to strengthen tradition and endow it with a greater value and prestige by tracing it back to a higher, better, more supernatural reality of initial events.

Myth is, therefore, an indispensable ingredient of all culture. It is, as we have seen, constantly regenerated; every historical change creates its mythology, which is, however, but indirectly related to historical fact. Myth is a constant by-product of living faith, which is in need of miracles; of sociological status, which demands precedent; of moral rule, which requires sanction.

We have made, perhaps, a too ambitious attempt to give a new definition of myth. Our conclusions imply a new method of treating the science of folk-lore, for we have shown that it cannot be independent of ritual, of sociology, or even of material culture. Folk-tales, legends, and myths must be lifted from their flat existence on paper, and placed in the three-dimensional reality of full life. As regards anthropological field-work, we are obviously demanding a new method of collecting evidence. The anthropologist must relinquish his comfortable position in the long chair on the veranda of the missionary compound, Government station, or planter's bungalow, where, armed with pencil and notebook and at times with a whisky and soda, he has been accustomed to collect statements from informants, write down stories, and fill out sheets of paper with savage texts. He must go out into the villages, and see the natives at work in gardens, on the beach, in the jungle; he must sail with them to distant sandbacks and to foreign tribes, and observe them in fishing, trading, and ceremonial overseas expeditions. Information must come to him full-flavored from his own observations of native life, and not be squeezed out of reluctant informants as a trickle of talk. Field-work can be done first- or second-hand even among the savages, in the middle of pile-dwellings, not far from actual cannibalism and head-hunting. Open-air anthropology, as opposed to hearsay note-taking, is hard work, but it is also great fun. Only such anthropology can give us the all-round vision of primitive man and of primitive culture. Such anthropology shows us, as regards myth, that far from being an idle mental pursuit, it is a vital ingredient of practical relation to the environment.

The claims and merits, however, are not mine, but are due once more to Sir James Frazer. *The Golden Bough* contains the theory of the ritual and sociological function of myth, to which I have been able to make but a small contribution, in that I could test, prove, and document in my field-work. This theory is implied in Frazer's treatment of magic; in his masterly exposition of the great importance of agricultural rites; in the central place which the cults of vegetation and fertility occupy in the volumes of *Adonis, Attis, Osiris*, and in those on the *Spirits of the Corn and of the Wild*. In these works, as in so many of his other writings, Sir James Frazer has established the intimate relation between the word and the deed in primitive faith; he has shown that the words of the story and of the spell, and the acts of ritual and ceremony are the two aspects of primitive belief. The deep philosophic query propounded by Faust, as to the primacy of the word or of the deed, appears to us fallacious. The beginning of man is the beginning of articulate thought and of thought put into action. Without words, whether framed in sober rational conversation, or launched in magical spells, or used to entreat superior divinities, man would not have been able to embark upon his great Odyssey of cultural adventure and achievement.

6

MYTH AS A DRAMATIC DEVELOPMENT OF DOGMA

WALKING THROUGH one of the suburbs of Innsbruck, the visitor might come upon a church not yet quite finished in one of the side streets; it stands in a backyard of a small suburban villa. Sometimes he might encounter people carrying bricks and other building material; if as an amateur ethnographer he were to stop and enquire, he would find that these are not professional masons and brick-layers but pilgrims—peasants and townspeople often coming from distant places who supply the material as well as the devotion and faith necessary for the construction of a new church. This is dedicated to St. Theresa and erected on a spot recently become renowned for its miraculous proper-ties. The miracle started with a sensational event of no mean importance; its traditions, though recent, have already grown into the dimensions of a minor myth. A woman gave birth to twins: they came into the world practically still-born, the faithful say they were already dead on arrival. The mother, a pious woman, offered them to St. Theresa, prayed and made a vow that if they were restored to life she would worship the saint in a little wash-house in her backyard. The saint acceded to her vows and prayers, the twins lived, grew and prospered; minor miracles followed the principal one. The Church often indifferent and sometimes hostile to new-fangled miracles took cognizance of this.[1] The wash-house was trans-formed into a small chapel: its miraculous properties became known, the services were attended to overflowing, and finally a collection was made to build a large church.

This is a recent, well-attested and typical process by which among a religious people, a new minor cult, a new rallying point for belief and a new tradition spring up simultaneously. It is a close parallel to Lourdes,

---

The typescript of this article is designated "Lecture I"; however, there is no indication in the records of when and where it might have been delivered. It appears to be a draft of an incomplete address.

[1] One has only to remember the case of Joan of Arc and the early hostility of the Church to the claims of Bernadette Soubirous at Lourdes. A few years ago the press reported throughout the world an interesting case from Hungary where three saints appeared to the faithful, drew large audiences and performed miracles. For some reasons of its own the Catholic Church refused to associate its authority with these miracles. The gendarmerie were summoned and finally the fire brigade were called and turned their hose on the faith-ful. The fire of enthusiasm of the faithful, deemed inapt by State and Church, was thus finally quenched.

Loretto, to Santiago de Compostela and to the innumerable shrines, altars and places of miraculous power at which we Roman Catholics worship God through his saints: we believe that on the very spot in connection with a statue, a picture or a relic, miraculous grace can be attained.

Roman Catholicism does not stand alone. A visitor to Salt Lake City will naturally inspect the Tabernacle and the row of houses in which Brigham Young and his wives lived; he will admire the wonderful energy, social organisation and moral strength which created a flourishing community out of a desert. He would understand how a powerful religion can create a vigorous community and lead to great works. A scrutiny of the foundation of this faith sooner or later discloses the most interesting myth which tells of how God revealed to Joseph Smith the foundation of a new faith and a new social order. Again we have a new myth, a new ritual, a new morality growing as it were out of one event simultaneously and in close inter-relation. Whether we take Christian Science with its sensational birth in a miraculous cure and revelation or the Society of Friends with its almost complete denial of miracles, yet with its sacred tradition of the Founder and his supremely ethical personality, we would find everywhere that the works of religion and its beliefs must have sacred tradition as its groundwork, and that the miraculous element whether in a purely ethical or magical form must have precedence to be believed.

All this seems common-sense enough to escape being seriously questioned. It may, in fact, appear so simple as to be hardly worth consideration as an important scientific contribution to the comparative study of human religion. And yet the implication of the simple truth that myth must be studied in its social, ritual and ethical effects rather than as an imaginative and pseudo-scientific tale has been almost completely disregarded in the study of the subject. This I shall briefly show in the following pages.

For the present let me just indicate that the ethnographer, working among primitive people, will find everywhere similar conditions. Among the Palaeolithic inhabitants of Central Australia all the elaborate ritual of magic and religion is intimately bound up with the sacred body of tradition which might almost be called the totemic gospels of these people. Exactly as we carry out our ritual of baptism because of our doctrine of original sin, and believe in this dogma because of what we are told in the Book of Genesis, so they have to initiate their young in order to make them full human beings. And their belief is born from their primitive gospels where man was changed from an incomplete and uncircumcised creature into full bodily and spiritual man by the will of a benevolent totemic spirit. Among the Pueblo Indians, as we shall see, a rich mythology dictates the belief that fertility can be obtained by dramatic representation of ancestral doings, by a ritual appeal to those forces of nature which once upon a time were revealed in a personified form in great miraculous events of the part. In some parts of Melanesia magic performs miracles to-day because it is a repetition of spells and rites which once upon a time created the great miracles of the Golden Age.

A Sociological Definition of Myth

What is then the fact of a myth? Briefly, that all the principal tenets of religious belief have a tendency to be spun out into concrete stories; in the second place, these stories are never mere accounts of what happened in the past. Every act of ritual, every artistic representation of religious subjects, in the worship of relics and sacred places in short, in all the visual signs of past sensational acts of grace every theme is revivified. The events of the mythological past play also a leading part in moral conduct and social organisation.

That myth is in a way a mere unfolding of dogma even a cursory glance at any religion will show. The belief in immortality, the dogma of individual survival, has given rise to the innumerable stories of how once man was made to live for ever on earth, how through a mistake of a supernatural messenger, or through his own sin, or through a mere technical error, man lost his eternal life.[2] The belief in Providence and in the great architect of the universe is embodied in numberless mythological cosmologies. On the shores of the Pacific and on its many islands, we are told how the world was fished out of the sea or moulded out of slime; or again, from other continents, we have stories relating how out of chaos the various parts of the universe have been shaped in succession, or how the earth was hurled from space, or out of darkness, by a divine maker. The wide range of beliefs which are usually labelled "nature worship" again have a rich mythology of totemic ancestors: of the early appearance and miraculous, though not always moral, behavior of nature gods, of the early contacts between man and his Guardian Spirit. In the analysis which follows of Australian totemic mythology, of the tales and sagas connected with Pueblo nature worship as well as the specimens of Melanesian mythology, I supply full documentation of this statement.

Wisdom, like charity, ought to begin at home. The principle here stated can be best appreciated by anyone, in relation to his own religious convictions. I suggest that if we were to take any of the living dogmas of our own religion, we would find that they are founded on our sacred traditions. The Roman Catholic may lay a greater stress on the teaching

[2] *See Sir James George Frazer, Folk-Lore in the Old Testament* [abr. ed., 1923], "The Fall of Man."

of the Church, the Protestant may go straight through the Bible, but in the long run it is the sacred tradition, oral or written, which supplies the foundation of all belief; the sacred tradition, of course, including the theological interpretation and additions.

I have already mentioned the dogma of original sin; the dogma of atonement is expressed in the whole of the New Testament and centered on the sacrifice on Mount Calvary; the dogma of real or symbolic presence in the sacrament has to be interpreted by reference to accounts of the Last Supper. The belief in the constitution of our Trinity, the three persons in their real relationship—a point on which a good deal of theological dispute and human blood has been spilt—finds its ultimate sources in the several events of the Bible. To indicate my own naive conviction from the time when I was a believing, practising Christian, I always thought at the Creation, God, the Father, acted in his private capacity, that later on, somehow, God, the Son, appeared on the stage, at first foreshadowed in the Old Testament, then as the full personality in the gospels. The Holy Ghost, to me always a somewhat shadowy, unsubstantial part of divinity, seemed to hover in the distance, present, no doubt, even when "darkness was on the face of the deep." In fact, I somehow felt that "when the spirit moved on the face of the waters" it might have done so most conveniently in a winged form—that of a dove. And aided, I think, by some pictures, I perceived the ship of God, the Father, floating above the dark waves of the primeval ocean. I am putting all this on record because I know from personal experience that no abstract dogma is sufficient substance for living belief. Belief, in its live form, turns to the real figures of sacred history as the act and word establishing salvation. Take, then, one living dogma after another. Whether we be Catholic or Protestant, Jew or Gentile, Buddhist or follower of Mrs. Eddy, Spiritist or Mormon, follow it up to its living roots and we will find that it leads back to some sacred events, or, at least, to some implication of a great picture emerging out of a story, of creation, of fall, of the tribulation of a chosen people, or of the fervent visions of the prophets.

It might not be so easy, perhaps, to do the reverse, to take an incident, even an important incident, in our holy writings, and to show how it has crystallised into a specific doctrine of faith, into a moral precept, or into a dogma of social behaviour. But of such an examination the results would be astonishing. The Flood, for instance, seems a first sight to be nothing but a dramatic tale. In reality—and here I speak again largely from personal experiences of living faith—the Flood is a mythological proof in vindication of God's moral vigilance. When humanity went completely astray, God was there to chastise men and women and to award one exception. The Flood was a miracle, and a miracle with a moral implication;

it stands as testimony of God's interest in moral behaviour and to his supreme justice.

It is easier, perhaps, to treat Christianity in the anthropological spirit than to approach savage and primitive religions with a truly Christian mind. The un-Christian attitude displayed by many of us towards primitive beliefs, our conviction that they are just idle superstitions and gross forms of idolatry, has deeply affected the study of primitive religions by Europeans. Savage tales of a sacred character have often been taken as mere idle fiction. Had it been recognised that they are the counterparts of our own sacred writings, those who have collected them might perhaps have studied more fully the ethical, ritual and social influence of primitive mythology. Thus, ethnographic evidence has to be largely vitiated by a false theoretical approach to the subject. Again, in the study of some historical religions, of Egypt, Vedic India, Mesopotamia, of the ancient orient, we have a full documentation of their sacred writings, a much more limited account of their ritual, and hardly any data available of how their religions were actually lived in morals, social institutions and public life.

I am saying all this in order to draw the intelligent reader's attention to the fact that the best understanding of religion can be obtained by an objective view of what we believe in practice in our own society. The next best can be achieved by a really scientific study of exotic religions as they are practised to-day by non-Christian communities. The understanding of dead religions of which we have only scattered data and fragmentary documents and monuments is not the royal road for the comprehensive study of religion.

The point of view here developed has then as its main philosophic basis the principle that the most important thing about a religion is how it is lived. "Faith apart from works is barren." Since myth is an inevitable background of faith, its very backbone indeed, we have to study myth as it affects the life of people.

In anthropological jargon, this means that myth or sacred story has to be defined by its function. It is a story which is told in order to establish a belief, to serve as a precedent in ceremony or ritual, or to rank as a pattern of moral or religious conduct. Mythology, therefore, or the sacred tradition of a society, is a body of narratives woven into their culture, dictating their belief, defining their ritual, acting as the chart of their social order and the pattern of their moral behaviour. Every myth has naturally a literary content, since it is always a narrative, but this narrative is not merely a piece of entertaining fiction or explanatory statement to the believer. It is a true account of sensational events which have shaped the constitution of the world, the essence of moral conduct, and determines the ritual contact between man and his maker, or other powers that be.

It may be well at this point of the argument to pause for a moment and draw the attention of the reader, especially if he be a layman, to the fact that we are not elaborating a commonplace. It is maintained here that myth is an intrinsic part in the make-up of any religion, more precisely that it supplies the charter for ritual, belief, moral conduct and social organisation. This implies that myth is not a piece of primitive science, nor yet a primeval philosophic allegory of a semi-poetic, rhapsodic nature, nor yet a strangely garbled historic account. Hence the primary function of myth is neither to explain, nor to recount past historical events, nor express the fantasies or crystallised day-dreams of a community. This view is not new or revolutionary; I have formulated it at an earlier period, more clearly, as it seemed to me then, too emphatically as was said by some of my colleagues, but the whole approach is an actual outcome of modern humanistic trends. The whole emphasis on the social aspect of religion, first recognised by Robertson Smith, later developed by Durkheim, by Hubert Morse and Radcliffe-Brown, brings near to us the question of the social aspect of mythology. The emphasis laid on behaviour and conduct in modern social sciences would also lead us to enquire whether mythology does or does not affect the ritual and moral behaviour of man. The psycho-analytic connection of myth with dreams and day-dreams, with fantasies and ideals, distorted though it might appear in many points to the unanalysed and uninitiated average citizen, does emphasise the dynamic aspect of myth, its connection with the constitution of the human family in its pragmatic aspect. But above all, the so-called functional approach, in the treatment of cultural phenomena, leads us directly to the study of myth through its cultural function. This approach insists on the fact that ideas, ritualised activities, moral rules, do not lead, in any culture, an isolated existence in water-tight compartments; that Man acts because he believes and he believes because the truth has been revealed to him in a miraculous presentation; that sacred tradition, moral standards, and ritual ways of approaching Providence are not isolated but that they work one on another, seems an almost self-evident assertion. That this is not the case a rapid survey of some theories of myth, current or recently advanced, will readily convince us.

Previous Theories of Folklore

Every one of these last-mentioned views has at one time or another dominated the scientific or pre-scientific conception of myth. Euhemerists, ancient and modern, hold that myth always centres round a kernel or core of historical truth, misrepresented by false symbolism and literary embellishments. Euhemerism still survives in all those approaches which used primitive tradition to establish historical fact. There is a great deal of truth in this view; the legends of Polynesia do contain undoubtedly a historical kernel. The reinterpretation of oriental mythology by Elliot Smith, Perry and [A. M.] Hocart has contributed to our knowledge of certain phases in the diffusion of culture. At the same time it is certain that the search for the historical kernel in the tribal tradition of the community touches but one aspect of the problem and probably not the most essential. It certainly does not define the actual sociological function of mythology. The main object of sacred tradition is not to serve as a chronicle of past events; it is to lay down the effective precedent of a glorified past for repetitive actions in the present. The historical assessment of myth, useful as it may be in many cases, has to be supplemented by the sociological theory of myth for two reasons. First of all, if the views here developed are correct, it is of the greatest importance that the field worker should not merely study the text of a sacred story or legend, but also, above all, its pragmatic effects on the social organisation, religious practices and moral conduct of the living society. In the second place, the theoretical explanation of miraculous, obscene, or extravagant elements in the myth cannot be achieved by treating such elements as distortions of historical facts. They, as well as many other motives of historical narratives, can only be understood by reference to ritual, ethical, and social influences of the story on present day conduct.

The theory that the nature of myth consists in an allegorical presentation of natural phenomena is associated in this country with the name of Max Müller. Here again, it would be wrong to reject his contribution en bloc. For there is no doubt that men's interest in certain phases of nature, above all in the growth of plants and in the reproduction of animals, has been expressed in religious rites, and these, as we know, are connected with mythology. But nature symbolism, especially as it is practised up to this very day by certain schools of thought in Germany, has short-circuited the problem by eliminating the intermediary link of ritual, prayer and religious belief. It has instead introduced two false concepts. One of them is the view that the real nature of myths is completely misconceived by those who now tell them and believe in them. In other words, that the allegoric or esoteric meaning of the combats, of the ordeals, of the crimes, triumphs and heroic deeds—which in reality are but cryptic accounts of the courses of the sun, of the phases of the moon, of the growth and decay of vegetation—corresponds to a primitive or a mythopoeic phase of humanity. This, our learned colleagues would tell us, can only be elucidated by a sound intuition, which allows us to guess at the inward meaning of the allegory. To the present writer, it is quite clear from his personal experience in the field, as well as from his perusal of literature, that this assumption of an entirely different mentality which created myths, and of another which practised them, is unsatisfactory. The events recounted in myths are so closely related to what human beings are doing now, albeit on a magnified, miraculous scale, that no esoteric explanation is satisfactory to account for the nature of myth. The other weakness in this type of explanation lies in their assumption not only that the whole substance of a mythological narrative is symbolic, but that all the symbolism refers to one or to another process of nature. Thus, according to some writers, all myths can be reduced to the course of the sun, and nothing else; or, according to others, to the phases of the moon; yet others see in them the processes of growth and development of plants or beasts only. But if the view here presented is right, and mythology follows belief, ritual and morality, then even these references to natural processes or astronomic events, which we find actually in myths, must differ from tribe to tribe and from region to region. Where climate and soil allow men to develop agriculture, the magic and religion of the people will centre round the life of plants, and myth will contain references to the growth and decay of crops, to the influences of sun, wind and rain. Hunter's moon, in any case, is important, because it regulates tribal life through its place in the calendar. Without underrating, therefore, the role of nature worship in religion and of references to natural processes in mythology, I would like to insist that both must be studied through the three-fold approach of religious dogma, ethics and ritual.

In combatting the allegorical interpretation of Max Müller, Andrew Lang developed the aetiological theory of primitive myth. In one way this was an advance because it assigned a more business-like role for myth in primitive culture. Yet it was vitiated by the way in which its sponsor formulated it. Let me quote his own words: "Savage men are like ourselves in curiosity and anxiety, causas cognoscere rerum, but with our curiosity they do not possess our powers of attention. They are as easily satisfied with an explanation of phenomena as they are eager to possess an explanation." "The savage stage of thought" which for civilised observers resembles a "temporary madness" (Müller) seeks an explanation of phenomena which presents itself "and that explanation he makes for himself or receives from tradition, in the shape of a myth. . . . Savage mythology, which is also savage science, has a reply to questions" (of the origin of the world, of man and of beasts).[3] Now the fact is that, on the whole, neither we, nor the savages, have a natural curiosity for the knowledge of causes. This curiosity in civilised man resides exclusively

[3] Article on "Mythology," by Andrew Lang, Encyclopædia Britannica, 12th Edit., 1922, pp. 131–32.

in the highly technical and differentiated scientific interest which is a product of a far-reaching division of labour. On the other hand, savages, like ourselves, must possess a sound, empirical, and practical knowledge which they need in all their technical processes, economic pursuits and collective activities on a large scale, such as war, sailing and trekking. To equate savage mythology with savage science is one of the greatest acts of violence perpetrated in the theoretical treatment of human culture. It has given rise to the later theories about the entirely different mentality of primitive man, about the prelogical mentality of savages and about the incapability of scientific or empirical thinking. The very fact that we have our own mythology quite as developed as a primitive for fulfilling the same function might have taught all the theorists of myth as an outcome of a different earlier mind, that their theories, to say the least, were insufficient. Yet all these views still influence modern scientific thought.[4] The somewhat eclectic and vague statement of the subject by Professor Ruth Benedict in the *Encyclopaedia of Social Science*, vide "Myth" and "Folklore," shows an advance from previous theories of myth. In this last-named article we find the following summing up: "Modern folklorist study is freeing itself from preconceptions and of far-fetched allegories and is founding itself upon the importance of folklore as a social phenomena, and as a means of expression by a social group of its own attitudes and cultural life. By regarding folklore as a cultural trait like technology, social organisation, or religion, any special consideration of communal authorship is made unnecessary, since myths are as much or as little due to communal creation as marriage or fertility rites. All cultural traits, including folk tales, are in the last analysis individual creations determined by cultural conditioning" (p. 291, 1931). And again, in article s.v. "Myth": "Myth is among some peoples the keystone of the religious complex, and religious practices are unintelligible, except by way of their mythology" (p. 180). But she considers that "The origin of religion is not

---

[4] Compare, for instance, the two last editions of *Notes and Queries in Anthropology*. In the last but one edition, we find the definition of myth as "stories which are intended to explain an abstract idea or vague and difficult conception," page 210. This is, of course, Andrew Lang with a vengeance. In the last edition, the substance of the theory here advanced was accepted completely; indeed, large chunks from a previous publication of mine are included (unfortunately without acknowledgements, without inverted commas, and without my permission). On page 329, lines 19 to 23 are the verbal repetition of a sentence on pages 119 to 120 of my *Myth in Primitive Psychology*, lines 24 to 33 are word for word with only slight abbreviations taken over from *Myth in Primitive Psychology*, page 124. Again the article on "Myth" in the 12th Edit. of the *Ency. Brit.* was written by Lang and contains a clear statement of the aetiological theory of myth. The 14th, the last one to contain a new article on myth, gives a brief summary of various theories and ends up with a statement of the functional and sociological interpretation of myth, and contains the quotation from *Myth in Primitive Psychology* by the present writer.

to be sought in mythological concepts, nor the origin of myth in religion, but the two have constantly cross-fertilised each other, and the resulting complex is a product of both primary traits." The view taken that folklore *expresses* social attitudes or that mythology and religion cross-fertilised each other does not reach the clear recognition of the specific social function of myth as a charter of ritual belief, ethics and social organisation. In fact, Professor Benedict explicitly criticises the views advanced by myself in her article on myth. She denies that the functional nature of myth as a charter of social organisation, religious belief, and ritual practices is universal.

We can therefore conclude that the view here advanced is making headway, but that it has not yet been universally accepted or clearly recognised. Yet it is by no means a new or original theory of the present writer. As in many other matters we owe the first flash of insight to that great Scot scholar Robertson Smith. Robertson Smith was perhaps the first clearly to recognise the sociological aspect in all human religions and also to emphasise, at times perhaps to over-emphasise, the importance of ritual as against dogma (*Religion of the Semites*, 3rd ed., 1927). Religion, according to him, is rather a fixed body of practices than a system of dogmas. There may perhaps be a slight exaggeration in his statement that "antique religions have, for the most part, no creed; they consisted entirely of institutions and practices" (*op. cit.*, p. 16). For in another place he is more correct in saying that "mythology takes the place of dogma. . . . The rite, in short, was connected, not with a dogma but with a myth" (p. 17). If we are correct in stating, not that each myth contains a dogma, but that most dogmas have their foundation in myth, we see that Robertson Smith has anticipated fully the point of view here, that "so far as the way of thinking expressed in a myth is not already expressed in the ritual itself, it had no properly religious sanction; the myth, apart from the ritual, affords only a doubtful and slippery kind of evidence." In this, Robertson Smith recognises clearly that any narrative has to be assessed by the function that it plays in organised religious behaviour. I would say that a myth that is not expressed in ritual is not a myth but merely an old wives' or an old men's tale. In other words, any definition or classification of folklore that ignores its influence on ritual and also on social organisation must remain barren. This is implied already in Robertson Smith's view that "religion was the body of fixed religious practices . . . and practice preceded doctrinal theory" (p. 19). At present we do not worry so much over the prius-posterus, but we retain the principle that doctrinal theory and traditional practices are two aspects of the same thing; that they grow up together and that to study one without the other is a fundamental error of method.

Robertson Smith's view has influenced many subsequent writers; Dr.

E. A. Gardner, writing on myth, in *Hastings' Encyclopaedia of Religion and Ethics*, [states] that "mythology, by its explanations and illustrations of the nature and character of the gods or other powers, would help man to keep his relations with them on the right basis." This might seem like a compromise between Andrew Lang and Robertson Smith, but as long as explanation is meant as a code and a charter for the correct carrying out of ritual practices, the essence of myth is correctly stated. The two volumes of Frazer's monumental work on the cults and myths of Adonis, Attis and Osiris contain a documentation of the point of view here developed, pervaded throughout as they are by the principles of Robertson Smith and the great insight of the author of *The Golden Bough* himself.

But where the inadequacy of the present state of anthropological knowledge makes itself most felt and the emphasis on the cultural function of myth is most necessary, is in the actual technique and methods of field work. A few first-rate writers, notably those whose work will be used in the subsequent pages, i.e., Spencer and Gillen, Fewkes, Cushing, A. R. Brown, Elsdon Best, as well as the younger field workers in the functional schools, Dr. Raymond Firth, Dr. I. A. Richards and Dr. H. Powdermaker, have supplied us with adequate data. But in many, even excellent, books, it would be difficult to find the co-relation between folklore and religion which would allow us to test and document the leading principles of Robertson Smith and his followers.

The final test of any theory in a branch of learning which claims to be scientific lies in its empirical value. Does the view here advanced open up new avenues of empirical research; does it force us to observe new facts and new relations between facts? Perhaps I can best bring home to you the significance of the present theory of myth by recounting briefly how I was forced to adopt this point of view in my field work. When I went out to New Guinea, I was already acquainted with the universally influential aetiological explanation of myth. This theory has, as we have seen, the fatal implication that we have to collect stories and regard them as self-contained documents of primitive science. I had to learn the lesson of functional co-relation between myth and ritual in the field.

PART FOUR

RELIGION AND MYTH IN

MODERN TIMES

7

THE FOUNDATIONS OF FAITH AND MORALS

Preface

ANTHROPOLOGY is the comparative science of human cultures. It is often conceived as the study of man's savagery and of his exotic extravagances. Modern developments in the world's history, however, have made us uncertain whether we can trace a sharp line of distinction between *culture* and *savagery*. The student of human institutions and customs is, as a matter of method, also feeling less and less inclined to confine himself to the so-called primitive or simple cultures. He draws on the savageries of contemporary civilization as well as on the virtues and wisdom to be found among the humbler peoples of the world. By this very fact the Science of Man has a lesson to teach.

But the specifically scientific task of anthropology is to reveal the fundamental nature of human institutions through their comparative study. An inductive survey establishing the intrinsic similarity which underlies fortuitous variations discloses the nature of law and religion, of property and co-operation, of credit and moral confidence; it also yields the correct definition of such institutions as human marriage, family, Church, and State. What is common to all of them, *quod semper, quod ubique, quod ab initio*, constitutes obviously their essential character. In all this the Science of Man is gradually falling into line with other sciences, above all with the exact and natural disciplines.

To many a thinking man and woman one of the most important questions of the day is the place of religion in our modern culture. Is its influence on the wane? Has it failed us, say, in the last war and in the framing of the ensuing peace? Is it gradually receding from the dominant place which it ought to occupy in our public life and private concerns? The attacks on religion nowadays are many, the dangers and snags innumerable and obvious. Yet, here again, the comparative study of civilization teaches that the core of all sound communal life has always been a strong, living faith. What about our own civilization? Is there not a slight shifting of the function and substance of religious belief? Do we not observe the infiltration of extraneous dogmas, political and economic, into the place

The following articles comprised the Riddell Memorial Lectures delivered before the University of Durham at Armstrong College, Newcastle-upon-Tyne, February 1935, and were published as a booklet by the Oxford University Press, London, in 1936.

of the spiritual truths on which Christianity is based? Is it true that some modern political movements, Communism or Fascism, the belief in the saving power of the totalitarian state and of new Messiahs, brown-, red-, or black-shirted, are becoming, in form and function, the effective religion of the modern world?

From the scientific point of view we must first arrive at a clear conception of what religion is. And this can be best achieved by a comparative study of religious phenomena, carried out in the anthropological spirit. Such a survey will show that, as regards religion, form, function, and substance are not arbitrary. From the study of past religions, primitive and developed, we shall gain the conviction that religion has its specific part to play in every human culture; that this is fundamentally connected with faith in Providence, in immortality, and in the moral sense of the world; and that this faith in turn demands a technique for its expression, a technique which offers possibilities of communion and prayer, of revelation and miracle; finally, that every religion implies some reward of virtue and the punishment of sin.

The argument which will be presented in these lectures will carry to the thoughtful reader the lesson that substance and expression are deeply interwoven in all religious manifestations. It is a tragic error, therefore, to apply religious technique to ends which are extraneous to true faith, to ends which are partisan, political, or economic. A sound social life must be based upon a truly religious system of values, that is, one which reflects the revelation to us of the existence of spiritual and moral order. This does not mean that all the members of the society controlled by religious belief and ethics should be bigoted sectarians, or even practising believers. To plead for the application of ethical principles and the recognition of spiritual values in public life and national policy is not tantamount to the declaration of one's own adherence to any metaphysical or dogmatic system.

I, personally, am unable to accept any revealed religion, Christian or not. But even an agnostic has to live by faith—in the case of us, pre-war rationalists and liberals, by the faith in humanity and its powers of improvement. This faith allowed us to work in freedom of thought and independence of initiative for the progress of science and for the establishment of a commonwealth of free human beings. It allowed us to exercise our intellectual and artistic faculties, safeguarded as we were by democratic institutions, looking forward, as we were able, to the welfare of generations to come. This faith has been as rudely shaken by the War and its consequences as that of the Christian. Science has suffered. It has become enslaved and subordinated to political and partisan ends. Science, too, like Christianity, has failed us as a foundation for ethics and for constructive action. So that as a rationalist and a believer in the development of human personality and of a liberal commonwealth of free men, I find myself in the same predicament as that of a believing Christian. It is high time that the old, now essentially unreal, feud between science and religion should be ended, and that both should join hands against the common enemy. The common enemy, in my opinion, is the planned misuse of force on a large scale, and the national organization for an aimless and destructive struggle between the members of what is really one commonwealth, united by economic, cultural, and ethical interests.

For some time past I was working on the foundations for a full and reasoned statement of my belief in the value of religion. Keeping to my anthropological last, I was engaged in the collection of material for a book or a memoir, in which I proposed primarily to analyse the technique of religious expression in myth and dogma, in ritual and ceremonies, in ethics and the social influence of faith.[1] When I was invited to give the Riddell Memorial Lectures for the Session 1934–5, I felt that the scope of my inquiries fitted well into the terms of the Charter: "The subject-matter of the Lectures is to be the relation between Religion and contemporary development of Thought . . . with particular emphasis on and reference to the bearing of such development on the Ethics and Tenets of Christianity." I decided to submit a preliminary statement of my results, and thus to demonstrate the integrative function of Christianity in our own culture. The text of the lectures here presented must be regarded as a preliminary statement of my conclusions, documented by the most relevant and most telling facts. I have to thank the Committee of the Riddell Memorial Lectures for the permission granted me to republish, at a later date and in a fuller form, the material and conclusions here outlined. Since, however, the more extensive publication will be of a strictly technical character, and will be addressed primarily to the specialist in anthropology and comparative History of Religion, the lectures as they stand will in no way be superseded.

Department of Anthropology   B. M.
    University of London

I
The Three Aspects of Religion

Religion is a difficult and refractory subject of study. It seems futile to question that which contains the answers to all problems. It is not easy

[1] In the collecting of the extensive material, only part of which is incorporated in this pamphlet, I was greatly helped by Miss Iris Harris and Miss N. Cohen, whose assistance was made possible by the generosity of the Rockefeller Foundation.

to dissect with the cold knife of logic what can only be accepted with a complete surrender of heart. It seems impossible to comprehend with reason that which encompasses mankind with love and supreme wisdom.

Nor is it easier for an atheist to study religion than for a deeply convinced believer. The rationalist denies the reality of religious experience. To him, the very fact of religion is a mystery over which he may smile, or by which he may be puzzled, but which, by his very admission, he is not qualified to fathom; it is difficult seriously to study facts which appear merely a snare, a delusion, or a trickery. Yet how can even a rationalist lightly dismiss those realities which have formed the very essence of truth and happiness to millions and hundreds of millions over thousands of years?

In another way the believer, too, is debarred from impartial study. For him one religion, his own, presents no problems. It is the Truth, the whole Truth, and nothing but the Truth. Especially if he be a fundamentalist, that is, unable to understand the foundations of human faith, he will simply disregard most religious phenomena as "superstitions" and will uphold his own views as Absolute Truth. And yet every one, the bigoted fundamentalist always excepted, might well pause and reflect on the way of his Providence which has vouchsafed the Truth to a small part of humanity, and has kept the rest of mankind in a state of perpetual darkness and error and thus condemned them to eternal perdition. Yet there may perhaps be room for a humble approach to all facts of human belief, in which the student investigates them with a sympathy which makes him almost a believer, but with an impartiality which does not allow him to dismiss all religions as erroneous whilst one remains true.

It is in this spirit that the anthropologist must approach the problems of primitive religion if he is to be of use in the understanding of the religious crises of our modern world. We must always keep in sight the relation of faith to human life, to the desires, difficulties, and hopes of human beings. Beliefs, which we so often dismiss as "superstition," as a symptom of savage crudeness or "prelogical mentality," must be understood; that is, their culturally valuable core must be brought to light. But belief is not the alpha and omega of religion: it is important to realize that man translates his confidence in spiritual powers into action; that in prayer and ceremonial, in rite and sacrament, he always attempts to keep in touch with that supernatural reality, the existence of which he affirms in his dogma. Again, we shall see that every religion, however humble, carries also instructions for a good life; it invariably provides its followers with an ethical system.

Every religion, primitive or developed, presents then three main aspects, dogmatic, ritual, and ethical. But the mere division or differentiation into three aspects is not sufficient. It is equally important to grasp the essential interrelation of these three aspects, to recognize that they are really only three facets of the same essential fact. In his dogmatic system, man affirms that Providence or spirits or supernatural powers exist. In his religious ritual he worships those entities and enters into relation with them, for revelation implies that such a relation is possible and necessary. Spirits, ancestral ghosts, or gods refuse to be ignored by man, and he in turn is in need of their assistance. The dependence on higher powers implies further the mutual dependence of man on his neighbour. You cannot worship in common without a common bond of mutual trust and assistance, that is, of charity and love. If God has created man in His own image, one image of God may not debase, defile, or destroy the other.

In discussing dogmatics, especially in primitive religions, we shall be met by what might be described as the mystery of myth. In all religions, Christianity and Judaism not excepted, we find that every tenet of belief, every dogmatic affirmation, has a tendency to be spun out into a long narrative. In other words, the abstract system of dogmatic principles is invariably bound up with a sacred history.

Minor characteristics, extravagances, and peculiarities of mythology have mostly attracted the interest of the student in the past and aroused his passion to explain them. The stories are at times crude, in some cases even obscene. This, within the general scope of our analysis, we shall not find difficult to understand: religious beliefs enter deeply into the essential facts of life, of which fertility and procreation are an essential part. Another peculiarity of myth is the frequent reference to natural phenomena, to features of the landscape, to quaint habits of animals and plants. This has often been accounted for in learned theories by the assumption that mythology is primitive science, and that its main function is to explain natural phenomena and the mysteries of the universe. Such theories we shall to a large extent have to dismiss or at least to correct. Primitive man has his science as well as his religion; a myth does not serve to explain phenomena but rather to regulate human actions.

The main problem of myth is in my opinion its relation to dogma; the fact that myth is an elaboration of an act of faith into an account of a definite concrete miracle. Why is this necessary? In the course of our analysis I hope to show that this is due to the very nature of life and faith. Faith is always based on primeval revelation, and revelation is a concrete event. In revelation God, or ancestral spirits, or culture heroes create and mould the universe, manifest their will and power to man. All this is a temporal process, a concrete sequence of activities, a set of dramatic performances. Man in turn reacts to this manifestation of supernatural power, he rebels and sins, gains knowledge, loses grace and regains it once more. Small wonder, then, that most of the dogmatic systems of mankind occur as a body of sacred tradition, as a set of stories stating the beginning of things and thus vouching for their reality. Again, since in myth we have an account of how Providence created man and revealed its reality to him, we usually find that myth contains also the prescription of how man has to worship Providence in order to remain in contact with it.

Thus the discussion of myth leads us directly to the riddle of ritual. Here, again, we shall not tarry over the sensational peculiarities of detail. We shall proceed at once to the central and fundamental problem: "Why ritual?" We may start here with the extreme Puritan's scorn and rejection of all ritualism, for this represents the voice of reason against the sensuous, almost physiological attitude of naïve faith. Incense, pictures, processions, fireworks are as incomprehensible, hence repugnant, to the highly refined and reflective type of religious consciousness as they are to the anti-religious rationalist. Ritualism is to reason, pure, or sublimated in religious feeling, always a form of idolatry, a return to magic. To the dispassionate student of all religions, who is not prepared to discount Roman Catholicism because he feels a deep admiration for the religion of Friends, nor yet to dismiss totemism because he appreciates its distance from the religion of Israel, ritual still remains a problem. Why has man to express such simple affirmations as the belief in the immortality of the soul, in the reality of a spiritual world, by antics, dramatized performances, by dancing, music, incense, by an elaboration, richness, and an extensiveness of collective action which often consumes an enormous amount of tribal or national energy and substance?

Here, again, our argument will not be a mere tilting at windmills. The usual scientific treatment of ritual, primitive and civilized, does not seem to me to be quite satisfactory. The conception, for instance, of primitive magic as "a false scientific technique" does not do justice to its cultural value. Yet one of the greatest contemporary anthropologists, Sir James Frazer, has to a certain extent given countenance to this conception. Freud's theory that magic is man's primitive belief in the "omnipotence of thought" would also dismiss primitive ritual as a colossal piece of pragmatic self-deception. The views here advanced will be that every ritual performance, from a piece of primitive Australian magic to a Corpus Christi procession, from an initiation ceremony to the Holy Mass, is a traditionally enacted miracle. In such a miracle the course of human life or of natural events is remodelled by the action of supernatural forces, which are released in a sacred, traditionally standardized act of the congregation or of the religious leader. The fact that every religious rite must contain an element of the miraculous will not appear to us an outgrowth of human childishness, of primeval stupidity (*Urdummheit*), nor yet a blind alley of primitive pseudo-science. To us it represents the very essence of religious faith. Man needs miracles not because he is benighted through primitive stupidity, through the trickery of a priesthood, or through being drugged with "the opiate for the masses," but because he realizes at every stage of his development that the powers of his body and of his mind are limited. It is rather the recognition of his practical and intellectual limitations, and not the illusion of the "omnipotence of thought," which leads man into ritualism; which makes him re-enact miracles, the feasibility of which he has accepted from his mythology.

The enigma of ethics, the question why every religion carries its own morals, is simpler. Why, in order to be decent and righteous, must man believe in the Devil as well as in God, in demons as well as in spirits, in the malice of his ancestral ghosts as well as in their benevolence? Here, once more, we have a host of theoretical conceptions, or misconceptions, dictated by hostility to religion or by the partisanship of sectarians. In order to safeguard ourselves against the superficial view that a sadistic priesthood has invented hell-fire so as to cow believers into doing what it wishes, we shall have to make an attempt at a real understanding of the phenomena. For, with all our sympathy for the religious attitude, we shall also have to reject the theological view that morality must be associated with dogma, because both have been vouchsafed to mankind by the One True Revelation. The correct answer to our problem lies in the social character of religion. That every organized belief implies a congregation, must have been felt by many thinkers instructed by scholarship and common sense. Yet, here again, science was slow to incorporate the dictates of simple and sound reason. Tylor and Bastian, Max Müller and Mannhardt treat religious systems as if they were philosophical or literary productions. The initiative in putting the sociological aspect of religion on the scientific map came from the Scottish divine and scholar, Robertson Smith. It was elaborated with precision, but also with exaggeration, by the French philosopher and sociologist, Durkheim.

The essentially sound methodological principle is that worship always happens in common because it touches common concerns of the community. And here, as our analysis will show, enters the ethical element intrinsically inherent in all religious activities. They always require efforts, discipline, and submission on the part of the individual for the good of the community. Taboos, vigils, religious exercises are essentially moral, not merely because they express submission of man to spiritual powers, but also because they are a sacrifice of man's personal comfort for the common weal. But there is another ethical aspect which, as we shall see, makes all religions moral in their very essence. Every cult is associated with a definite congregation: ancestor-worship is primarily based on the family; at times even on a wider group, the clan; at times it becomes tribal, when the ancestor spirit is that of a chief. The members of such a group of worshippers have natural duties towards each other. The sense of common responsibility, of reciprocal charity and goodwill, flows from the same fundamental idea and sentiment which moves clansmen, brothers, or tribesmen to common worship. I am my tribesman's brother, or my clansman's totemic kinsman, because we are all descended from the same being whom we worship in our ceremonies, to whom we sacrifice, and to whom we pray. We have only to change the word *descended* into *created* in order to pass to those religions which maintain as a fundamental principle the brotherhood of man, because he owes his existence to a Creator whom he addresses as "Our Father which art in Heaven." The conception of the Church as a big family is rooted in the very nature of religion.

These conclusions may seem simple, once they are stated directly. Fundamental scientific truths in physics and biology, as in the science of man, are never sophisticated. Yet, as I shall show later, even now anthropologist and missionary alike deny ethics to the heathen.

I hope that the perusal of the following lectures will supply the reader with what might be called a sound theoretical framework for the appraisal of other religious phenomena, primitive and civilized, ancient and modern, healthy and pathological.

II
A Sociological Definition of Myth

The central problem of myth has already been raised, and its answer foreshadowed. The problem is why dogma has a tendency to develop into a story; the answer suggested was that, since all dogmas are revealed, the story of the revelation has to be told so that the truth of the dogmas be founded in real historical fact. Turn to a collection of material such as Frazer's *Golden Bough* or his *Folk-Lore in the Old Testament* and you will find our contention fully documented. The belief in Providence and in the Great Architect of the universe is embodied in numberless mythological cosmologies. On the shores of the Pacific and on its many islands we are told how the world was fished out of the sea or moulded out of slime; or again, from other continents, we have stories relating how out of chaos the various parts or elements of the universe have been shaped in succession, or how the earth was hurled from space, or out of darkness, by a divine maker. The wide range of beliefs which are usually labelled "nature-worship" again have a rich mythology of totemic ancestors, of the early appearance and miraculous, though not always moral, behaviour of nature gods.

There is no doubt that all the stories of creation, of the first appearance of man, of the loss of worldly immortality and the translation to another world after death account to a certain extent for the existence of the world, of man, of after-life. But they are not scientific explanations. They are not taken as items of ordinary knowledge. They are regarded by the people as sacred; they are enacted by them in religious mysteries, sacrifices, and ceremonies; and they form the foundation, not only of faith, but also of religious law. To tell how God created the world is to affirm that God is not only the cause but also the end of all existence, the giver of all that is good and the source of all the laws of life. To tell how man lost eternal life on earth, and then was given an after-life, is to impart the dogma of the immortality of the soul, and through this to give the foundation of ancestor-worship, as well as the ritual of burial and mourning. To describe how man at one time descended from the animals gives a charter of totemic relationship for the members of a clan, who are still regarded as related to the animal species and can therefore control that species through ritual and magic.

Right through we can see, even at a cursory glance, how myth is a living reality, is active in ritual and in ethics, and is dramatically convincing as the foundation of dogma. The best way, perhaps, to bring home the significance of myth as a charter of belief, ritual, and ethics, is by analysing one example fully. It will provide us with what I understand is called, in the technical language of the moving pictures, a "close-up." I shall briefly show how I was forced to adopt this theory in the course of my experiences in field-work in Melanesia.

When I first went there I knew that every good ethnographer must collect "folk-lore." By the time I was able to use the vernacular, I was eagerly writing down any story which was told to me by a native. I collected tales about ogres and flying canoes, about malicious stepmothers and daring sailors, about the beginnings of magic and the queer pranks of an avaricious harlot. Gradually, however, it dawned on me that the natives themselves were aware of points in the performance which I was constantly missing; for I was collecting texts but disregarding contexts. In the course of time, I realized that the manner of telling a story and the way in which it was received, the circumstances under which the story was told and its immediate and also indirect influence, were quite as important as the text itself.

I missed not only the context of situation but very often the context of further elaborations and commentaries on the part of the natives.[2] After telling me some important or sacred story, the narrator would often con-

---

[2] The reader acquainted with the present writer's *Coral Gardens and their Magic*, 1935, and especially with the linguistic arguments of Vol. II, will understand what is meant by the term "context of situation" and the theoretical importance of this in the ethnographic treatment of human speech and folk-lore.

tinue into what seemed to me entirely irrelevant verbosities. I still can remember the first time I was told the myth about the brother and sister incest.[3] After the tragic account was finished, my friend, who belonged to the community which "owns" this myth, began to boast: he told me how they and they alone have the power to enact properly the love-magic which is associated with the myth; how they have the right to levy toll on neighbouring communities; how certain spots in the territory are important for the correct carrying out of the magic. Feeling that the narrator was "rambling," I cut him short and told him that if the narrative was not finished he ought to continue it, but that if he had nothing more to tell of the story, I was not interested in his bragging. It was only later that I realized that in this very bragging lay what was perhaps the most important aspect of myth. My informant, in a characteristically boastful manner, was simply stating how the myth acts as a warrant for the correct performance of the magic; how it gives a right of ownership and control to the natives of the community where the magic originated, and from whence it draws its miraculous powers. He was, in short, giving me the sociological function of myth, in his naïve, concrete, and strongly personal manner. In the course of my work I discovered that such epilogues or appendixes to a narrative very often contain new and unexpected side-lights on ritual, on the rank or privileges of the communities, clans, and individuals, and on the way in which the very validity of magic was established in native belief.

In fact, with a better knowledge of the vernacular, I was forced to discriminate between several categories of folk-lore, and I had to base my discrimination not so much on differences in text, but rather in cultural setting.[4] I found that there is a class of stories which might be called fairy-tales or folk-tales. The natives call them *kukwanebu*. These are told during the rainy season when people are largely confined to the villages and, especially in the evenings, have nothing to do. They are told entirely for entertainment. Their subject-matter consists of grotesque, miraculous, and often bawdy events which appear in the same light to the natives as to the European listener. These stories definitely form what may be called tribal fiction—tales told for mere entertainment—and they do not convey any important truths, moral precepts, or ritual directions.

A second class, called *libogwo*, consists of historical legends, believed to be true, and usually told to enhance or define the status of a community, clan, or family. These stories as a rule contain little or nothing that is actually miraculous or extravagant, although they are not always free from exaggerations in the heroic line.

[3] Compare the last chapter of *Sexual Life of Savages*, and Part 2, Chapt. IV, of *Sex and Repression*.

[4] Compare *Myth in Primitive Psychology*, pp. 24–36.

There is a third class of story, told for a very serious purpose, and connected with religious belief, social order, or moral issues, and last but not least with ritual. These stories, like the fairy-tales, have a strong tinge of the supernatural. But here the supernatural is not a mere trick of fancy, not an idle satisfaction of day-dreaming, but a miracle which is firmly believed in, a miracle, moreover, which, as likely as not, will be re-enacted in a partial and modified form through the ritual of native magic and religion.

Thus there exists a special class of story regarded as sacred, embodied in ritual, morals, and social organization, and constituting an integral and effective part of religion and magic. These stories do not live by idle interest; they are not narrated as historical accounts of ordinary facts. They are to the natives a statement of a higher and a more important truth, of a primeval reality, which is still regarded as the pattern and foundation of present-day life. The knowledge of the mythological past supplies man with the incentive, as well as with the justification, for ritual and moral action; it furnishes him with a body of indications and directions for the correct performance of the sacred acts.

If I wanted to convince you briefly of the correctness of my conclusions, and if I had the opportunity of transporting you to the Trobriand Islands for a short visit, I would first make you participate in a typical social gathering at which fairy-tales are recounted. You would find yourself among a hilarious gathering of people, invariably at dusk or at night, sitting round the fire, at times engaged in some manual work and listening to stories which they all know almost by heart, but to which they always respond with interruptions, repartees, and laughter. Many a man or woman "owns" a number of fairy-tales, that is, tales which he or she has appropriated by custom and practice. Such tales are often punctuated by ditties in which the other natives join in chorus. The jokes are often ribald and the audience responds or caps them with additional remarks.

It would have been an entirely different setting in which you would hear a native legend told naturally and spontaneously in the course of tribal life. We would have to visit some distant community, and there, perhaps at an historic spot, or in reference to the rights of ownership of another village, or in order to flatter the pride of a subclan, we would be told a tale which has all the hall-marks of an historical account. Stories of that nature would also be related at times of overseas sailing, or, in olden days, during a war between two groups of villages. We would then hear about famous exploits, shipwrecks and rescues, victories and fierce battles.[5]

---

[5] Some such stories the reader will find in my *Argonauts of the Western Pacific*, in Professor Seligman's *Melanesians of British New Guinea*, and in Dr. Fortune's *Sorcerers of Dobu*.

But it is when tribal festivities or magical ceremonies are to be performed that the time for telling the most sacred tales is at hand. Thus, during the sacred season of harvest rejoicing, the younger generation are reminded by their elders that the spirits of their ancestors are about to return from the underworld and visit the ancestral village. The dogmatic substance of Trobriand belief about the fate of the soul after death, the nature of the underworld, and the various forms of communion between the living and the dead, are stated at that season more frequently than at any other time. The reality of the spirit world would also be present both in the mind and in the conversation of the natives on the occasion of death or when a big ceremonial distribution of wealth occurs to commemorate a recently deceased person.[6]

Thus during harvest and after, at the season of Milamala, when the spirits come for a few weeks and settle again in the villages, perched upon the trees or sneaking about the houses, sitting on high platforms specially erected for them, watching the dancing and partaking of the spiritual substance of the food and wealth displayed for them, the knowledge of the whole dogmatic system concerning spirits is necessary, and it is then imparted by the elder to the younger. Every one as yet uninformed is told that after death the spirit has to go to Tuma, the nether world associated with the small island of that name. He has to pass through a narrow cleft in the rocks which is the entrance to the nether world. On the way he encounters Topileta, the guardian of the spirit world, who must be offered gifts, the spiritual substance of the valuables with which the body is covered at death. After he has passed the entrance and satisfied the guardian of the dead, the spirit is received by friends and relatives to whom he tells news of the world of the living. And then he settles down to a second life, built very much on the pattern of the previous existence.

In order to keep in touch with the supernatural realities and happenings of the Milamala, it is necessary for every one to be instructed in the ways of spirits and on their behaviour: how they manifest their existence and how they can be reached by the living; how they show their anger and their pleasure. On the whole, adherence to custom and tradition pleases the ancestral ghosts, while neglect angers them. The rules of conduct of man towards spirits and their reactions to them are given, not in the form of abstract principles and precepts, but by telling the story of an occurrence. This is at times a recent event, at times very ancient, but it always points a moral and establishes a precedent. These stories have

[6] A fuller documentation of the native belief in the spirit world will be found in an article entitled "Baloma, Spirits of the Dead in the Trobriand Islands," in the *Journal of the Royal Anthropological Institute*, 1916.

very often only a local currency. In one village I was told that three years ago the spirits spoiled a whole feasting and dancing season by inducing bad weather, destroying the crops, and sending sickness on the people, because the community had not obeyed its chief who wanted them to carry out their fishing magic according to old custom. Elsewhere, it was the unsatisfactory performance of a big mortuary feast, due to the meanness of the headman, which had irritated the spirits and made them show their displeasure by sending a set of calamities.

III
The Spirit World in Myth and Observance

But over and above such local minor myths there exist one or two stories referring to very ancient times and defining several of the fundamental tenets of native belief. The very existence of the other world and its place beneath the surface of the earth, in a different dimension, so to speak, is established by the story which might be called the Trobriand "myth of myths" about the first arrival of human beings on earth. Humanity, once upon a time, led an existence similar to that which the spirits now lead underground, in a shadowy world different from the present one. From thence they ascended to earth by crawling out through places of emergence, "holes" or "houses" as they are called.

The fact of broken existence, that is, the fact of death and continuance afterwards, is embodied in a tale of original immortality, of its loss, and of its partial retention in the survival after death. Originally every one was able to rejuvenate by the process now observed in snakes and other reptiles, by sloughing the skin. This might have continued up to the present, but for an original error or lapse of an innocent girl. It happened in the village of Bwadela. An old woman who dwelt there with her daughter and granddaugthter went out one day for her regular rejuvenation trick. She took off her skin and threw it on the waters of a tidal creek, which, however, did not carry it away, as it was caught on a bush and stuck there. Rejuvenated, she came back as a young girl and joined her granddaughter, who was sitting at a distance. But the girl, instead of welcoming her grandmother, failed to recognize her, was frightened, and drove her away—a very serious insult among Trobrianders. The old woman, hurt and angry, went to the creek, picked up her old skin, donned it again, and came back in her wrinkled and decrepit form. From that moment, and in the fulfilment of the curse which the old woman put on her daughter and granddaughter, the rejuvenation process was lost once and for ever. It is characteristic here that we have, in a matrilineal society, one of the most important and dramatic occurrences in human history taking place between women of three generations. It is also characteristic that a small localized event has cast its blight upon the whole of humanity, even as an event happening in a small garden somewhere in Mesopotamia has blighted the life of that vast branch of humanity who believe in the Old Testament. This story obviously receives its full significance only when we place it within the context of belief about death, immortality, and the communion between the living and the dead.

On this last point the story is supplemented by another myth. For, though human beings lost immortality and eventually died, yet the ghosts remained in the villages and took part in ordinary life, even as these spirits now do on their annual return after harvest. It was only when one of the poor invisible ghosts, sneaking in at meal-time and snatching the crumbs of the living, was scalded with hot broth, that a new crisis arrived. After the spirit has expostulated, she, for it again was a woman, was told by her daughter, "Oh, I thought you were away, I thought you were only returning after harvest." The old woman, with insult and mortification added to injury, retorted, "Good, I shall go to Tuma and live in the underworld." From that time on, the spirits have dwelt in their own realm and returned only once a year.

There is another set of beliefs, essential to our understanding of the Trobrianders' attitude towards life and death and survival. These natives might be said hardly to recognize death as an inevitable event, inextricably bound up with the process of life and setting a natural term to it. Although they will admit that some people might die of old age or of an accident, yet in the course of my inquiries I never came across a single concrete case of "natural death." Every form of disease was conceived as the result of witchcraft. An old man may be more susceptible to witchcraft, but the real cause of his death is always a specific act of sorcery, to which also are attributed all the fatal accidents. Here, once more, we have a rich mythology. A number of stories are told of how witchcraft was brought upon mankind. These, perhaps, are less primeval in their nature, for the Trobriander believes that witchcraft always existed outside his district, and he feels only the necessity of relating how it came to the Trobriand archipelago. One story tells how a crab flew through the air from a southern island nearer the mainland of New Guinea, and came down on a spot on the north of the main island of the Trobriands, in a district which now enjoys the reputation for most efficient sorcery. This crab taught the members of the local clan how to bewitch others and kill them, and this knowledge is still retained by the clansmen of to-day. On the south of the island, again, we are told how a bad and malicious being travelled in the hollow of a bamboo, and was stranded on the southern tip of the main island. In another story we hear about a big tree, in which malignant demons resided. When it was felled its tip touched the southernmost point of the Trobriands, which became immediately peopled with carriers of sorcery.

The mythology of witchcraft accounts for the fact that Black Art flourishes in its most efficient form in the two districts, the one where the crab fell and the other where the evil beings were conveyed from the south. But the story does not contain merely an explanation. It is a sociological charter for the local inhabitants, who derive part of their income and most of their prestige from the fact that they are the accredited sorcerers of the district. They also teach sorcery to others for a substantial payment.

I have briefly summed up the main stories which refer to the phenomena of death and its causes, to survival and immortality, and to the communion between living and dead. Take one of these stories alone, and at first sight it might appear as if it were just a tale told in "explanation" of the loss of immortality, of the removal of spirits to another world, of the occurrence of witchcraft, of sickness and of death. This to a certain extent is true, for, if our theory is right, the essential nature of myth is that it serves as a precedent, and every precedent contains an element of explanation, for it is a prototype for subsequent cases.

But a precedent is not an explanation in the scientific sense; it does not account for subsequent events through the relation of cause and effect, or even of motive and consequence. In a way, it is the very opposite of scientific explanation, for it relates a complete change in the order of the universe to a singular dramatic event. It shows how the outburst of passion in the heart of an insulted and injured woman makes her throw away the benefits of immortality, undergo the ordeal of decrepitude and death, and all this in order to be able to curse posterity with the loss of eternal life. In short, myth is not a pseudo-science of nature; it is a history of the supernatural. It invariably refers to a unique break in the history of the world and mankind.

It is only by the ambiguous use of the word "explanation" that we could defend the aetiological theory of myth. Once this ambiguity is recognized there is no harm in fully illuminating how far and to what extent myth really satisfies the craving for explaining or accounting. The answer is that myth explains in so far as a precedent establishes new procedure; or as a creative act brings forth a new reality; or as a miracle accounts for something which is unaccountable on the basis of scientific knowledge. Mythology, then, is definitely the complement of what might be called the ordinary knowledge or science of primitive man, but not its substitute. It is true that the appearance of the Holy Virgin to Bernadette Soubirous explains the miracles of Lourdes, but we must distinguish this explanation from the axioms of biology, the generalizations of bacteriology, and the empirical rules of medical knowledge. Those who mistake primitive mythology for an equivalent of science should reflect on the relation of our own myth to our own academic disciplines. Perhaps the greatest shortcoming of the aetiological theory of myth is its denial of primitive knowledge. The so-called primitives do distinguish between natural and supernatural. They explain, not by telling a fairy-tale, but by reference to experience, logic, and common sense, even as we do. Since they have their own science, mythology cannot be their system of explanation in the scientific sense of the word. If in turn we try to define more clearly the exact manner in which myth *accounts for* the order of the universe and the life of man, we see immediately that the function of myth is specific: it serves as a foundation for belief, and establishes a precedent for the miracles of ritual and magic.

We can draw another conclusion from our analysis. It is incorrect to take one incident from a narrative or even one narrative in isolation from the others. It is only when we treat the whole cycle of stories connected with the fact of death and survival, and when we place this cycle within the context of native ritual behaviour and their moral attitudes, that we do justice to the cultural character and role of myth. The theory of myth, then, here propounded, implies a different treatment of empirical reality; it assigns to myth a different function from that of either explanation or allegory; it shows that the whole complex of cultural practices, beliefs, and myths expresses man's pragmatic reaction towards life and its vicissitudes; it refers to his emotions, forebodings, and to the ritualized behaviour in which these mental attitudes are expressed.

Let me further substantiate this by a brief summary of other types of Trobriand mythology. If I am correct in my theoretical handling of the facts, we ought to find sacred stories whenever there is an important dogma, a vital ritual, or some fundamental ethical process at stake. Apart from health, disease, and self-preservation, man is perhaps most concerned about two things: the satisfaction of his hunger and of his erotic impulses. As regards the first, the complex and elaborate system of food-providing processes intervenes between nature and man's square meal. The Trobrianders procure their food in several ways, of which two are primarily important. First, the fruits of the jungle are collected and the tubers of the gardens cultivated; second, the fish of sea and lagoon are caught. Now, as regards vegetable food, agriculture is highly developed and supplies them with their staple sustenance. Agriculture, therefore, constitutes for them the primary interest in life, since success in gardening means plenty and wealth, while failure means misery and starvation. There is a twofold set of activities connected with the raising of crops, the rational and the magical. In connexion with magic, there exists a mythology telling how a culture hero, Tudava, originally apportioned different measures of fertility, together with spells and rites, for the raising of crops. Those districts where he received a warm welcome were given good gardens, those who received him with hostility were penalized by arid soil and meagre gardens. This mythology serves to buttress the natives' confidence in their magic. Side by side with the main myth about the culture hero there exist also minor local myths, sometimes extremely brief and succinct but very important, myths in which the members of a community relate how their own local system came into being and why it is so very effective. But I need not enter into this aspect of magic and myth, for I have elaborated it elsewhere.[7]

Fishing, again, has an elaborate system of magic, and, connected with it, myths telling how the fishing of red mullet was instituted, again by Tudava, the culture hero; also how shark-fishing and its magic came into being in one of the villages of the north shore. In the matter of fishing, an interesting correlation can be established in the Trobriands. Wherever the pursuit is dangerous and its issues uncertain, there we have a highly developed magic and, connected with it, a mythology. Where, as in fishing by poison, there is no question about success and no tax on human skill, endurance, or courage, we find no magic and no mythology. And when it comes to minor economic pursuits, such as arts and crafts, hunting, the collection of roots, and the gathering of fruit, again neither magic nor mythology is to be found.

Returning once more to the main source of sustenance, that is, the soil and its products, one condition of fertility is essential, the right incidence of rain and sunshine. Since in this part of the world there is never danger of too much rain, while droughts occasionally occur, it is the timely arrival of rain which is the main source of anxiety. If rain fails for more than a year, the whole district suffers drought and famine sets in. Historical accounts of terrible years of starvation are told by the natives; and drought with its incident famine is always assigned to magic. The magic of rain and sunshine is vested in one person and one person only, that of the Paramount Chief of the district. It makes him the general benefactor of the whole tribe when things go well, even as he is the dispenser of punishment when his subjects have given him grounds for displeasure. The complex and elaborate system of rain and drought magic is again based upon a myth. This tell us how rain was born of a woman; how it had to be stored in one or two sacred spots, ever since important in magical ritual; and how the privilege of using this magic became finally vested in the family of the Tabalu, the paramount rulers of the district. In many ways this magic is the ultimate source of the chief's political power and of his personal prestige.

The most ambitious seafaring enterprise of the natives, the circular

---

[7] *Coral Gardens and their Magic*, 1935.

trade of valuables called *kula*, also has a system of magical practice and a number of myths associated with it.[8]

Love, like hunger and the fear of death, is always fraught with strong emotions, and anxieties, and forebodings. Nor does the course of love ever run smoothly. We are not surprised, therefore, to find a mythology and a magic associated with love. Here, the story of how an incestuous love-adventure between brother and sister was caused by the accidental misuse of magic supplies not the explanation of the existence of love, nor yet of the use of magic. It establishes a powerful precedent and gives a certain community the charter for its performance.

The "close-up" of Trobriand mythology has allowed us to appreciate the cultural nature of myth on one example. Mythology, the system of sacred stories, constitutes the charter of social organization and the precedent of religious ritual. In this, mythology supplies the foundations of all belief, especially the belief about life after death and about the miraculous powers of magic and ceremonial. The sacred stories of the Trobrianders reveal how humanity has experienced the greatness of ancestors and culture heroes; how through dramatic events a new order became established or new principles introduced into human life; how the power of magic was given to men, how it was used or misused. Our analysis has proved to us also that, in Melanesia at least, myth must be studied within the context of social life. Since myth does not live by myth alone, but in so far as it influences art and dancing, social organization and economic activities, directly or indirectly through the ritual connected with them, the life of myth is not in its telling, but in the way it is fully enacted in tribal custom and ceremonial.

IV
The Sacred Story and Its Context of Culture

Let us for the moment look up and away from the narrow technicalities of ethnography, and see what our conclusions mean as regards the nature of religion in general. First of all, our facts teach us one truth regarding the structure of Trobriand religion. Myth, ritual, and ethics are definitely but three facets of the same essential fact: a deep conviction about the existence of a spiritual reality which man attempts to control, and by which in turn man is controlled. Dogma, ritual, and ethics are therefore inseparable. Take the facts presented above about the mythological cycle of death, immortality, and the spirit world. We started from stories, but

---

[8] Compare *Argonauts of the Western Pacific*, where a full description of the *kula* and its magic has been given.

we were immediately led into a discussion of action directed towards the subject-matter of these stories, that is, a discussion of ritual. At Milamala we see how the ritual of give and take, the sacrifices to the spirits and their response, are the expression of the truth contained in mythology. And here ethics come in immediately, because the spirits and their re-action are determined by moral principles. You give offerings to the spirit of your own kindred, and they show their pleasure or displeasure by su-pernatural symptoms. But the spirits expect not only material gifts but also good behaviour. The spirits are in general conceived of as guardians of tradition. They will be satisfied when people follow custom, scrupu-lously carry out magic and observe taboos, conform to rules of family life, kinship, and of tribal organization. The two stock answers always given to the question why custom is observed and tradition followed are: "It has been ordained as of old," or else, "The spirits would be angry if we did not follow custom." If you press further as to who it is that has "or-dained of old," reference will be made immediately to a specific myth; or you will perhaps be told, "Our ancestors in olden days always did that. They live now as spirits in the other world. They like us to behave as they did. They become angry and make things bad if we do not obey custom." In other words, the general principle of the observance of cus-tom has its spiritual backing. It is directly connected with the whole body of tradition, and with the ritual enactment of this tradition. Take away from the natives the belief in the reality of their sacred lore, destroy their sense of the spirit world as it exists and acts upon them, and you will undermine their whole moral outlook.

The consideration of the norms and practices connected with death, burial, and mourning shows the close correlation between moral behav-iour towards living and dead, ritual practice, and dogmatic belief. At the death of an individual a whole system of mortuary duties devolves on his immediate relatives.[9] The essence of these duties, from the sociological point of view, is that they reaffirm the bonds of marriage and the duties of children towards parents. In short, in its moral aspect, mortuary ritual is the religious extension of the ethical rules of conduct as between the members of the family, of the wider kindred group, and of the clan. Later on, when the spirits enter into a permanent or periodic and seasonal communion with the living, the family bonds and other social relations contracted in life become extended to the spirits beyond.

Such a communion between the living and the dead, based upon the pattern of earthly existence, is to be found wherever there is a belief in spirits, or any form of ancestor-worship or Manism. In Christian Europe on All Souls' Day, when people according to sect and nation commemo-

---

[9] *Sexual Life of Savages*, Chapt. VI; *Crime and Custom*, pp. 33–34.

rate at graves or carry out memorial services in the church, there exists this spiritual interaction between a man and the dead ones of his own family. The dead depend upon the prayers, masses, or, at least, on the loving memory of the survivors. The living turn to the dead for intercession in Heaven. The African, again, lives in a world determined for good and evil by ancestor spirits, the dispensers of good fortune and adversity alike. Health and disease, affluence and famine, victory and defeat are generally attributed to the goodwill of ancestral ghosts or to their displeasure respectively.

The relation between living and dead is realized in three ways. In every form of ancestor-worship, the belief is founded on that specific mythology which consists in family tradition, the knowledge of ancestral names, the personalities and exploits of the forebears in direct line, especially in the miraculous aspect. The ritual of sacrifices and devotion to ancestors is essential. Ritual, in turn, is necessarily permeated with ethics: the ancestors in spirit form, as the living parents, punish for bad behaviour and disrespect, and reward for good conduct and dutiful services. In all this we have gone beyond the Trobriands: our conclusions hold good for the Communion of Saints in Christianity, or for ancestor-worship in China or ancient Rome, in Bantu Africa or among the Pueblo Indians, in Australia or the Egypt of the pharaohs.

And here we can see how the substance of religious belief is not arbitrary. It grows out of the necessities of life. What is the root of all the beliefs connected with the human soul, with survival after death, with the spiritual elements in the universe? I think that all the phenomena generally described by such terms as animism, ancestor-worship, or belief in spirits and ghosts, have their root in man's integral attitude towards death. It is not mere philosophical reflection on the phenomena of death, nor yet mere curiosity, nor observations on dreams, apparitions, or trances, which really matter. Death as the extinction of one's own personality, or the disappearance of those who are near, who are loved, who have been friends and partners in life, is a fact which will always baffle human understanding and fundamentally upset the emotional constitution of man. It is a fact about which science and rational philosophy can tell nothing. It cuts across all human calculations. It thwarts all practical and rational efforts of man.

And here religious revelation steps in and affirms life after death, the immortality of the spirit, the possibilities of communion between living and dead. This revelation gives sense to life, and solves the contradictions and conflicts connected with the transience of human existence on earth. Religion, moreover, does not merely affirm an abstract truth as an idle comfort for thought and emotion. Through the revealed truth, and on its foundations, religion tells man how to behave, how to enter into relationship with the dead, how to better their existence and to gain their favour and assistance in turn. Mortuary ritual is the enactment of the truth of immortality. And, since the relations between living and dead are based on the moral principle of give and take; since they carry over the affection and mutual assistance from this world across the dividing line, they supply the supernatural sanction for family ethics. The affection of parents for their children, founded as it is in the physiology of reproduction, receives an additional dimension. Parents value their children and have to look after them with an additional concern, because, after death, they will be dependent on their services. The children grow up in a system under which parents and forebears are not only the dispensers of the good things of this world, but even after death will be able to assist or to harm with a supernatural might.

I have enlarged upon the one aspect of religion, illustrated by perhaps the most important myth of the Trobrianders and their most elaborate ritual, because I am convinced that the concern in the immortality of the soul is one of the two principal sources of religious inspiration. This belief is not in its essence a philosophical doctrine. It does not encroach upon the domain of knowledge. It is the outcome of the deepest human cravings, the result of that desire for continuity in human life and the traditional relationship between the generations, which is the very essence of human culture. Ceremonies and rites which immediately follow the death of an individual, services at burial, the commemoration of and the communion with the dead, are universal and are perhaps the most conspicuous phenomena of human religions. They are all the expression of this one main source of human faith, the desire for immortality.

What about the other myths and ceremonies which we have met in our brief survey of Trobriand religion? They consist mostly of mythology connected with magic—magic of love and of gardens, of war and of ceremonial exchange, of hunting, fishing, and sailing. Here we have an entirely different dogmatic element. The affirmation contained in this type of myth refers to a primeval power which man wielded over the unconquered and unconquerable forces of nature. Thus in one myth we are told that, since rain was born of a woman, she and her kindred, being of the nature of rain, were able to control it completely. The birth of rain was a miracle, and through this miracle man in a certain lineage was given the power of re-enacting minor miracles. In the same way, some people brought the magic of love with them. The myth tells us how the force of its magic was once revealed in breaking through the strongest prohibition, that of incest between brother and sister. That miracle, dreadful and wonderful at the same time, is the pattern on which at present the minor miracles of love-magic are believed to be possible. In pursuits where there is well-founded knowledge and where practice and hard work achieve part of the results, magic is resorted to in order to overcome those forces and elements which are governed only by chance. Thus in agriculture, in hunting and fishing, in war and in dangerous sailing, magic effects in a spiritual manner that which man cannot attain by his own efforts. Here the relation of mythologically founded dogma and ritual is as close as in the case of the communion between living and dead. It is only because man is in need of magic wherever his forces fail him that he must believe in his magical power, which is vouched for by myth. On the other hand, the primeval myth of the magical miracle is confirmed and repeated in every act of subsequent magic.

What is the common measure of all these beliefs in man's magical power, primeval and present? They are of the same substance as our belief in Providence. In almost every myth which has a charter of magical efficacy we have the affirmation of a fundamental bond of union between man and the forces of nature and destiny. The mythology, which assigns common parentage to a particular lineage of man with rain or the fertility of plants, an animal species or wind, establishes a common measure between man and the relevant aspects of his environment. It submits those forces of rain, weather, fertility, vegetation, and fauna, which man needs, yet cannot practically master, to a superadded, supernatural control. Whether we call this type of belief totemism or zoolatry, or the religion of Mana, or preanimism, they achieve one main end. They humanize the outer world; they put man in harmony with his environment and destiny; they give him an inkling of a working Providence in the surrounding universe.

Here again it is very important to realize that the whole substance of Trobriand magic—and this is also true of Central Australian totemism, or of the fertility ritual of the Pueblo Indians, or of the rain ceremonial of the divine kings of Africa—remains completely outside the legitimate domain of science. It is an indispensable complement or counterpart of man's practical activities, but it never confuses or stultifies them.

V

Totemic Miracles of the Desert

We must, however, turn to some other ethnographic area and look at the facts more in detail once again. Unfortunately, few cultures have been studied with the all-round interest so indispensable to all functional analyses, that is, analyses of the mutual influence of religion and ordinary life, of magic and economics. We know a great deal, however, about the beliefs and practices of a small group of people in Central Australia, thanks mainly to the pioneering work of Spencer and Gillen.

Their ordinary existence, common to men and women, and concerned with the obtaining of food, with amusements, and the daily round of camp life, is based upon a different type of tradition. There is a body of rules, handed from one generation to another, which refers to the manner in which people live in their little shelters, make their fire by friction, collect their food and cook it, make love to each other, and quarrel. This secular tradition consists partly of customary or legal rules, determining the manner in which social life is conducted. But it also embodies rules of technique and behaviour in regard to environment. It is this aspect of secular tradition which corresponds to knowledge or science. The rules which we find here are completely independent of magic, of supernatural sanctions, and they are never accompanied by any ceremonial or ritual elements. When the native has to produce an implement, he does not refer to magic. He is strictly empirical, that is, scientific, in the choice of his material, in the manner in which he strikes, cuts, and polishes the blade. He relies completely on his skill, on his reason, and his endurance. There is no exaggeration in saying that in all matters where knowledge is sufficient the native relies on it exclusively. If you want to appreciate the amount of such knowledge, as well as the practical skill necessary for the production of the technological apparatus of the Central Australians, study chapters xxvi and xxvii in volume II of *The Arunta*, by Spencer and Gillen. The authors refer to the judicious choice of material suitable for a ground axe, or again for a chipped one. They tell us that in one case the "shape and finish is simply a question of material available," or again, we find that the hafting, in technique and material, depends on the purpose for which it is made. That this secular tradition is plastic, selective, and intelligent, and also well founded, can be seen from the fact that the native always adopts any new and suitable material. "Even amongst tribes that have had very little intercourse with white men, iron is beginning to replace stone." We might add that bottle-glass is rapidly ousting quartz or obsidian, woven materials are used instead of animal skins or bark-cloth, and kerosene-tins in Australia, as elsewhere, have become the most widely used water-vessels.

In his organized hunting the native also obeys an entirely secular tradition. He displays a great deal of skill, but also a considerable amount of knowledge, in stalking the kangaroo or wallaby, in following the emu and the euro. He knows the habits of the game, their watering-spots, the characteristics of the terrain. His capacities for finding his way where the European would get lost, in discovering hidden water or food-supplies inaccessible to the white man, are well known from the history of early exploration in Australia.

In short, the Central Australian possesses genuine science or knowledge, that is, tradition completely controlled by experience and reason, and completely unaffected by any mystical elements. I am emphasizing this because, in order to understand the supernatural, we have to see how the natural is defined in a given culture. The distinction, I believe, is universal. It is a mistake to assume that, at an early stage of development, man lived in a confused world, where the real and the unreal formed a medley, where mysticism and reason were as interchangeable as forged and real coin in a disorganized country. To us the most essential point about magic and religious ritual is that it steps in only where knowledge fails. Supernaturally founded ceremonial grows out of life, but it never stultifies the practical efforts of man. In his ritual of magic or religion, man attempts to enact miracles, not because he ignores the limitations of his mental powers, but, on the contrary, because he is fully cognizant of them. To go one step farther, the recognition of this seems to me indispensable if we want once and for ever to establish the truth that religion has its own subject-matter, its own legitimate field of development; that this must never encroach on the domain where science, reason, and experience ought to remain supreme. To-day this truth is important, not so much perhaps in the clash between science and religion, but rather in the encroachment of political, economic, and pseudo-cultural doctrines of the Fascist and Communist types upon the preserves of legitimate religion.

The Stone Age primitives whom we are considering, the Central Australians, do not make such a mistake. Their sacred tradition is concerned only with those things where experience and reason are of no avail. The Central Australian may be guided by his own excellent knowledge in hunting and collecting, in finding water and in preparing his implements, but one thing he cannot control, and that is the general fertility of his environment, which depends upon the rainfall. If this be adequate, then "as if by magic, the once arid land becomes covered with luxuriant herbage"; plants, insects, marsupials, and birds abound, and the native's prosperity sets in. If, on the other hand, the rainfall fails, the species do not multiply, and he is faced with starvation and misery.

Now in order to appreciate the essential difference between the technique of magical and ceremonial life on the one hand, and that of ordinary economic activities on the other, let me once more describe one totemic ceremony in detail. Were we to arrive at the proper time of the year, before the beginning of the rains, somewhere near Alice Springs in Central Australia, we could witness a typical ceremony, that of the witchetty grub totem, and observe the behaviour of the men, which is not that of ordinary everyday routine. Those who are about to take part in the ceremony have to leave the camp quietly; they slink out to a meeting-place which is not far off, but which is not supposed to be known to any one who does not belong to the totem group. Only a few of the older men of this group will remain in the camp, to keep an eye on what is happening there. The performers are thus a group united by the bonds of totemic identity; they are all reincarnations of mythological ancestors, who once roamed the country and used to perform ceremonies identical in substance with the ones which their descendants are performing now. The group is organized; there is a leader; there are distinctions according to age, degree of initiation, and of traditional knowledge.

The men adopt a behaviour, costume, and a mental attitude entirely different from that of ordinary life. No one is allowed to carry weapons or decorations; they must go quite unarmed, naked, discarding even the hair-girdle, which is the one constant article of clothing worn by men. Only the very old men are allowed to eat; the others, we are told, must on no account partake of any food until the whole ceremony is over. Even if some game is caught, this must be handed over to the old men. It is not only the season which is determined, but also the time of day. They start at dusk, so that they can spend the first night at a special camp. Place, like time, is strictly defined by tradition, which in this, as in everything else, follows mythological precedent.

In fact, since the whole country has been created with close reference to the concern and interests of man, above all to his ceremonial preoccupations, there exists what might be described as a totemic geography or, at least, topography of specially sacred spots, which have been defined as the result of ceremonial activities of the past.[10]

> Every prominent, and many an insignificant, natural feature throughout this strip of country—the most picturesque part of the great central area of the continent—has some history attached to it. For example, a gaunt old gum tree, with a large projecting bole about the middle of the trunk, indicates the exact spot where an Alchera man, who was very full of eggs, arose when he was transformed out of a witchetty grub (*The Arunta*, p. 327).

It is in this scenery, impregnated with traditional memories of ancestral acts, that the ceremonies take place.

Each ancestral act was a creative miracle producing either a permanent feature of the landscape, or a sacred implement, or else directly producing animals or plants. For the time of the totemic ancestors was largely

---

[10] Cf. *The Arunta*, Vol. I, Chapt. V, where the formation of the landscape by the creative acts of the original world-makers is described. On pp. 88–91 a minute description with plans and diagrams is given of the spot at which the present ceremony takes place. This should be collated with the account of the ceremony in Vol. I, pp. 148–53. The mythological story of how both landscape and ceremony originated will be found on pp. 326–34. I am giving this information, since the writers do not cross-reference. The fact that they are apparently not aware how important is the parallelism between myth, ceremony, and the spiritual essence of the landscape increases the documentary value of their material.

taken up with the enactment of totemic miracles, ceremonies through which individuals belonging to plant or animal species were created. And the rites of to-day are nothing else but repetitions, as exact as possible, of the ancient miracles, the tradition of which is preserved from generation to generation, not merely in memory, but also by the very fact that year after year they are performed, and their dramatic substance thus perpetuated in the behaviour of man.

The aim of the ceremonies is the same as it was; the technique is identical, and so is the social organization on which they are based. For, as already mentioned, even the members of the present-day group are the incarnations of individuals who lived in the Golden Age. Only the ceremonies have abated as regards miraculous intensity. To-day the totemic people cannot create mountains or canyons, cannot produce fresh animal species or individuals, cannot change the shape of man or nature. The only thing which they can achieve is to contribute towards the fertility of their own totemic species.

Let us once more join our witchetty grub local clan and follow their ceremonial behaviour on the morning when they start their beneficent ritual. First of all they have to provide themselves with the liturgical implements; the men have to pluck twigs from the eucalyptus, while the leader carries a small wooden trough. This latter represents the *meimba*, the sacred vessel in which the culture hero, called Intwailiuka, carried his store of spirits and sacred bull-roarers. Here again the mythological implement, the original *meimba*, was miraculous in the extreme; its counter-part to-day still carries, as we shall see, some of its magical power. Provided with their liturgical implements, the natives now follow, with their leader in front, the path traversed by Intwailiuka, the totemic ancestor, who first created the ceremony and also the landscape. They reach the Great Cavity, high up on the western wall of the ravine. In spite of its name, it is only a shallow cave with a large block of quartzite surrounded by smaller stones. The culture hero was of course also responsible for producing these stones miraculously, and they represent the large body of the witchetty grub, which is the totemic animal of the group, whilst the small stones are the eggs. The head man of the group begins to sing, tapping the stone with his wooden trough, while the other men tap it with their twigs, and also chant songs. We are not given the text of these, but the authors tell us that the burden of them is an invitation to the animal to lay eggs. Complicated manipulations follow: the ceremonial stones are tapped with twig and trough; the leader takes up one of the smaller stones and strikes each man in the stomach, telling him, "You have eaten much food." The tapping of the stone produces grubs; the magical songs invite the animal to lay eggs; the anatomical ritual refers to the satiety which follows the plentiful supply of grubs, which again is the theme of the magic.

We cannot follow in detail all the acts. We should have to chant further with the natives at a place where the totemic ancestor used to cook, pulverize, and eat the grub. He was a great producer and also apparently a Gargantuan consumer of his totem. Then we should have to repair to the drawings (*op. cit.*, Fig. 44, facing p. 141), which were placed on the rocks, not by Intwailiuka, the totemic ancestor, but by Numbakulla, the First Creator. These drawings, as a matter of fact, also refer to subsequent events by one of those proleptic or prophetic acts of creation by which the First Creator anticipated the future. The totemic ancestor Intwailiuka used to stand here, throwing up the face of the rock numbers of sacred bull-roarers, and this is imitated now by the leader of the performing group. Although we are not told so explicitly, this also obviously contributes towards the fertility of the grub. A number of other ceremonial spots are visited; once more they chant, carrying on ritual activities in imitation of ancestral acts; over and over again the leader repeats the words, "You have eaten much food," thus magically anticipating plenty. There seem to be some ten of such spots, and at each of them the ceremony is carried out again. The totemic group of performers then move back towards the main camp, and not far from it they are met by the rest of the local population, men and women alike, who henceforth play a small and collateral part in the rest of the proceedings.

One element of these latter must be mentioned. While the totemic performers had been away, a long, narrow hut had been built, which is intended to represent the chrysalis case from which the fully developed insect emerges. When the party return, the people of the other moieties and the women assemble behind this hut-chrysalis. They range themselves, men of the other moiety in one group, the women of the same moiety in another, the women of the other moiety in a third. The totemic and class differentiations come always very much to the fore in such ceremonies. Now, in and around this hut-chrysalis, an important stage of the ceremony is performed, the men wriggling in and out, chanting songs about the animals in their various stages and about the sacred stones with magical import, created in ancestral, mythological times.

The most characteristic feature of the subsequent phase of the ceremony, where others participate, is the kind of ceremonial or magical give and take. This can only be understood by referring it to the social organization of these natives and to certain economic principles of their ceremonialism. The rites for the multiplication of the totemic species can be performed only by the members of the clan. It is not only their privilege, but also their duty towards the community as a whole, to carry out such rites. The natives believe deeply that the fertility of animals and plants depends on the magical co-operation of the totemic clans. Most totems are edible animals and plants, and apparently there is no important food-supply but is represented on the totemic list. There can therefore be no doubt that, in the aborigines' economic conception of the world, totemic co-operation is indispensable to human existence. The essence of this as a system among the Arunta consists, therefore, in each clan carrying out the ceremonial for the benefit of the rest. Although a man is not absolutely forbidden to eat of his totem, he eats sparingly, usually not at all, and he is debarred from eating the best part of his totem animal, when this is large and succulent, as the emu, the kangaroo, or the wallaby.[11] The clan as a whole, therefore, derives little if any benefit from its ceremony.

The ceremonial by-play which now takes place must be considered against the background of this totemic co-operation. The performing party are expected by the others; they are welcomed by them, and at certain stages they receive food, which has been cooked for them, while they in return distribute some of their ornaments to the other people. The leader says: "Our increase ceremony is finished, the *Mulyanuka* (men of the other moiety) must have these things, or else our increase ceremony will not be successful, and so harm will come to us." Then the men of the other moiety approach, and the objects are divided among them.[12]

The dependence of present-day religious ceremonial on the supernatural reality of the Golden Age manifests itself in every detail of the above account. As regards the nature of the acts, that is, the magical rites, we can see at once that they have nothing to do with any practical work. To describe that sort of magic as pseudo-science, or the primitive counterpart of science, is not correct. There is in many details of the ceremonial an element of imitation, but the imitation is not of the animal, nor is it based of natural history. It is the imitation of ancestral behaviour, and it is based on the sacred tradition of myths. The native identifies himself with his totemic animal, but here again the identification is not between man as he is to-day and the kangaroo, emu, or grub as it now exists. In his ceremonial life, man becomes Alchera, that is, totemic ancestor, and he acts as an Alchera. The witchetty grub man goes back to the Golden Age, in which men and women of this clan were supposed "to have been full of eggs which are now represented by rounded water-worn stones," many of which, as we have seen, are actually manipulated in the sacred ceremony. Every act of this, and of any other, totemic ceremony in Central Australia is not an imitation of the animal species, but an imitation of the primeval, supernatural, half-animals half-men of which mythology teaches, and which were the ancestors of the present-day clan.

[11] Cf. *The Arunta*, pp. 80–87.

[12] The full account of this ceremony will be found in *Native Tribes*, pp. 170 *sqq.*, and in *The Arunta*, Vol. I, pp. 148 *sqq.* Comparing the latter, which is also the later book, the student will be interested to note that the amplifications emphasize even more strongly the dependence of ritual on tradition.

The Alchera were creative in a supernatural sense; the powers and influence of magic are again creative and supernatural in the very same sense, but with enormously reduced intensity. The supernatural, to the Arunta, is that power which the totemic ancestors fully possessed, since they were able to create the world, transform the landscape, make men, animals, and plants, and institute social order, customs, and ceremonies. Of this power man participates only in those activities which are ceremonial, and which have been handed down from the Alchera. In all other things man can only achieve what he produces by hard labour, by skill, and on the basis of his empirical knowledge.

In the analysis of the Central Australian tribes we have again found a confirmation of our theory of myth and sacred tradition. We were able to arrive at conclusions which emphasized the profound difference between acts achieved by magic and religion, on the one hand, and those based on knowledge, on the other. This distinction is necessary for our theory of myth; it also implies this theory. Sacred tradition, we perceive more and more clearly, does not explain things; it tells us how they were created. This is not a scientific explanation, but a religious truth.

Let us go one step farther. What is the place of ceremonial or magic or ritual or religion, or whatever you like to call it, within the scheme of culture? What does the whole totemic ritual contribute to the tribal life of a Central Australian? From one point of view, we have to class it as a delusion or superstition, following in this the footsteps of Tylor. But there are elements in it which must be appraised in an entirely different manner. Taking native mythology and ritual together, we see that they contain two elements. From the dogmatic point of view, the creation of the world, the natural affinity between men and animals and plants, the reinterpretation of the landscape and all the natural features in terms of human interest, one and all establish a deep bond between man and his environment. Here, once more, we find a belief closely akin to our idea of a beneficent Providence, even as we have found another counterpart in the Trobriands. The Central Australian, living as he does in an arid, inhospitable, hostile country, has developed a system of beliefs which humanize the environment. Above all, the mythology and its dogmatic contents establish a close affinity between the socially organized groups of the natives and the vast range of animal and plant species, including most, probably all, of those which are useful to man. The limited knowledge of the Central Australian allows him to collect plants, grubs, and small marsupials, and to hunt the bigger animals. It allows him to produce the implements which he needs for this purpose, and the clothing and ornaments necessary in that climate. Where his knowledge fails him, where his scientifically logical and empirically orientated mind tells him that no effort of his body or mind will bring any results, there sacred tradition steps in.

Pragmatically speaking, this tradition helps him in the effective carrying out of his practical work. At the time when rains are due to come, and favourable weather may either fulfil his great expectations or adverse drought blight all his hopes, the native, instead of merely waiting in idle and demoralizing anxiety, marks time in carrying out his totemic ceremonies. Mythology teaches him that these ceremonies will contribute towards the fulfilment of his hopes. Far from being a harmful delusion which diverts his energies from useful pursuits, totemism brings about an integration of the individual mind, and an organization of collective activities, both directed towards the desired end. Magic is a system of collective suggestion, which at that critical season tells the Central Australian that all will be well, on condition that man obeys the behests of tradition and enters into communion with the supernatural essence of his world.

We have seen above that the totemic increase ceremonies are based on the ethical principle of co-operative services rendered by each totemic group to the whole community. That the benefits are, from the rational point of view, illusory does not diminish the ethical elements contained in this work done unselfishly for the benefit of others. It would be possible to go even farther and to show that the totemic ritual of the Central Australians exercises an important influence on the development of purely economic virtues. The ceremonies foster foresight, regularity, and organization of effort; they involve, perhaps, the greatest quantity of collective labour carried out by these natives. The fact that purely religious ceremonial creates labour-gangs, trained to work systematically, to obey the leadership of one man, to work for the benefit of the community as a whole, with direct reference to practical ends, is of no mean importance for economic evolution.[13]

I am enlarging on this, because the real importance of the so-called functional method in modern anthropololgy consists in the parallel study of mutually dependent phenomena or aspects of tribal life. The functional principle teaches that if you want to understand magic, you must go outside magic, and study economic ritual within the context of those practical activities in which it is really embedded. This principle, the theoretical importance of which I first conceived from the excellent material of Spencer and Gillen, I have later applied in field-work.

In the appreciation of Melanesian magic there is perhaps no more important truth to be recognized than its influence upon practical activities and the way in which it is determined by them. Those who glance over

[13] This was the thesis of my earliest essay, written in English and published under the title "The Economic Aspect of the Intichiuma Ceremonies," in *Festskrift tillagnad Edvard Westermarck*, Helsingfors, 1912.

the pages of one or two of my books (*Argonauts*, but especially *Coral Gardens*) will find that magic is essentially an integrating and organizing force. It provides that spiritual strengthening of the individual mind and that discipline and preparation of the group which are necessary whenever the natives are confronted with a task difficult and not altogether controllable by knowledge and skill. Take their sailing, for instance. In the construction of their canoes, the organization of their crew, their choice of season, route, and sailing technique, they depend on a rational tradition. But the vicissitudes of sailing—wind and weather, reefs and calms—are beyond the control of Trobriander and European alike. So also, to a certain extent, is the reliability of the material from which a canoe is built, and the human element which the Trobriander will meet at the other end of his expedition. For these unaccountable, uncontrollable elements, there exists magic: of mist and of wind, of shipwreck and of malevolence, of success in trading, and of benevolence of potential enemies. Individually, this magic means for every man confidence, optimism, preparedness. Socially, this magic emphasizes the prestige of its master. It gives him additional power and adds an element of strength to the social organization of the crew and of the whole body of the sailing expedition.

In agriculture, as I have shown with an almost tedious elaboration of detail, the same also obtains. Magic never encroaches on rational and practical work. The domain of intelligent effort and enlightened persistence on the one hand, of good luck on the other, are mutually exclusive. But magic adds to the zest and beauty of work: it introduces rhythm, punctuality, discipline, and order into the collective activities of the gardening team; it provides this team with a leader.

While the Australian evidence shows that economic virtues may be developed by magic in anticipation of their subsequent utility in organized production, the conditions in the Trobriand Islands present us with the economic function of magic fully established. An intermediate stage in this development we might perhaps find in the fertility ceremonies of the Pueblo Indians, with which we shall deal very briefly, only showing that the functional nature of myth and ritual in that area falls within the scope of our analysis.

VI

The Evidence of Other Ethnographic Areas

In a brief and simple statement of anthropological theory it is always best to demonstrate the principles by giving one or two examples, taken from well-known and fully documented areas. I have based my conclusions on

Central Australia because our material is exceptionally good, and on the Trobriand Islands because I know this region from personal experience. What about the wider validity of the present theory?

I have been attempting to demonstrate that the substance of religion, that is, its subject-matter, is not arbitrary. The twin beliefs in immortality and in Providence grow out of the necessities of human life. They step in as all-powerful, beneficent cultural forces, integrating the individual mind and organizing social grouping. The two beliefs, moreover, as we have seen, would not be alive if they were mere abstract formulae. They are believed because they are human experiences present and past. All religion is founded on revealed truth because man had to experience the reality of the supernatural in order to accept it. This revelation may be contemporary: miracles must occur, and do occur, in every live religion. As a rule, however, the great miracles of religion come from the past. They are handed down through an age-long, venerable tradition. Conformity, whole-hearted submission to traditional biddings, is perhaps the most important moral force in any healthy society, primitive or civilized. The existence of such ethical influence we have fully established both in Central Australia and in the Trobriand belief in spirit life and magical power. The other active and pragmatic manifestation of every religious belief is the enactment of limited miracles of magic and ritual.

In one way, perhaps, it is the concept of miracle which forms the core of my theoretical approach. The word "miracle" is, in theology, restricted to more spectacular events, above all to the tangible, concrete, sensuously appreciable workings of supernatural force, which fall outside the established course of nature. Thus the theologian would class the production of wine at Cana, the multiplication of bread and fishes, the resurrection of Lazarus, as miracles, but he would refuse the title of miracle to the supernatural processes which take place in the Sacrament.[14] For the theologian regards these events as falling under the law of nature of the supernatural.

I submit, however, that the anthropologist, or any scientific student of the history of religions, must redefine the crude, popular language which, in this case, the theologian seems inclined to accept. To the scientific mind any event in which supernatural forces manifest themselves, whether to the bodily eyes or to the vision of faith, must belong to the same category. The transformation of the earthly substance of bread and wine into the real body and blood of Jesus Christ, for instance, is a miracle in so far as the Real Presence is assumed. Again, the complete change of the substance of the human soul in the sacrament of the remis-

[14] Cf. the articles s.v. "Miracles" in *Hastings' Encylopaedia* and the *Roman Catholic Encyclopaedia*.

sion of sins is as genuine a miracle as a complete change in bodily metab-
olism produced, let us say, by the water of Lourdes. In one way, the
scientific approach is here more religious and reverent than that of the
theologian. The anthropologist dissociates himself resolutely from doubt-
ing Thomas and the theologian alike; he places the spiritual reality assumed by religious faith on the same level as the material reality acces-
sible to the senses. Actually, what the scientist follows in his classification
is the whole cultural setting and attitude of the faithful. He draws the
line of distinction, not by the naïve, crude criteria of sight, sound, touch,
or smell, as opposed to mystical experience. The line of demarcation
must be scientifically drawn between phenomena where nothing but
physical events occur, and those were supernatural forces enter as cause
or effect.

Let me exemplify my point by the miracle of Bolsena. Here we have a
genuine myth, not only attested by Catholic writers, but embodied in
one of the most magnificent churches of Christendom, and in some of the
most famous paintings, notably the *Stanza* of Rafael. Those who have
seen the latter, especially the detail of the bleeding Host, those who have
visited the Cathedral of Orvieto, where the miracle is confirmed by the
sacred relic and represented in fresco and enamel work, will realize how
myth becomes monumentally translated into works of art. The story itself
tells how a Bohemian priest, sceptical as to the doctrine of transubstantiation, became convinced by a miracle which occurred between his own
fingers while he was celebrating the Holy Mass in the town of Bolsena.
In the very act of consecration, and between the words, he had an access
of doubt, and then the miracle happened. Blood overflowed in the chal-
ice; the Host became covered with drops of blood; the whole congregation saw this. Indeed, the whole of Christendom was so impressed by
this visible manifestation of the Real Presence that the Pope not only
ordered the building of the Cathedral of Orvieto, but also instituted the
festival of Corpus Christi. We have here in one event the ritual consequence of the myth.

But what is really important here is the relation between the ordinary
miracle of consecration and its spectacular manifestation at Bolsena.
From the religious point of view it would be worse than heresy to affirm
that the true miracle of our religion, the Real Presence of the body and
blood of Jesus Christ, was any more genuine, or real, or factual on that
one occasion than on any other.[15] The miracle did not change anything in
the true substance of the mystical reality. It was merely a sign; but even
this sign to the truly faithful is unnecessary, since the sacrament itself is

[15] I am writing this, of course, as a good anthropologist, from the strictly Roman Catholic
point of view, in which, moreover, I was brought up.

the sign. Where does the miracle then reside? Its reality lies in the invisible grace which makes the sacrament of transubstantiation the very epitome of everything that the Catholic believes: the incarnation of the Second Person of the Trinity, His sacrifice on Calvary, and the institution of the sacrament by which He perpetually reappears on earth and unites Himself with every believer in the Sacrament of the Communion.

From this one example we can see that the only scientifically correct definition of miracle is as an event in which supernatural realities are created by ritual acts. The miracle of magic, the utterances of words, and the performance of gesture are supernatural forces which, through a supernatural mechanism, bring about natural events. In the miracles of sacrifice or sacrament we have again words and gestures which bring about events as real and true, but supersensuous because spiritual in nature. The reality of both has to be vouched for by experience: we know that the Sacrament of Communion is true because it was instituted by Jesus Christ during the Last Supper, and also because at every Communion the believer mystically experiences the divine grace which comes from the union with God. We know that the miracles at Lourdes are true, because there is a running tradition of miraculous healing, but above all, because the Virgin Mary appeared to the poor shepherdess.

And here we come immediately upon the very essence of myth: it is above all, as has been so often emphasized, the affirmation of primeval miracles. I think it would be interesting to survey from this point of view other examples of belief and ritual. There is no doubt that in some religions the element of the miraculous is almost negligible. Let us take an area known to me from a four weeks' visit, in which I was, however, conducted by an expert anthropologist who had remained there two years, Dr. I. A. Richards, to whom I am entirely indebted for the following information, given me both in the field and in London. The religious life of these people, the Bemba of Northern Rhodesia, is almost completely devoid of anything which would fall into the category of the directly miraculous. They very seldom even ask for a specific result of prayer, sacrifice, or rite. The ancestral spirits are asked for blessings in general, for peace, health, and prosperity of the land. "May we go in peace, give us life, give us children." The spirits are begged in general to promote the welfare of the group, heal sickness, or bring rain.

Consequently, since there is no definite request or attempt to bring about a specific effect, there is very little need for an empirical testimony of clear-cut results. The mythology of the Bemba is accordingly extremely poor. But even they have a legendary cycle connected with the first man who, from the north-west, entered the territory at present occupied by the tribe. This man, Lucelenganga, received the knowledge of medicine and of magic from the High God. Before that, "All the magical trees and herbs were in the country, but we did not know how to use them." The tradition was carried on because Lucelenganga selected the most intelligent men living and taught them the magic of healing medicine. This legendary background is not a mere story, but lives in ritual. The witch-doctor, *shinganga*, to-day calls upon Leza the High God when digging his herbs and roots, and addresses Lucelenganga by name when mixing his medicines or divining. A witch-doctor utters these words: "You, Lucelenganga, who left your footsteps on the rock and the footsteps of your dog, give strength to my medicine." Or else he repeats the same initial words and says ". . . make the words of my divination true." A witch-doctor has also to add the names of the actual ancestors or predecessors from whom he has bought or learnt the use of the medicine. The footsteps mentioned in the incantation refer to a natural feature in the landscape which the natives still show, and which they atttribute to the heavy tread of Lucelenganga as he first passed through the country.

We have here, therefore, not a complete absence of mythology, but rather mythology reduced to a bare outline. In its sober and limited way, we have the same appeal to the continuity of tradition, the same reference to the divine sources of supernatural power. The mentioning of names of predecessors and of ancestors is, incidentally, a very prominent feature of the Melanesian language of magic.[16]

From my very rapid and rather superficial survey of East African tribes, I have come to the conclusion that mythology is not completely absent, though it plays a far more limited part than in Melanesia or in Central Australia. But here only very careful analysis of the character of ritual and its supernatural context, with direct reference to what might be called the historical records of the efforts of ritual, can give a satisfactory answer. For mythology flourishes not only in the dim, distant past: there is also the living, current mythology of contemporary miracle or supernatural manifestation of divine power. In Lourdes such mythology is recorded in the scientifically attested chronicle of miraculous healings. Manifestations of the supernatural power of saints are recorded again in the chronicles of Roman Catholic hagiology. Such records have to be kept, because the canonization of saints is contingent on the occurrence of at least two well-attested miracles. Christian Science, spiritism, faith healing, palmistry attract and retain their faithful, or their customers, by alleged empirical proof or claim of miracles achieved.

Once we define myth as a sacred tradition which exists in order to attest the reality of any specific vehicle, channel, or mechanism by which the supernatural can be tapped or moved, it becomes quite clear that, on

---

[16] Cf. the present writer's *Coral Gardens and their Magic*, Vol. II, part vi, "An Ethnographic Theory of the Magical Word," and part vii, "Magical Formulae."

the one hand, it is idle to argue whether there are myths unconnected with religion. On the other hand, it is equally barren to study any religious ritual or ethics without seeking to discover how far the dogmas involved have that empirical and historical background of attested occurrences which we define as the only legitimate sphere of mythology or sacred tradition.

The point of view, therefore, here adopted with regard to myth really turns on the question whether we define myth in a purely mechanical and formal way, or functionally, that is, by the role it performs in culture. As long as the purely formal approach dominates, we shall have in ethnography collections of "folk-lore" and descriptions of "ritual" and "ceremonialism" entirely unrelated to each other, and it will be difficult to prove the point of the present theory, or to appreciate the living reality of religion in such artificially dissected material. The formal point of view of which I am complaining still does predominate. Even a competent American anthropologist tells us that it is quite impossible "to generalize as to the degree to which myth is dynamic in religion."[17] This misconception is based simply on a formal and, to me, barren definition of the term "myth." This writer, incidentally, affirms that the "dairy ritual of the Todas seems unsupported in myth, and the gods mentioned in the prayers are on the level of mere abracadabra" (*loc. cit.*). Yet the student who turns to the source, the book by W. H. R. Rivers on the Todas, can see from pp. 182 *sqq.*, and also p. 246, that a knowledge of their mythology is indispensable in order to understand the ceremonies and the prayers connected with the dairy or with the village. The prayers contain "references to various incidents in the lives of the gods, and many of the clauses would be unintelligible without a knowledge of these lives." The Toda god is distinctly anthropomorphic, lives the same life as the present-day Toda, and tends his dairies and buffaloes. So close is the relation between present-day life and the mythological background that the Todas regard their sacred dairies as the property of the gods, while the dairymen are looked upon as priests. Indeed, Rivers tells us that there was "a period when gods and men inhabited the hills together. The gods ruled the men, ordained how they should live and originated the various customs of the people"; and again, "According to tradition, the most sacred dairies . . . date back to the time when the gods were active on earth and were themselves dairymen."

This is, I think, sufficient to show how badly my critic has selected her negative example to prove the inadequacy of my theories. Were we engaged in a specialized anthropological discussion, it would be possible

[17] Dr. Ruth Benedict in the article on "Myth" in the *Encyclopaedia of Social Sciences*, New York, 1933.

and also advisable to scrutinize the material presented by Rivers about the Todas more in detail. It would confirm our theory of myth and its relation to ritual, and the essential correlation between ethics and religion. We might discuss some of the interesting material collected by Professor Radcliffe-Brown on the mythology and religious ritual of the Andaman Islanders, and their influence one on the other. I should have liked to join issue with this author in his theoretical interpretation of myth. For he regards myth as a form of primitive philosophy by which early man establishes his system of social values. These latter, however, Radcliffe-Brown does not attempt to correlate with practical activities.

Polynesian mythology and its place in religion would lend itself especially well to a functional analysis of the ethical and cultural influence of tradition.

The area, however, to which I should like to refer the specialist, and about which I should like to say a few words to the general reader, is that known in ethnography as the Pueblos. To the popular imagination they have been made attractive by the writings of D. H. Lawrence and Aldous Huxley, by the glamour of their archaeological past still surviving in mighty ruins, and by the legendary stories which have hung round them ever since the early Spanish explorations. We have also some really good anthropological material on these people, and, what is useful to the layman, one or two excellent summaries of their main cultural and social characteristics.[18]

The religion of these Indians is dominated completely by their dependency on rain and sunshine, by their interest in their fields, and also by their desire for the fertility of women. The religion is carried out partly in the form of public ceremonies, partly by private prayers and offerings. These are directed to superhuman beings associated with such natural phenomena as the sun, the earth, fire, and water. It is about these beings that a very rich mythology flourishes.

There is, however, another class of supernatural beings, the Kachinas,

[18] A good, brief, and comprehensive account of one of the groups of the Pueblos is given by G. P. Murdoch in *Our Primitive Contemporaries*, New York, 1934. The chapter on the "Pueblos of New Mexico" in *Patterns of Culture*, London, 1935, by Dr. Ruth Benedict, gives a very vivid picture, based partly on her own observations. My own brief survey was enriched by information generously given me by Mrs. Robert Aitken (Miss Barbara Freire-Marecco), who has intensively studied the Tewa on the First Mesa. During a short visit there and among other settlements of the Pueblo, I was able to gain a concrete impression, and had the good luck to be present at one of the Kachina dances at Oraibi. The writings of Fewkes, of Voth, and of Curtis, valuable though they are, suffer from the "false anatomy," the complete severing of mythology from ritual and the treatment of the latter as if it were performed by marionettes. A good compensation for that is to be found in the short but excellent monograph by Dr. H. K. Haeberlin, *The Idea of Fertility among the Pueblo Indians*, 1916, which is one of the pioneering works in functional anthropology.

who are regarded as ancestors, and of which the visible representation appears during the ceremonial season in the form of masked dancers. Most of the ceremonial is, from the social point of view, connected with the organization of the Pueblos into religious fraternities or priesthoods. These are often named after animals and objects of worship, and they claim mystical affinities with snake and with fire, with antelope and with lightning, affinities again recorded in the stories of native mythology.

A brief outline of the nature of Hopi religion will best be given in the words of Dr. Murdoch, who, without any theoretical preconceptions in favour of our thesis, yet summarizes the state of affairs almost in the terms adopted in the present essay.

> An agricultural people inhabiting a cool and arid region needs, above all things, warmth and rain for the growth of its crops. It is understandable, consequently, that Hopi should worship a Sky God who brings rain, an Earth Goddess who nourishes the seed, and a Sun God who matures the crops, as well as a special Corn Mother and a God of Growth or Germination. Moreover, the essential summer rains fall only in sudden torrential thunderstorms at irregular and unpredictable intervals; sometimes they fail entirely, or an unseasonable frost or severe windstorm blights the crops. Thus man's very existence depends upon an element of chance which manifests itself in ways so violent and seemingly arbitrary that they suggest the agency of supernatural powers as capricious as they are mighty. It is but natural, therefore, that the Hopi should bend every effort to control these unseen powers through propitiation and coercion.[19]

It remains only to add that all the efforts to control the Unseen Powers are carried out according to prescriptions mostly derived from the mythological past.

The function of Hopi religion, therefore, is identical with that which we established on the basis of the Trobriand material and which we also discovered in Central Australia. For these natives too have conceived of a vast supernatural world, superimposed on their empirical reality. To propitiate this supernatural world by ritual, to establish concord between man and the Universe by the observance of ethical rules, occupies half of the Pueblos' existence. For the ethical element is prominent in Pueblo religion. ". . . the Pueblos show a great advance over many primitive tribes in that their legends and their priests reiterate constantly that 'prayer is not effective except the heart be good' ".[20]

---

[19] *Op. cit.*, p. 348.

[20] M. R. Coolidge, *The Rainmakers (Indians of Arizona and New Mexico)*, 1929, p. 204. The same writer speaks also about the goodness, unselfishness, truth-telling, respect for property, family and filial duty of the natives, and affirms that these virtues are "closely connected with religious belief and conduct, but not their principal object." With this latter

In scanning the detailed descriptions of Pueblo ritual contained in the many volumes of Curtis, Fewkes, or [Henry R.] Voth, we can see that this inner purity of heart is actually obtained by following a whole system of lustrations, of abstinences, and by keeping a strict control of passions. "One of the obligations that rest upon every priest and official during the time when he is actively participating in religious observances is that of feeling no anger."[21] Virtue and morality in ordinary conduct of life are also enjoined under supernatural sanctions. The failure of crops is attributed to adultery quite as much as to insufficiency in ceremonial. And here it is interesting to note that such moral precepts are based on mythological foundations. For one of the main culture heroes of the people, Alosaka, is described in one of the myths as being so thoroughly disgusted when his wife was seduced and the people ravished women and attacked the old, that he departed from this earth together with the miraculous bounty he had brought, and returned to his mother, the Earth Woman. The ethical *motif* can be found throughout Pueblo mythology. Politeness, goodwill, offerings on the part of the culture heroes towards gods are rewarded; evil deeds are punished.

I cannot enter, however, into the details of myth and ritual, and must remain satisfied with the brief indication that, in Pueblo culture, not only are myth and ritual closely connected with each other and with ethics, but the whole religion is a by-product of man's adaptation to his environment.

VII

Conclusions on the Anatomy and Pathology of Religion

From our brief ethnographic survey we can conclude that the scientific analysis of religion is possible, for there are common elements in all religious systems as regards substance, form, and function. Every organized faith, we have seen, must carry its specific apparatus, by which it expresses its substance. There must be a dogmatic system backed by my-

---

part I would agree, but it is the connexion of ethics with religious belief and ritual which is too often overlooked in ethnographic theories and observations.

[21] R. Benedict, *op. cit.*, p. 61. This author adds that "anger is not tabu in order to facilitate communication with a righteous god who can only be approached by those with a clean heart. It is rather a sign of concentration upon supernatural affairs, a state of mind that constrains the supernaturals and makes it impossible for them to withhold their share of the bargain. It has magical efficacy." I cannot follow this argument. The very fact that a complete concentration of mind is necessary and that all passions must be excluded when we approach God is essentially a moral rule. The fact that, in order to attain magical efficacy, we must pay undivided attention to our spiritual communion, demands what every theologian as well as the anthropologist or the man in the street would call "a clean heart."

thology or sacred tradition; a developed ritual in which man acts on his belief and communes with the powers of the unseen world; there must also be an ethical code of rules which binds the faithful and determines their behaviour towards each other and towards the things they worship. This structure or form of religion can be traced in totemism and animism, in ancestor-worship as well as in the most developed monotheistic systems.

We find, moreover, that there exists an intrinsically appropriate subject-matter in every religious system, a subject-matter which finds its natural expression in the religious technique of ritual and ethics, and its validation in sacred history. This subject-matter can be summed up as the twin beliefs in Providence and in Immortality. By belief in Providence we understand the mystical conviction that there exist in the universe forces or persons who guide man, who are in sympathy with man's destinies, and who can be propitiated by man. This concept completely covers the Christian's faith in God, One and Indivisible though present in Three Persons, who has created the world and guides it to-day. It embraces also the many forms of polytheistic paganism: the belief in ancestor ghosts and guardian spirits. Even the so-called totemic religions, based on the conviction that man's social and cultural order is duplicated in a spiritual dimension, through which he can control the natural forces of fertility and of the environment, are but a rude version of the belief in Providence. For they allow man to get in touch with the spiritual essence of animal or plant species, to honour them and fulfil duties towards them, in return for their yielding to his needs. The belief in Immortality in our higher religions is akin to that of primitive creeds, some of which only affirm a limited continuance after death, while others assume an immortality consisting in repeated acts of reincarnation.

The substance of all religion is thus deeply rooted in human life; it grows out of the necessities of life. In other words, religion fulfils a definite cultural function in every human society. This is not a platitude. It contains a scientific refutation of the repeated attacks on religion by the less enlightened rationalists. If religion is indispensable to the integration of the community, just because it satisfies spiritual needs by giving man certain truths and teaching him how to use these truths, then it is impossible to regard religion as a trickery, as an "opiate for the masses," as an invention of priests, capitalists, or any other servants of vested interests.

The scientific treatment of religion implies above all a clear analysis of how it grows out of the necessities of human life. One line of approach consists in the study of sacraments, that is, those religious acts which consecrate the crises of human life, at birth, at puberty, at marriage, and above all at death. In these religion gives a sense and a direction to the course of life and to the value of personality. It binds the individual to the other members of his family, his clan or tribe, and it keeps him in constant relation with the spiritual world.

Another empirical approach shows how magical and religious phenomena are directly dictated to man by the stresses and strains of life, and the necessity of facing heavy odds; how faith and ritual must follow the darker, more dangerous, and more tragic aspects of man's practical labours. Here the material foundations of man's life ought to be scrutinized. Agriculture, with its principal condition of rainfall and sunshine, leads to the magic of fertility, to an elaborate ritual of sowing, flowering, harvest, and first-fruits, and to the institution of divine kings and chiefs. Primitive food-gathering produces ceremonies of the Intichiuma type. Hazardous pursuits, such as hunting and fishing, sailing and distant trading, yield their own type of ritual, belief, and ethical rules. The vicissitudes of war and love are also rich in magical concomitants. Religion, no doubt, combines all these elements in a great variety of designs or mosaics. It is the object of science to discover the common elements in them, though it may be the task of the artist or of the mystic to depict or to cherish the individual phenomenon. But I venture to affirm that in not a single one of its manifestations can religion be found without its firm roots in human emotion, which again always grows out of desires and vicissitudes connected with life.

Two affirmations, therefore, preside over every ritual act, every rule of conduct, and every belief. There is the affirmation of the existence of powers sympathetic to man, ready to help him on condition that he conforms to the traditional lore which teaches how to serve them, conjure them, and propitiate them. This is the belief in Providence, and this belief assists man in so far as it enhances his capacity to act and his readiness to organize for action, under conditions where he must face and fight not only the ordinary forces of nature, but also chance, ill luck, and the mysterious, ever incalculable designs of destiny.

The second belief is that beyond the brief span of natural life there is compensation in another existence. Through this belief man can act and calculate far beyond his own forces and limitations, looking forward to his work being continued by his successors in the conviction that, from the next world, he will still be able to watch and assist them. The sufferings and efforts, the injustices and inequalities, of this life are thus made up for. Here again we find that the spiritual force of this belief not only integrates man's own personality, but is indispensable for the cohesion of the social fabric. Especially in the form which this belief assumes in ancestor-worship and the communion with the dead do we perceive its moral and social influence.

In their deepest foundations, as well as in their final consequences, the two beliefs in Providence and Immortality are not independent of one another. In the higher religions man lives in order to be united to God.

In the simpler forms, the ancestors worshipped are often mystically identified with environmental forces, as in totemism. At times they are both ancestors and carriers of fertility, as the Kachina of the Pueblos. Or again the ancestor is worshipped as the divinity, or at least as a culture hero.

The unity of religion in substance, form, and function is to be found everywhere. Religious development consists probably in the growing predominance of the ethical principle and in the increasing fusion of the two main factors of all belief, the sense of Providence and the faith in immortality.

The conclusions to be drawn with regard to contemporary events I shall leave to the reader's own reflection. Is religion, in the sense in which we have just defined it—the affirmation of an ethical Providence, of immortality, of the transcendental value and sense of human life—is such religion dead? Is it going to make way for other creeds, perhaps less exacting, perhaps more immediately repaying and grossly satisfactory, but creeds which, nevertheless, fail to satisfy man's craving for the Absolute; fail to answer the riddle of human existence, and to convey the ethical message which can only be received from a being or beings regarded as beyond human passions, strife, and frailties? Is religion going to surrender its own equipment of faith, ritual, and ethics to cross-breeds between superstition and science, between economics and credulity, between politics and national megalomania? The dogmatic affirmations of these new mysticisms are banal, shallow, and they pander directly to the lowest instincts of the multitude. This is true of the belief in the absolute supremacy of one race and its right to bully all others; the belief in the sanctity of egoism in one's own nationality; the conviction of the value of war and collective brutality; the belief that only manual labour gives the full right to live and that the whole culture and public life of a community must be warped in the interests of the industrial workers.

Those of us who believe in culture and believe in the value of religion, though perhaps not in its specific tenets, must hope that the present-day misuse of the religious apparatus for partisan and doctrinaire purposes is not a healthy development of religion, but one of the many phenomena in the pathology of culture which seem to threaten the immediate development of our post-war Western society. If this be so, these new pseudo-religions are doomed to die. Let us hope that our whole society will not be dragged with them to destruction. Let us work for the maintenance of the eternal truths which have guided mankind out of barbarism to culture, and the loss of which seems to threaten us with barbarism again. The rationalist and agnostic must admit that even if he himself cannot accept these truths, he must at least recognize them as indispensable pragmatic figments without which civilization cannot exist.

FURTHER READING

Ellen, Roy, Ernest Gellner, Grazyna Kubica, and Janusz Mucha, eds. *Malinowski between Two Worlds: The Polish Roots of an Anthropological Tradition*. Cambridge: Cambridge University Press, 1988.

Firth, Raymond, ed. *Man and Culture: An Evaluation of the Work of Bronislaw Malinowski*. London: Routledge and Kegan Paul, 1957.

Langendoen, D. T. *The London School of Linguistics: Study of the Linguistic Theories of B. Malinowski and J. R. Firth*. Cambridge: MIT Press, 1968.

Malinowski, Bronislaw. *A Diary in the Strict Sense of the Term*. V. Malinowski, ed. New York: Harcourt, Brace and Jovanovich, 1967.

Mandelbaum, Maurice. "Functionalism in Social Anthropology" in *Philosophy, Science and Method*, Sidney Morgenbesser, Patrick Suppes, and Michael White, eds, 306-32. New York: St. Martin's, 1969.

Spiro, Melford E. *Oedipus in the Trobriands*. Chicago: University of Chicago Press, 1982.

Stocking, George W., Jr. "Special Review: Empathy and Antipathy in the Heart of Darkness: An Essay Review of Malinowski's Field Diaries." *Journal for the History of the Behavioral Sciences* 4 (1968): 189-94.

Stocking, George W., Jr., ed. *Malinowski, Rivers, Benedict and Others: Essays on Culture and Personality*. Madison: University of Wisconsin, 1986.

Strenski, Ivan. *Four Theories of Myth in Twentieth-Century History*. London and Iowa City: Macmillan and Iowa University Press, 1987.

Symmons-Symonolewicz, Konstantin. "Bronislaw Malinowski: An Intellectual Profile." *The Polish Review* 3 (1958): 55-76.

―――. "Bronislaw Malinowski: The Formative Influences and Theoretical Evolution." *The Polish Review* 4 (1959): 17-45.

―――. "Bronislaw Malinowski: Individuality as a Theorist." *The Polish Review* 6 (1960): 53-65.

Wax, Murray L. "Tenting with Malinowski." *American Sociological Review* 37 (1972): 1-13.

INDEX

Abstinence, 169

Abusive expressions. *See* Obscenity

Achilles, 12

Adam and Eve, xvii

Adonis, Attis, Osiris (Frazer), 115–16, 127

African tribes: the Bantu, 150; the Bemba, 164–65

Agnosticism, 132

Alchera, 159

All Souls' Day, 149

Alosaka, 169

Ancestors, 35, 91, 167–68

Ancestor worship, 149–50, 172

Ancestral act, 155–56, 158–59; as primeval reality, 114. *See also* Myth: as dramatic development of dogma

Ancestral mother, 60–61, 92

Ancestral spirits, 137, 164

Ancestral village, 142

Animals: cooperation with, 157–59; and magic, 158; in myths, 22, 39, 67, 156; and sorcery, 102–3; spirits changing into, 104; totemic significance of, 27, 60, 90, 156

Animism. *See* Manism

Anthropology: contemporary relevance of, xi n. 1, xii, xxix, 172; defined, 131; field-work in, 115, 127; and psychoanalysis, xxiv, 55–57

Argonauts of the Western Pacific (Malinow-ski), xxviii, xxx–xxxi, 72, 103, 161

Aristotle, xvii

Arthur, King, 12

Arunta, 159

Arunta, The (Spencer and Gillen), 153, 155 n. 10

Astrological influences, 31

Atheism, 134

Attis. See *Adonis, Attis, Osiris*

Atu'a'ine, Aturamo'a and Sinatemubadiye'i, myth of, 37–39

Australia, tribes of Central, 152–59 *passim*

Bantu, the, 150

Bastian, Adolf, 137

Behavioral functionalism, xxiii

Behavior, human, normative patterns of, 32–33

Belief in Immortality, The (Frazer), 77

Bemba of Northern Rhodesia, 164–65

Benedict, Ruth, 125–26, 166–67, 169

Bible, Christian dogma rooted in, 119–21

Biblical stories, 13, 80–81, 118

Biological functionalism, xvii–xix

Black magic, 62, 102–4, 107, 144–45. See also *Bwaga'u*

Blithe Spirit, xix, xxi, xxiii

Bodily experience, xxiii

Bolsena, miracle of, 163–64

Brothers, 37–39; younger, 21, 95

Brother-sister incest, 57–60, 69–72

Burne, C. S., 87

Bwaga'u, male sorcerers, 104

Campbell, Joseph, xi

Cannibalism, 62–63, 84; distinguished from noncannibalism, 25; origins of, 38

Canoe: construction of, 24, 26, 109; flying, 13, 21–29, 65–66, 139

Castration, xxv

Categorical imperative, 32

Celibacy. *See* Continence

Central Australian tribes, 152–59 *passim*

Ceremony. *See* Ritual

Chance, and magic, 35, 110, 152, 161, 168

"Charter," legal, 87, 93–94, 113, 148

Chiefs, 147, 171; rank of, 95–98; spirits of, 137

Christian dogma, 120, 132, 162

Christianity, xxxi–xxxii, 81–82, 132, 149. *See also* Jesus Christ; Roman Catholi-cism; Trinity

Christian Science, 71, 118, 132, 165

Christopher Columbus story, xxii–xxiii

Clans, 27, 67, 141; autochthonous, 93–94; mythical origins of, 26, 29, 90–99; rank-ing of, 90, 94–96; subclans, 98–99

Classical mythology, study of, 113–14, 120

"Collective Ideas" (Durkheim), 34

Colonial management, xxix; effects of, 41–43; Malinowski on, xxix; and morality, 43–44; of warfare, 44–46

MYTHOS: *The Princeton/Bollingen Series in World Mythology*